WILTSHIRE

The King's England

Edited by Arthur Mee

in 41 Volumes

Enchanted Land (Introductory Volume)

Bedfordshire and Huntingdonshire
Berkshire
Buckinghamshire
Cambridgeshire
Cheshire
Cornwall
Derbyshire
Devon
Dorset
Durham
Essex
Gloucestershire
Hampshire with the Isle of Wight
Herefordshire
Hertfordshire
Kent
Lake Counties
Lancashire
Leicestershire and Rutland
Lincolnshire
London
Middlesex
Monmouthshire
Norfolk
Northamptonshire
Northumberland
Nottinghamshire
Oxfordshire
Shropshire
Somerset
Staffordshire
Suffolk
Surrey
Sussex
Warwickshire
Wiltshire
Worcestershire
Yorkshire—East Riding
Yorkshire—North Riding
Yorkshire—West Riding

THE KING'S ENGLAND

WILTSHIRE

by

ARTHUR MEE

fully revised and edited by

C. L. S. LINNELL

Illustrated with new photographs by

A. F. KERSTING

HODDER AND STOUGHTON
LONDON SYDNEY AUCKLAND TORONTO

First published May 1939
Fourth impression 1950
New and reset edition 1965
Second impression 1973

ISBN 0 340 00107 0

Printed in Great Britain
for Hodder and Stoughton, Ltd.,
St. Paul's House, Warwick Lane, London EC4P 4AH
by Fletcher & Son Ltd, Norwich

For the former edition
the Editor was greatly indebted to
Miss JOAN BEGBIE and Mr J. B. JONES
for their help with this book

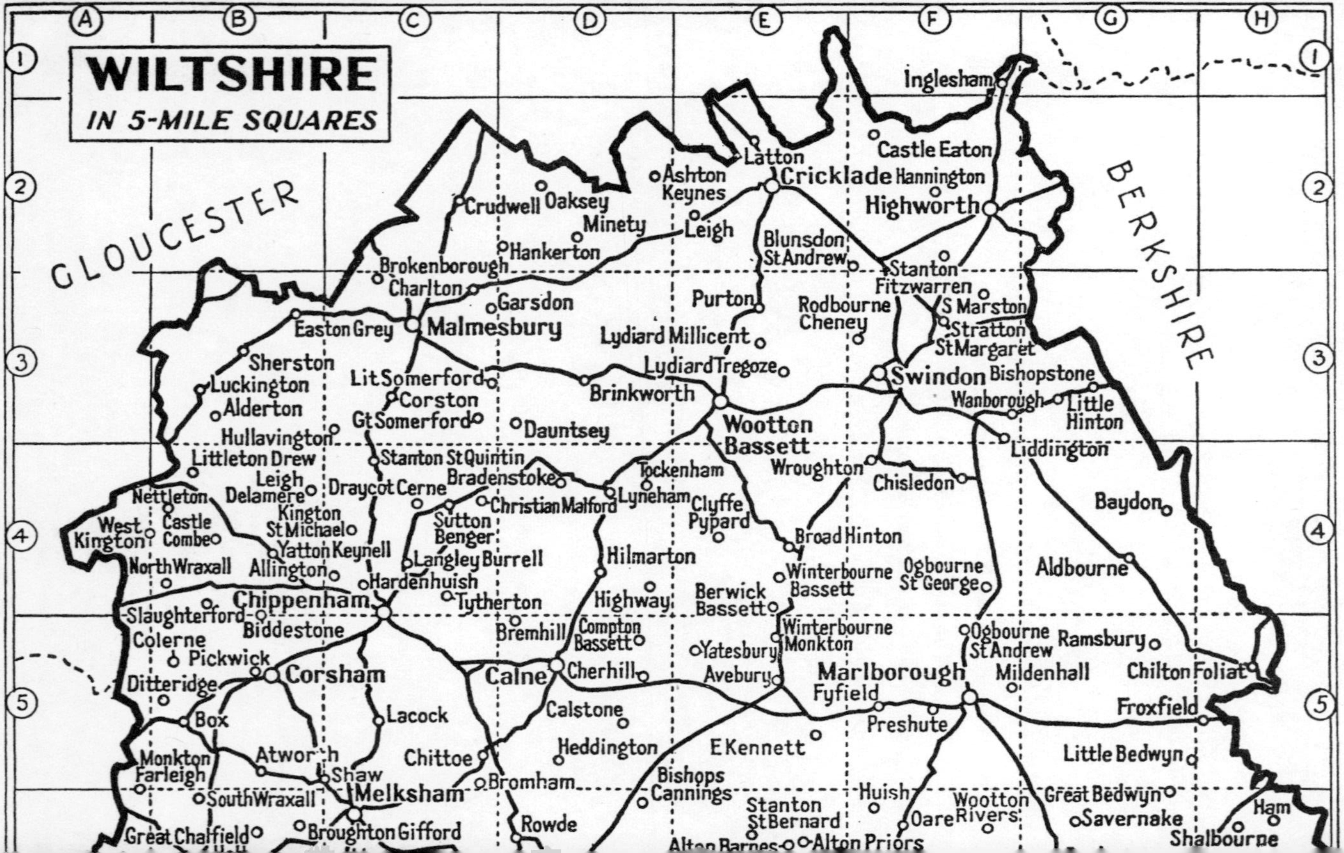
WILTSHIRE
IN 5-MILE SQUARES
GLOUCESTER
BERKSHIRE
Inglesham
Castle Eaton
Latton
Cricklade
Hannington
Highworth
Ashton Keynes
Crudwell
Oaksey
Minety
Leigh
Blunsdon St Andrew
Hankerton
Brokenborough
Charlton
Stanton Fitzwarren
Garsdon
Purton
Rodbourne Cheney
S Marston
Stratton St Margaret
Easton Grey
Malmesbury
Lydiard Millicent
Sherston
Luckington
Alderton
Lit Somerford
Corston
Gt Somerford
Brinkworth
Lydiard Tregoze
Swindon
Bishopstone
Wanborough
Little Hinton
Wootton Bassett
Dauntsey
Hullavington
Littleton Drew
Stanton St Quintin
Leigh Delamere
Draycot Cerne
Bradenstoke
Tockenham
Lyneham
Wroughton
Chisledon
Liddington
Nettleton
Kington St Michael
Christian Malford
Clyffe Pypard
Baydon
West Kington
Castle Combe
Sutton Benger
Yatton Keynell
Broad Hinton
North Wraxall
Allington
Langley Burrell
Hilmarton
Winterbourne Bassett
Ogbourne St George
Aldbourne
Hardenhuish
Chippenham
Tytherton
Highway
Berwick Bassett
Slaughterford
Biddestone
Bremhill
Compton Bassett
Winterbourne Monkton
Ogbourne St Andrew
Ramsbury
Colerne
Pickwick
Yatesbury
Corsham
Calne
Cherhill
Avebury
Marlborough
Mildenhall
Chilton Foliat
Ditteridge
Fyfield
Froxfield
Box
Lacock
Calstone
Preshute
Monkton Farleigh
Atworth
Chittoe
Heddington
E Kennett
Little Bedwyn
Shaw
Melksham
Bromham
Bishops Cannings
Huish
Wootton Rivers
Great Bedwyn
South Wraxall
Stanton St Bernard
Oare
Savernake
Ham
Great Chalfield
Broughton Gifford
Rowde
Alton Barnes
Alton Priors
Shalbourne

HAMPSHIRE
DORSET
RSET
North Bradley
Erlestoke
East Coulston
Edington
Great Cheverell
Market Lavington
West Lavington
Charlton St Peter
Upavon
Everleigh
Collingbourne Ducis
Chute
Ludgershall
Bratton
Westbury
Enford
Fittleton
Netheravon
Tidworth
Tilshead
Upton Scudamore
Imber
Figheldean
Corsley
Warminster
Orcheston St Mary
Orcheston St George
Milston
Durrington
Bulford
Bishopstrow
Chitterne
Shrewton
Norton Bavant
Heytesbury
Stonehenge
Horningsham
Longbridge Deverill
Knook
Winterbourne Stoke
Rollestone
Cholderton
Sutton Veny
Upton Lovel
Codford St Peter
Amesbury
Newton Tony
Hill Deverill
Codford St Mary
Wilsford
Boyton
Fisherton de la Mere
Berwick St James
Allington
Maiden Bradley
Brixton Deverill
Sherrington
Steeple Langford
Boscombe
Monkton Deverill
Stockton
Wylye
Stapleford
Durnford
Kilmington
Kingston Deverill
Little Langford
Woodford
Idmiston
Great Wishford
Winterbourne Gunner
Stourton
Stratford-sub-Castle
Hindon
Berwick St Leonard
Winterslow
Barford St Martin
Old Sarum
Teffont Magna
Zeals
Mere
Fonthill Gifford
Chilmark
Wilton
Teffont Evias
Dinton
Baverstock
Burcombe
East Knoyle
SALISBURY
Farley
Tisbury
Fovant
Compton Chamberlayne
Bemerton
Sutton Mandeville
W. Harnham
Britford
Semley
Ansty
Fifield Bavant
Stratford Tony
Alderbury
West Grimstead
Donhead St Andrew
Bishopstone
Coombe Bissett
West Dean
Odstock
Broad Chalke
Standlynch
Donhead St Mary
Alvediston
Ebbesborne Wake
Whiteparish
Berwick St John
Downton
Tollard Royal
7
8
9
10
11
A
B
C
D
E
F
G
H

INTRODUCTION TO THE REVISED EDITION

In preparing the new edition of The King's England care has been taken to bring the books up to date as far as possible within the changes which have taken place since the series was originally planned. In addition the editor has made his revisions both in text and illustrations with a view to keeping the price of the books within reasonable limits, in spite of greatly increased production costs. But throughout the book, it has been the editor's special care to preserve Mr Arthur Mee's original intention of providing something more than just another guide book giving archaeological, ecclesiastical, and topographical information.

In the case of every town and village mentioned in the King's England Series, it has been the intention not only to indicate its position on the map, but to convey something of its atmosphere. And the biographical selections about people who are ever associated with that part of the country in which they lived, or who are commemorated in the parish church—which was such a popular feature of the former edition—have been retained and in some cases supplemented.

For this new edition of *Wiltshire* the editor is most grateful for the assistance he has received from Mr E. T. Long.

C. L. S. Linnell

LIST OF ILLUSTRATIONS

WILTSHIRE

WILTSHIRE

A CHALK giant sprawls across the southern half of England. His head rests against the pillow of the Cotswolds. He dabbles his toes in the sea at Cromer and at Dover. His body is in Wiltshire, in the Marlborough Downs spreading into Berkshire, in the 300 square miles of Salisbury Plain and in the southern group of Downs touching on Hampshire, reaching from Salisbury to Tollard Royal and continuing on into the Dorset heights.

From the earliest times men have found the giant congenial. They have dwelt upon his back and his body is pitted with their graves; and it is in Wiltshire that prehistoric men have left two of the most impressive of their memorials in the monoliths at Stonehenge and in the Circles at Avebury with the extraordinary "avenue" of stones leading away towards Silbury Hill, that most amazing and mysterious monument of all.

The roads are few across the Downs but the tracks are numerous and are probably as old—if not older—than the monoliths and the barrows and time which antiquates antiquities and hath an art to make dust of all things has spared these minor monuments which have been trodden by men ever since there have been men to tread. Many of these upland paths gather about Avebury and the visitor who would understand something of the prehistory of Wiltshire might well start from this place. Stay an hour in Avebury and one cannot avoid feeling something of the spirit of this extraordinary place. Spend the night and walk in the gloaming round that mysterious circle, nearly a mile in extent, and one feels very near—perhaps almost unpleasantly near—the men of more than a hundred generations ago who raised these stones for a purpose we do not understand.

Avebury is a good starting point to explore Wiltshire. Southwards to Salisbury through the Vale of Pewsey, or a longer detour through the Savernake Forest, or even a longer way round through Devizes not forgetting to have a look at the Wansdyke which has two beginnings at Inkpen Beacon and Ludgershall, meeting at Great Bedwyn and then passing for 60 miles across into Somerset and which can be seen to the best effect behind the White Horse at Cherill and on the heights above the Devizes road. This way to Salisbury, through Devizes, passes close to Stonehenge and visitors to this, one of the most remarkable prehistoric monuments in the world, should not forget that near by, at Durrington, there was also a Woodhenge, of which there is little to see, for wood is less enduring than stone, but which has been proved to have had the same orientation as Stonehenge and may have been a wooden prototype for its stone neighbour, as the wooden Saxon Churches were the forerunners of the churches in stone.

Both the Saxons and Normans left their mark upon Wiltshire. At Bradford-on-Avon is the most beautiful little Saxon Church in all England, at Limpney Stoke the arcades of the church show as fine Saxon workmanship as can be found anywhere. Old Sarum was the headquarters of the first Saxon settlement. Wilton was the capital of the Saxon Kingdom of Wessex, remained so for long after the Norman Conquest and eventually gave its name to the Shire itself. The work of the Normans is to be found everywhere but nowhere better than at Malmesbury Abbey, which, though a fragment of its former glory, must be accounted as one of the great Norman Churches of England.

To our medieval ancestors the work of the Saxons and Normans appeared primitive and old fashioned and wherever possible they adapted it to the Gothic, and in some places replaced it with an entirely new building as did Bishop Poore, who demolished the Norman Cathedral at Old Sarum and started to build the new Cathedral at Salisbury, the apogee of the thirteenth century style and one of the most remarkable and beautiful Gothic buildings in the world. It is an amazing testimony to the strength, originality, and architectural abandon of the Gothic age that the famous spire (404 ft high and the tallest in England) was never thought of in the original plan but was added afterwards on top of a tower that was raised in height, and all poised for 700 years on piers which were never intended to carry it!

The body of the great chalk giant is scored by little streams, the Wylye, the Nadder, the Ebble and the Bourne which feed the Salisbury Avon running southwards to the English Channel; in the northern part of the county the Kennett carrying the waters from the northern downs into the Thames, which in its infancy is a Wiltshire boundary stream, and in the west the Bristol Avon.

It is in the valley of the Bristol Avon that one realises that Wiltshire is not all Downs but also a land of meadows and pastures providing dairy produce and the famous Wiltshire Bacon. As it winds its way westwards the Bristol Avon cuts its way through rocks which are older than the chalk. Beneath the surface lie fine building stones, the Bath oolite of which that city and most other old buildings of that area were constructed and the Chilmark stone used for Salisbury Cathedral and elsewhere in the south of the county; and it was from the clay that is older than the Downs that the 19th and 20th century builders made the bricks for the houses in Swindon, Wiltshire's largest town.

Wiltshire is one of the most thinly populated counties in England and only three towns have a population of over 10,000. The medieval villages and townships—a dozen of them Market Towns—over 250 of them and all of them worth seeing, gather in the valleys. But in the days when the valleys were waterlogged and undrained, and the woodlands on the lower slopes more dense, prehistoric men preferred the back of the chalk giant and what are now the wide unpopulated expanses of the Downs—in which is the true spirit and atmosphere of Wiltshire—were once the scene of an abundant life and one of the most populous parts of Britain.

Aldbourne. It stands on the hilly Berkshire border between Marlborough and Wiltshire's chief industrial town, Swindon. So old that in a barrow on Southward Hill was found an incense cup with a pierced cover made in the Bronze Age. Thousands of years more recent are the steps and shafts of an ancient cross on a patch of grass below the church.

Gargoyles look down from the splendid 15th century tower, with an embattled parapet, pinnacled buttresses, and a noble arch; among its eight bells two are medieval, one with a prayer for Richard Goddard and for "Elizabeth and Elizabeth his wives." Over a window in a transept wall is a hideous stone face of a man with long hair and his tongue out.

The 15th century church has a Norman doorway with a boldly carved arch round which run small flowers. The roofs are old and new, and rest on 20 stone faces below the clerestory windows. An arch facing the door has two extraordinary little heads, one a goggle-eyed dog and the other a curious little man. There is a richly carved Jacobean pulpit and just behind it is a winged and crowned angel. Two brothers who saw 180 years of life between them have a tomb which must have been a brilliant spectacle in Shakespeare's day. Edward Walrond who was 96 and his younger brother William of 84. They kneel on cushions of red, green, and gold, both with ruffs and both with beards, both in armour but with no swords. In front of their tomb is a gaily painted frieze of flying dragons.

There is a painted monument of Thomas Goddard, bearded and in 16th century armour, kneeling with a daughter and three bearded sons, looking into the beautiful panelled arch of a medieval chapel. The father's helmet hangs above him. In one of the aisles is the brass portrait of an ancestor who gave the ancient bells, Richard Goddard of 1482. His brass shows him with his wife. On the floor of the chancel is a brass of a priest of 1508, Henry Frekylton, in Mass vestments.

But the glory of this place is the tomb by the altar in which lies John Stone, the priest who was here before Henry Frekylton. The top of his stone tomb is a magnificent piece of alabaster in which the portrait of John Stone (1501) is deeply engraved, showing him over six feet high lying in his vestments, holding a chalice. His head is on a cushion and he is surrounded by exquisite carving.

Oldest of all the possessions of the church are the nave arcades in which the Norman stones were used again in the 13th century. The roodloft stairway is still inside the buttress, the old chest has survived the centuries, and even those old friends of the village the 18th century fire wagons are cared for in this church. They stand in one of the aisles, two small wagons with solid ironshod discs for wheels, made in Ratcliffe Highway, London.

Alderbury. It lies on the hills near Salisbury with the river running below, and has a gabled inn known to Charles Dickens, for in *Martin Chuzzlewit* he sent Mark Tapley there to stay. But as the nearest village to the Forest of Clarendon it has a place in many important pages of our history.

A small farm here is on the site of a vanished priory, and in the walls of the house called Ivychurch are fragments of carving which must have been familiar to the monks of many generations. In the garden is what is left of a Norman arch on a round pillar with a carved capital. Across the way from the 19th century church is Alderbury House, built of grey stone from the old belfry of Salisbury Cathedral. On a hilltop are fine clumps of beeches from which we have a wonderful view of the Salisbury Spire.

The story of Clarendon, a mile or two away, is one of the most thrilling chapters of excavation in our time. Here was one of the least known of our historical royal palaces, begun as a hunting-box for Norman kings and growing into a favourite country home for the Plantagenets. It was built on a hill in the forest two or three miles east of Salisbury, and for centuries all that remained of it was a ruined gable and buttresses covered with ivy. It was reached by a picturesque walk from the modern stone house built in the park of 300 acres with a lake of 18 acres. In the last few years excavations made by Dr Tancred Borenius have revealed the ruins of a site hardly less captivating than Old Sarum itself, for this place is not only interesting as an ancient court of kings, as the scene of the drawing-up of some of the earliest laws regulating relations between church and state, but it has a unique value because it is the first royal palace known that was never fortified. When a monarch took his pleasures here it was a sort of declaration that his kingdom was at peace. We must regard it as the beginning of the domestic manor house.

It is about 400 years since Clarendon Palace passed into oblivion, being finally abandoned in the days of Henry the Eighth. Thomas

Becket rode down the old track that still leads to it to take part in the conference which established what are known as the Constitutions of Clarendon. Henry the Second wished to limit the powers of the Church Courts. He met Archbishop Becket there and they agreed on Sixteen Points regulating the conduct of the clergy and limiting their powers. They were not allowed to appeal to Rome without the king's consent, or to excommunicate tenants, or to ordain the sons of peasants without consent, or to leave the country without permission, and if charged with crime they were to be handed over to the secular court.

The life of the palace developed under Henry the Third, who is believed to have made it a place of great beauty. The first known kiln for making tiles apart from a monastery has been found here, and among the thousands of tiles discovered (making this the richest site known in England for medieval tiles) are some showing Richard Lionheart on horseback, fighting Saladin. Other tiles have on them lions rampant, griffins, and dragons, all with the fleur-de-lys. Much of one floor of inlaid tiles has been found intact in a room occupied by the queen of Henry the Third, and a mass of tiles has been found which crashed through the private chapel of that king into what is called the Antioch Chapel below. From these it has been possible to reconstruct a circular floor with a Latin inscription, a floor that has no parallel in England. Most of the tiles are from the 13th and 14th centuries, and an immense number of faulty ones have been found, as is natural at a kiln.

The palace covered about eight acres and had one of the biggest aisled halls in the kingdom, 80 feet long by 50 feet wide, built in the 12th century. The cloisters were largely of wood and appear to have been burnt down at the end of the 14th century and not rebuilt. The Black Prince's son Roger of Clarendon was born here. There have come to light some remains of new kitchens built in the 15th century opposite the King's Apartments, and they have a pathetic interest, for it is believed that they may have been built in 1453, when Henry the Sixth was at Clarendon and was attacked by madness, so that he was not in a fit state to dine in the great hall.

The treasure discovered on this site has been mostly found on the rubbish heap behind the kitchen quarters, but among the things that have come to light is what is believed to be the first bradawl ever used in England, an example of the earliest known window glass ever set in a lead frame, a small angel's wing exquisitely wrought in stone with its original gilding and red paint, and, most notable of all, the sculptured head of a young man of 700 years ago when English art was in its earliest stage. It is thought the head may have been part of a door ornament in the king's apartment, and it comes from the period of the fine tiled floor found in the queen's room. The head is splendidly modelled, the hair is coloured a light brown, the lips are faint pink, and the detail of the teeth is remarkable.

It was from Clarendon that Edward Hyde took his title in 1661.

Alderton. In the beautiful country on the Gloucestershire border, it has fine trees and a big pond, a churchyard with a splendid line of cut box and Irish yews with a Wellingtonia towering up, and a simple 13th century church with a Norman doorway, a stone spire, and rather terrifying sculpture on its wall.

There is a fine oak screen, pews with old carved ends, six choir stalls with neat heads, a stone almsbox on a pillar and many little stone corbels, and a charming face at each end of the nave arcade. On one of the stones we read of a benefactor,

Loved by the rich, the poor did bless
Her as their sovereign almoness.

But it is for a tragic little tale that we remember this small sanctuary, filled with the monuments of the Gores, lords of the manor in the 17th century. On the chancel floor is the grave of Lydia Gore, whose five children all died young. A brass tablet has a verse asking us to weep for her, nor fear that our tears will fall alone, for "floods are due unto this stone."

The eldest of this tragically young family, the six-year-old Charles, kneels at prayer in a recess of the wall. He wears a long skirt of green and gold with gilded spurs on his riding boots, a black cap on his head, a sword held in place by a gaily striped bow. On the wall behing him is sculptured the big black hat he wore, with a white feather curled over the crown and one side of the brim caught up by a gold ornament.

All Cannings. Peeping over a high wall decorated with a little stone urn is a rectory, which was the delightful home of Anthony Methuen, rector for 60 years. He was a friend of the poet Coleridge, who came to stay with him two years after Waterloo, and on the 50th anniversary of this visit the rector and his sons rebuilt the chancel as a memorial to their "happy home," the home which Coleridge had shared with them for a time.

The Methuen initials are on a row of tiles before the altar steps, their tablets on the walls, and a steel engraving of the rector hangs in the vestry.

The 15th century tower of the church has a tall turret. There are ten richly coloured fragments of old glass in some of the windows; a dainty little organ; a Jacobean cover on the 15th century font; two sculptured Norman capitals; 15th and 17th century roof beams; and upper and lower doorways to the old roodloft, the stairway being inside a pier.

There are two big wall monuments of the 16th and 18th centuries, one about 12 feet high, to the Ernle family. The older monument is the more beautiful, a fine piece of work though a trifle gruesome. Three eagles crown it, and below is written: "Wheresoever a dead carkas is, even thither will the eagles resorte." Below in a panel with pillars, surrounded by quotations from the Bible, is a beautiful heraldic carving with roses round. The tomb of William Ernle, who died in 1581 and lies with his son John. The other monument is topped by a curly-haired head wearing a cap like a jester's ending in tasselled strings. Under it sleeps Sir John Ernle, who died as rector here in 1734, and is with his wife and their babies.

From the little bridge here can be seen the white horse on the hills above Alton Barnes, cut about the time of Waterloo.

Allington. A hamlet on the road from Old Roman Silchester to Old English Sarum, with the famous Wansdyke earthwork at the top of St Ann's Hill. The small flint and stone church is 19th century, and has a small chancel arch only eight feet wide with a line of bead moulding running along the wall on either side and passing round its capitals. There is a plain old cup-shaped font with a pierced wood cover.

Allington. Time has brought great changes to this lonely corner near Chippenham. Here is a stable that has become a church. Here is a great house that has become a barn. Here are burial mounds in which lie ancient warriors.

The great house was the home 300 years ago of Sir Gilbert Prynne; we see one of his beautiful stone windows blocked up near the roof. We come through his stone doorway, but the old front door that he opened is now the farmer's back door, and on it is the old knocker with which callers knocked 300 years ago when they would see Sir Gilbert Prynne. Few barns that we have seen are so elegant as this. In the farmyard is the old ox-house which has been a church since about 1860, and a little farther up the road is one of the loveliest homes in Wiltshire, Bulidge House. It has a stately front, and two charming garden houses flanking the gate.

When one of these prehistoric mounds was opened hugh stones were found inside which were set up as a cromlech, with a mass of bones which were taken out and arranged so that they made a figure of a giant, about seven feet high.

Alton Barnes. It lies under that fine line of Downs known as the Marlborough Hills, with the fruitful Pewsey Valley spreading out before it, and the fine tumulus known as Adam's Grave above it.

On one of the hills is a high-stepping horse. He was cut out of the turf three years before Waterloo. He can be seen from Old Sarum 22 miles away, for he is 180 feet high and 165 feet long. It is said that a farmer paid £20 to have the horse cut out of the turf, so that his village should not be behind the dignity of Marlborough and Cherhill.

Old as he is, the church was here 800 years before him. The nave is only 25 feet long and 15 wide, and has deeply splayed windows, ancient roof beams, a panelled gallery, and a charming old font on a slender stem with a domed cover. In one of the windows of the 18th century chancel is a lovely piece of heraldic glass in memory of a vicar who rebuilt the parsonage. The altar is older than the chancel, and by it are two handsome carved chairs and a pretty table with claw and ball feet, suggesting Chippendale's workmanship.

Two names well known in Wiltshire, and not unworthily known in literature, are on two of the many tablets crowding these walls. One tells us that William Crowe was vicar here; the other is in memory of another vicar, Augustus Hare. Of William Crowe we are told that he was a man of "rare genius and elegant learning." He was the poet of the Wiltshire hills, and his work was highly valued in his day, although he was so poor that he would walk miles from here to Oxford, where he was public orator of the University; often he was seen on these roads carrying his clothes over his arm, or sitting in a lane making notes for his orations and sermons.

Both these vicars must have preached from the Jacobean three decker pulpit.

Some letters from Maria Hare, the vicar's wife, give pictures of their life among the village folk. She shows us the vicar, careless of his own health, visiting and reading to his flock when they were suffering from a dangerous fever running rife among them. She draws attractive pictures of the gardener in his blue plush breeches, drab jacket, and fur cap, and though she bemoans the state of the roads as so bad that it took a gig an hour to do three miles, she once walked up to the great white horse and planted her stick in his tail. She tells us of a dark and ugly night when 200 peasants descended on the village to break up machines on the farms.

Alton Priors. It is set in a lovely scene among the rugged hills of Marlborough and the Pewsey Valley. The 15th century church has a chancel rebuilt in brick retaining the old windows.

It has two brasses, one of William Button on the sanctuary wall and one on the floor of a lady with a girdled gown from which a quaint ornament is hanging. She died in 1528, a generation before William Button, who lies in a 16th century heraldic tomb with the brass let into the back of it. Round the tomb are figures of a man with a moustache and a woman with long hair, both apparently rising at the sound of the trumpet, for on William's brass is an angel bursting through the clouds vigorously blowing a trumpet to wake William Button from his grave.

Alvediston. The hills about it, reaching 700 feet high, have splendid views of miles of rolling downs. On the way to the church we pass a grand avenue, mostly of limes. The church is 13th century, with a pinnacled tower and an old mass dial. Inside the tower arch ends with carved tasselled ornaments. The plain round font is Norman. In the vestry is an old panelled chest. A delightful little tombstone carved with a cross is let into the wall of the sanctuary. In the south transept under an arch lies a knight in armour, his feet on a dog and angels at his head. He is a member of one of the oldest families in England, the Gawens, who lived at the house called Norrington which is late 14th century with Elizabethan additions. It lies in the hills and is reached by a rough and winding downland road.

Amesbury. Lies in the south of Salisbury Plain, with the great stone circle of Stonehenge and the great timber circle of Woodhenge equally distant, half-an-hour's walk away. It lives, with these mysterious temples, in the dim beginnings of the faith that has raised temples like Winchester and Salisbury not far off, and it lives in the story of King Arthur and his Knights, for here it was, when Guinevere had fled the court, that she sat in the holy house of Amesbury. Here she lay at Arthur's feet and heard him say:

But hither shall I never come again . . .
See thee no more. . . . Farewell.

William Cobbett, who saw more of England than any man before his time, found nothing to please him like this valley of the Avon, which comes down to Amesbury from one stream near Devizes and another from the marvellous forest of Savernake, and runs on through the New Forest to join the sea near Christchurch Priory.

Here on the river banks we find the camp of Vespasian which was here before the world heard of the Caesars, an ancient church begun by the Saxons, and a modern house standing where the ancient abbey stood.

Through the shade of heavenly beeches we come into a churchyard filled with yews leading to a huge studded door which has been swinging on its hinges for 500 years and all the time this great key has been turning in the huge wooden lock.

The church was built by the Saxons and refashioned by the Normans, and the English builders made it the Cathedral of the Valley. There are fragments of a Saxon wheel cross in a glass case, and the Norman font has been rescued from under the floor and set on a carved base 500 years old; but it is a 13th century church that we look upon, crowned with 15th and 16th century roofs, beautiful with tracery and carved bosses. The aisle roof has a head carved in it which looks like one of the queerest ideas we have come upon in a church—Henry the Eighth as a cherub. The embattled roof of the nave has splendid tie beams.

In the aisle is a canopied piscina and aumbry together, with tiny carved heads and a stone shelf borne on leaves. In the timber roof of one of the transepts is a fierce monster of the 16th century devouring a man whose limbs dangle limply from between its teeth; in the other transept is the 13th century Jesus Chapel, with a stone vaulted roof over which is a priest's room, lit by a lovely little window divided by a group of small columns with leafy capitals. The candlesticks and cross of the chapel are made of old oak piles from under the tower.

In a 14th century window of great beauty in the chancel are fragments of original glass with the head of the Madonna wearing a golden crown. There is a graceful traceried screen of the 15th century, and by the altar is a stone table supported by lovely bosses from the old east window. Under a tall recess with a crocketed canopy was a seat in olden days for the abbess. On the high altar is a beautiful copy of a 12th century Irish cross, daintily wrought with silver thread and set with stones. On the wall is an embroidered purse from the battlefields of the Somme.

The 13th century arches of the tower form a noble group, and deep in the wall by one of them is the base of a Saxon pillar which has been here all the time. A fresco which has kept it company since medieval days is fading away by another arch. It has been a portrait of Saint Malor, the boy murdered by a cruel uncle and buried here.

The house still known as Amesbury Abbey, a modern stone building with a colonnaded front raised on five arches, stands in a fine park with the river flowing through. It is on the site of the abbey to which Guinevere came after the discovery that she had been false to the king, the abbey to which Arthur came to say Farewell.

Close by Amesbury is the ancient earthwork known as Vespasian's Camp. It stands on a wooded hill above the Avon, and encloses 39 acres. The Emperor Vespasian, when serving as a General under the Emperor Claudius, captured the Isle of Wight, followed the Avon up to Sarum and Amesbury and passed on into Somerset; but the camp had been there long before he came. It is early British, not Roman, in construction.

About the year 980 Queen Elfrida founded a nunnery at Amesbury in contrition for the murder of her stepson King Edward at Corfe Castle. The stone head in a niche is thought to be that of Queen Elfrida, and the base of a column of her old church was seen in the wall beside the north-west pier of the tower.

After the Dissolution of the religious houses the convent passed into the hands of the Protector Somerset, and in due course a great house was built by Inigo Jones. In the 18th century the house became one of the most hospitable in the land, under the rule of the handsome but eccentric Duchess of Queensberry, wife of the third Duke. It was her delight to know and entertain poets and other writers. She was a friend of Pope, Thomson, Prior, and Swift, though she only knew Swift through correspondence. John Gay spent nearly all his time either at the Abbey House at Amesbury or at the Queensberrys' London house, and Amesbury thought of him as belonging to the place, and still can point out where he sat in the rounds and wrote some of his Fables. The duchess was Matthew Prior's

Kitty beautiful and young,
And wild as cat untamed.

Ansty. In a wooded park stand the ruins of Wardour Castle, built in 1392, and destroyed in the Civil War by Lord Arundell, who blew up his own house because he could not eject General Ludlow (occupying it for the Parliament) in any other way. Lady Blanche Arundell held out heroically against the Parliament army, only capitulating when granted honourable terms of surrender, which were not kept.

The ruined castle stands on a green hill above a lake, with noble cedars growing about it, and a strange and lofty tropical ironwood tree with clustered stems springing up against it. Lord Baltimore brought this odd old tree from Maryland. It is 38 feet round, and 75 high. A line of lofty yews grows on the terrace above the ruins. Mullioned windows and charming doorways lie open to the sun and wind, peopled by birds and clothed with bushes and plants. We can sit by the well in the central courtyard and look up the vaulted stairs through a handsome archway with fluted columns. Over another doorway is a niche with a bust of Our Lord, and the inscription, Under thy name rest the family and the house. The family and the house have now moved across the lake to a new Wardour Castle, with an imposing 18th century front. Lady Blanche Arundell, the gallant defender of the old castle, lies at Tisbury close by.

In the small 13th century church are some lovely 17th century bench-ends from Salisbury Cathedral, carved with exuberant foliage. Three pointed arches lead into the chancel and the transepts. The altar is Jacobean, with a carved front. An old mass dial is still on the walls. There was a house of the Knights Hospitallers by the church; the remains are part of a farmhouse and the big barnlike workshop of a wheelwright.

Ashton Keynes. The shallow Isis flows past its charming stone cottages near Cricklade, spanned by little bridges leading to their gardens. There are three simple old crosses in the village and another by the church, to which an avenue of splendid elms brings us across the field.

Gargoyles look down from the 14th century walls of the church, and inside is a company of stone heads, all bearing up the timbers of the roof, with their carved bosses of flowers. The pointed arches of the nave with carved and moulded capitals are 13th century. The big Norman font is shaped like a drum and handsomely decorated with a belt of chevrons between rows of leaves and honeysuckle. Near the steps of the old roodloft doorway with an ancient coffin stone for a lintel is an arch with lovely canopied niches above. It leads into a 13th century chapel, lit by groups of lancets and a 15th century window. It has a canopied piscina.

The striking chancel arch, with beautiful mouldings and diaper work, has in it many of the original Norman stones. In the chancel is a canopied piscina. The founder of the church as we see it has a 15th century window in his memory, with a little of its ancient glass. Here they set him, clad in blue and white with gold-embroidered robes, holding a model of the church in his hand, with the Trinity before him.

A pathetic brass inscription tells of a little boy and his grandfather who died on the same day under the Commonwealth and were buried in one grave in the chancel. A marble wall monument of 1800 shows Charlotte Nicholas on her deathbed with her husband and children round her, one holding her hand.

The farmhouse by the church is all that is left of a vanished monastery. The moat still encircles some of the fields. One of the barns is medieval.

At Aston Keynes there has grown up what is known as the Cotswold Bruderhof, a community of various nationalities, but chiefly Germans driven from their own country. It was at Tytherton in Wiltshire that a church was founded in the 18th century by the Moravians. The Bruderhof is the first community of its kind in this country, a Brotherhood of peaceful-minded people (two or three hundred of them) who share a farm of 300 acres and live a self-contained life, receiving no wages and spending no money, but printing, book-binding, and doing all manner of work, even running a small power station for power and light. They have about 100 head of cattle, a hospital, a veterinary surgeon, and whatever is necessary for the life of a small community.

Atworth. In 1938 the remains were discovered of a Roman villa of 24 rooms and passages. There were signs that the house had had a suite of baths, four or five heating-chambers, and tessellated floors; and a flight of six stone steps has been uncovered. The house was roofed with sandstone tiles from the neighbourhood of Bristol, and in some cases the tiles have been found with the iron nails for fastening them to the battens still in position. Most interesting of all the discoveries are the earthenware tiles, some having on them the imprint of hob-nailed shoes, the paws of dogs, and the fingertips of men; on some of them are clear impressions of the finger-nails. There was charcoal from the Roman fires, scores of coins of the third and fourth centuries, and a perfect little jar which had been used for oil or wine. It is believed that this Roman house may have been destroyed by fire in the many raids between the departure of the Romans and the settling down of England under Saxon kings.

The old tower stands apart from the rebuilt church, linked to it by a passage. In the church is a stone pulpit with richly canopied panels, and on the green is a clock tower with four arches, the memorial for World War I.

Avebury. The character of the village and the downland about it is to be preserved for ever as one of the sacred possessions of our island, and it is right that it should be so.

The stones of Avebury are older than Stonehenge, and, though not so impressive today, they must have been greater to those who knew this ancient temple long ago.

It is best approached from Silbury Hill on the London road to Bath, the largest artificial mound in Europe, 1660 feet round at the base, 300 feet round at the top, and 130 feet high. This astonishing monument covers five acres and it has been said that this was a task comparable with the building of the Pyramids, and the mightiest piece of labour put forth by prehistoric man in Europe.

It was all part of some vast plan we do not understand, but we know that from this hill to the great circle of stones at Avebury was nearly a mile, and that from Overton Hill to the circle these builders raised an avenue of huge stones, two rows of about a hundred each. At the end of the avenue was the Great Circle made by a ring of stones sunk two feet into the chalk, some 20 feet high and some weighing 60 tons. There were about a hundred of them, and within the Circle were two small rings of upright stones.

All round the Great Circle is a deep trench dug into the solid chalk for 30 feet, and one can walk round this immense mound which is 29 acres in extent and nearly a mile round.

It was a temple of some prehistoric Baal, and from the pottery found it is thought to go back as far beyond the Crucifixion as we are on this side of it.

Excavation has shown that a section of the ditch at the Avebury end of the avenue from the Overton Woodhenge had never been dug, but formed a natural entrance causeway 24 feet wide. Hence one still enters the circle of Avebury by the entrance so planned by the prehistoric men who built the great monument. There have

Avebury: the stone circle, with its surrounding bank and ditch. *(National Trust)*

Avebury Manor.

Avebury Church: the medieval sc
with its roodloft.

Avebury Church: the font.

been excavations of Silbury Hill, but nothing has suggested any further reason for it. In 1723 they found a skeleton near the top, evidently a murdered traveller. In 1777 a hole was sunk down the middle of the ground and a piece of timber found, used by the builders as a working centre. In 1849 a tunnel was bored into the hill from one side and two pieces of antlers and some strands of twisted grass were found, the grass being probably the remains of a basket for carrying chalk. In 1886 about a dozen shafts were sunk, and in every shaft but one were found the bones of deer and oxen. In another a Roman coin was found; in another a black layer of clay, charcoal, and broken flints and bones suggested human occupation.

In recent years the avenue has been explored and carvings found on some of its stones, carved circles not met with before in southern England. Buried stones have been dug up and re-erected, and the holes from which others have vanished completely have been marked. Most important was the discovery of several graves, the remains in each case being in the socket-hole of a stone, the skeleton to the east of the stone. One of the dramatic discoveries made in our time has been the broken skeleton of a man who is thought to have been the village tailor. Some time 600 years ago he was helping to dig a pit to bury one of the big stones, and unhappily the huge boulder, weighing 35 tons, fell on top of him. There was no more news of him till 1938, when the excavators found his broken bones with silver coins and a pair of scissors he had worn on his belt. Further excavations have been made on Windmill Hill, on the other side of Avebury from Silbury; here were found a baby's skeleton, the earliest known skeleton of a domestic dog, and a piece of a bowl which a potter had ornamented by pressing on to it blackbird bones. The discoveries on Windmill Hill have shown the evolution of culture among the oldest people of our island who can be said to have been civilised.

A marvellous sight Old Avebury must have been, with its hundreds of upright stones, of which about 20 are left. The church is built of the broken stones; so is the old manor house with its barns and stables; so are many of the houses. In the midst of the village stands the church set back where the ancient temple stood, started by the Saxons, carried on by the Normans, and crowned with a new tower in the 15th century.

There was a church here before the Norman Conquest, the Saxon successor of a prehistoric temple. It is believed that Saxon children were brought to this font to be christened, but the carving round it is Norman; it shows a mitred bishop slaying a dragon coiled round his cross.

It may be said that Avebury is as interesting indoors as out, for this church, approached through a rich Norman doorway, has Saxon windows, Norman aisles, a peephole that we can walk through to the chancel, a 15th century screen with the roodloft still over it, and a feature in the nave which is one of the best witnesses we have to the ingenuity of our Saxon builders—a pair of round Saxon windows high up in the walls. Each opening is formed of a single stone pierced and splayed both ways, representing a clever idea of the Saxons for getting light through a rubble wall. It is obviously easy to pierce a solid wall, but how is a window to be set among rubble? The Saxon took his stone at Avebury and, having made his opening in it for the window, pierced small holes all round it through which he pushed thin willow sticks radiating outwards to carry on the splay right through the wall. He set plaster round these sticks which set solid, and the whole mass was then built into the rubble.

The chancel screen has 12 modern painted panels along the bottom, with an apostle in each panel; the canopy is beautifully carved, and the front of the roodloft is elegant open tracery.

Nobly set in this historic countryside, the ancient church has a noble house to keep it company. It is the Elizabethan manor house on the site of a monastery standing here 800 years ago. The house is 16th century and stands among lovely trees enclosed in its beautiful garden walls, and it has a round dovecot perhaps older than itself, with hundreds of nesting-places.

Barbury Camp. High above the Vale of the White Horse to the south of Swindon rise two steep heights of the Marlborough Downs, Liddington and Barbury, both crowned by camps. Barbury belongs to the far-off past of this most ancient county, but an act of devotion to two of Wiltshire's sons has brought it into our living present, for we found standing here an old Greywether of the Downs set up in our own time as a monument to two Englishmen who brought honour to a Wiltshire town. It is a great stone left standing when hundreds of others were moved down the hill for the Avebury Circle.

In our own days there have been added to these ancient monuments of the Downs memorials enshrining for all time the names of two nature poets of Swindon who loved these hills, Richard Jefferies and Alfred Williams. The memorial on Liddington is a simple plate fixed to the Ordnance Survey pyramid in November 1938; the memorial on Barbury is a three-ton sarsen stone moved from Overton Down. On this grey stone have been placed two plates with these words:

Richard Jefferies, 1848–1887.	*Alfred Williams, 1877–1930*
It is Eternity now.	*Still to find and still to follow*
I am in the midst of it.	*Joy in every hill and hollow,*
It is about me in the sunshine.	*Company in solitude.*

Richard Jefferies is known to English readers everywhere as one of the fine lovers of Nature among writing men; Alfred Williams was the railwayman, scholar, and poet, whose genius won him wide fame.

Barford St Martin. There are ancient earthworks on the Downs above it. Through the village of today the River Nadder runs. Near the church stands what is left of the old cross. The tower is 15th century, and has four pointed arches and a vaulted ceiling with carved bosses. Much of the church is 13th century; the nave is 15th. All the roofs have old beams.

The chancel has ancient panelling carved with flowers, and a fine massive altar of 1680 which was originally a chest; it is carved on the front with three figures. Two beautiful Jacobean chairs are carved with flowers and foliage. The font is 500 years old.

Set in a panelled and recessed tomb is a rare painted figure of a woman in a winding sheet, lying on a reed mattress. She died before the Spanish Armada, and is thought to have lived in the manor house. Facing her quaint portrait is a stone frame with a curious small relief of a woman in a quilted garment, kneeling by a pot piled high with loaves. There is a brass portrait of Alice Walker, another Barford lady who died when England was expecting the Armada; she is kneeling with her 11 children, all in Elizabethan dress, and her epitaph describes her as one

Whose soul (no doubt) has pierced the clouds
And scaled the empire sky.

A mile across the river is Hurdcott House, a fine 17th century stone structure with splendid views from its gardens, and on the downs is Grovely Wood, which has a chapter in the story of Wiltshire liberties. From time immemorial the ill-paid labourer was entitled to gather wood for firewood, but last century came a lord of the manor who, loving pheasants more than peasants, would have driven the labourer out of his domain. The men of the village were willing to succumb, but the women were not, and four of them determined to stand up for their rights. They set out on the long track to the forest, gathered their sticks, and were arrested and imprisoned. But Liberty was on their side. It turned out that the lord of the manor was wrong and the four brave women were right and they were set free.

Baverstock. The small 14th century church stands on a quiet green hill above the River Nadder, with sheltering trees about it. It has a low tower with pretty windows, a mass dial, a canopied niche, and an old font like an egg cup. In the sanctuary is a pair of old chairs, one carved with a fox and the other with a hound. An elaborate and heavy wall stone to John Henry Leech, of Hurdcott House, tells us that his short life was devoted to the science of entomology, to travel, and sport. In the graveyard sleep many English and Australian men who died in camp during World War I.

Baydon. Ermine Street runs past it, 750 feet up on the Berkshire border. To many of those who come its most interesting possession will be a small brick and flint house, among tumbledown barns and apple-trees. It is called Finche's Farm, and the house is said to have belonged to Sir Isaac Newton. The church is one of the many in which is chalk still good and strong after 700 or 800 years. It is in the piers of a 12th and 13th century arcade, and since the 15th century these chalk piers have borne the weight of the clerestory added in those days. Then also the tower was built with its queer doorway, having a rose and a lily carved in its spandrels. The oak beams of the roof are 500 years old, there is a font with sunk arcading, and some of the stalls have 17th century carving.

Bemerton. Ever memorable for being the home of George Herbert who was rector here for only three years, dying of consumption at the age of 40, but in that time made for himself the reputation of the model country parson, whose *Priest to the Temple* is one of the most famous devotional treatises in the English tongue.

He was the fifth son of Sir Richard Herbert of Montgomery Castle and the Lady Magdalen Herbert, a lady of great serenity and charm of whom Dr John Donne wrote:

No Spring, nor Summer beauty hath such Grace
As I have seen in one Autumnall Face.

After a brilliant career at Cambridge he surprised all his friends who predicted for him high honours in the service of the State as a diplomat, by taking Orders and shortly after his marriage (after three days of courtship) he became Rector of Bemerton.

Twice a week he would walk into Salisbury to attend the services in the Cathedral and to join a few friends when his skill on the lute and viol made him welcome.

The church, with its simple wooden bell turret, is much the same as when George Herbert knew it in the 17th century and still seems charged with his spirit:

Seven whole days, not one in seven
I will praise Thee.
In my heart, though not in heaven,
I can raise Thee.
Small it is, in this poor sort
To enrol Thee,
E'en eternity's too short
To extol Thee.

Near the altar are four windows given by admirers of George Herbert 300 years after his death. He is shown standing by Salisbury Cathedral with a lute under his arm, with his friend Nicholas Ferrar standing by his little church at Little Gidding in Huntingdonshire and holding the manuscript of Herbert's *Poems* which the author left to him to publish.

Berwick Bassett. Sheltered by Hackpen Hill, it lies in the fine country round Marlborough.

In the church the font, fashioned 600 years ago, has arcading with leaves springing from the capitals and unfolding on the cusps; the chancel screen, carved in oak by a 15th century carpenter has an archway with roses and fleur-de-lys and exquisitely carved spandrels, with a leaf pattern on the cresting; the delicate tracery is lovely and the screen is supported by panelled buttresses. In the floor of the chancel is a brass to William Bayley in Mass vestments. The tower is 14th century with an embattled top. The nave is a century younger, and its walls are built of broken sarsen stones, those hard greywethers scattered in thousands over the great prehistoric plain of Wiltshire, the stones we see at Stonehenge, and on which Windsor Castle stands.

Among the great barns by the church stands an old farmhouse shadowed by a fine ilex tree. The house is plastered, but under the plaster is the herringbone brickwork and timbering of Tudor times.

Berwick St James. The Normans built its church with flint and stone and gave it the central tower with round-headed windows. The Norman doorway in the porch has fine zigzag mouldings, scalloped capitals on the round pillars, and a straight stone carved with diamonds across the bottom of the tympanum. The font is also Norman. The stone pulpit has simple carved niches with shields in them; it is about 500 years old. The roof of the nave has fine moulded timbers resting on stone corbels carved with faces. The south chapel, built in the 13th century, is approached through a round arch, and has for its altar an old carved chest. A mass dial is on the walls.

A 13th century chalice belonging to this church is in the British Museum.

Berwick St John. Here on the Downs on a dark winter's night we may hear the church bell ringing; it is the idea of John Gane, a vicar who left a small bequest in the 18th century so that the bell could be rung for fifteen minutes every winter's night to guide lost travellers. On these bare downs is Winklebury entrenchment, an earthwork with a rampart 40 feet high, from which one can see into Hampshire and Dorset, and on a very clear day ships sailing in the Solent.

The 13th century church has a beautiful 15th century tower with pinnacles, gargoyles, and lovely pierced stone windows. The parapet is bçautifully panelled. A battered stone coffin lies in the churchyard. There is also a mass dial.

In the church are tombs with canopies, one with fine foliated decoration for Sir John de Hussey and Sir Robert Lucie. There is a wall tablet to one of the greatest seamen of our time, Admiral Fisher, who used to live here. By the altar is a carved chair, with birds pecking bunches of fruit.

Berwick St Leonard. A beautiful and stately sycamore tree, growing in the kitchen garden of a farmhouse near the little church, is all that is left to show where once stood the old home of the Howe family, under whose roof William of Orange spent one night in 1688 before he came to the English throne. In the church is an unusual marble wall monument, with reliefs of George Howe with his wife and their three children.

Biddestone. It has the very spirit of Wiltshire, for never was a county where the homes of the people fitted more perfectly into Nature's scene. Their walls and roofs are of the grey Cotswold stone, the old stone tiles, the heavy thatch, the little dormers and the stately gables, with here and there an oriel and here and there a group of lovely chimneys.

And Biddestone has builded well and laid itself out like a picture. It has a wealth of trees, a cross and a pond on the green, a village pump under a charming conical roof, a fine old barn, delightful houses everywhere and one set back from the road for all to see behind its sweeping lawn and its trimmed hedges.

The church has a Norman doorway, its capitals leaning a little and a cross carved within the arch. The deep font with faces sculptured at the base is also Norman, and the two chancel arches were made when the Norman influence in building was passing away. The nave is filled with box pews.

Bishop's Cannings. Running down the great road from Wansdyke to Stonehenge, the eye catches sight of the church spire rising from a hollow in the trees.

The church rises to a great height from the low grey-green roof of the aisles, its pinnacled battlements standing out against the sky. All round the battlements are sculptured heads. One facing west has a double face—one merry and one sad, as if to typify the two halves of the world. All over the walls are small faces and there is also an old mass dial. There is a tiny skull outside the porch and inside the nave more heads carved on the corbel brackets. In the south chapel, over a 16th century tomb, is a little figure carved in stone with a tasselled cap, seeming to spring from a mass of leaves, and over the altar close by is a helmet crested with a small bearded man like a pirate, a gold handkerchief with black bands round his head.

The church belongs to most of the periods of medieval architecture, the 12th century starting it, the 15th century crowning its tower with a spire 130 feet high. Below the spire are lancet windows with small heads above them, and grotesque creatures look down from the parapet.

The very fine entrance to the porch is rich in 14th century moulding and panelled pinnacles, and slender pillars with leafy capitals carry the plain arch of the doorway. The vaulted stone roof of the porch, carrying a room above, has an exquisitely carved boss in the centre. In the vaulting of the tower are dragons, birds, faces, and foliage.

The nave has fine arcades, borne on columns with a plain moulded ring and capitals of many patterns; and there are big traceried clerestory windows, a triple lancet window with leaf-crowned pillars and a dark timber roof borne on the heads of bishops and kings. The delicately beautiful lancets of the nave are repeated in the transepts, which are entered through lovely arches. On one of the lancets is an ape.

There is a queer old almsbox with three locks, set on a post, and a curious old chair like a small box-pew, with a high back on which is painted a hand with outstretched fingers and a Latin inscription which may be freely translated:

Thy heir will seldom do anything for thee . . .
Wealth shall vanish; what thou hast another shall have.

The long and low chancel has a stone-vaulted roof with rich floral bosses, the fragment of a canopy with a man's curly head once belonging to the sedilia, a piscina with two pillars supporting its basin, and a doorway into a sacristy lit by tiny lancets and leading up to a room above.

In the Ernle chapel, with an Elizabethan table for an altar, lie John and Edward Ernle, John with his arms carved on the top of a low canopy under which is a tiny face in an elaborate frame; Edward set amid columns and beautiful heraldic carving.

Bishop's Cannings owes its music every Sunday to a village boy who sailed round the world with Captain Cook; he was William Bayley, and an inscription on a wood panel relates that he gave the church its organ and endowed it with a small fund for an organist.

To those who love to seek and find our oldest monuments the most dramatic point in Bishop's Cannings will be by the solitary cottage known as Shepherds Shore, a point of the Marlborough-to-Devizes road where is seen the best section of Wansdyke, the marvellous earthwork probably built after the Roman occupation.

Mounting the slope towards Morgans Hill, with the solitary group of trees capping the Downs, one meets the abandoned road to Bath, and a few hundred yards farther, past two lonely barrows, a spot where the grandeur of the great earthwork suddenly comes upon us. At the foot is the site of a camp, with a bank round it. The depth from the parapet to the silted-up ditch must be thirty feet, and very steep. It is at this point that Wansdyke is more imposing than on any other road. Here its course can be traced both ways for miles over the Downs, with curve after curve until the great wall is lost in the distance. The Lansdowne Column which crowns the great natural amphitheatre of Cherhill is visible from here, but the white horse on which its shadow falls is on the hidden side of the hill.

Bishopstone. Under the great Downs near Wilton the River Ebble wanders through its meadows, turning the wheel of a small mill. Beeches screen the 14th century church.

The lofty chancel, almost as big as the nave, has a vaulted roof, the ribs spring in groups from carved corbels and spreading out to meet in beautiful bosses, sculptured with a bird in a nest, angels, foliage, and a bearded head of God the Father. The lovely east window has on each side a tall niche framed with wood. There is a sedilia with a rich canopy with heavy pinnacles and charming faces; and the handsome panelling behind the altar is pierced with two recesses. Over it are carved wood canopies. In the sanctuary is an old armchair carved with a tree. A delightful feature of the church is the number of carved faces of men and women indoors and out, and there is also a mass dial. The south transept has a fine stone roof with beautiful bosses. Here, too, are fine traceried windows, an exquisite canopied niche, and the elaborate tomb of a rector who gave the chancel its carved woodwork. He is remembered for his good life as well as for his sad death; he was killed by the falling of some vaulting in East Grafton church in 1842.

It was this rector, George Augustus Montgomery, who gave the remarkable pulpit, said to have come from Spain. In the north transept is a canopied piscina, a 14th century tomb, and in a recess the figure of a white-bearded man who died in 1612, wearing a black gown, cap, and ruff, and holding a handkerchief.

Outside the south transept, a little cloister with a vaulted roof.

Bishopstone. In a hollow of the Downs on the Berkshire border near Swindon. A village of thatch and trees with a pond filled from a stream flowing by the church. The church has a richly carved Norman doorway built up in the chancel wall and the village blacksmith's old clock kept in the tower. It keeps time no more, but it went on ticking for 238 years after the blacksmith made it. It would be telling the time for Charles Curtis, who died here about 100 years ago and crossed the Atlantic six times, living for 31 years in Antigua. Coming home he was nearly shipwrecked and we read that for his preservation for another 16 years "he daily offered up his thanks."

The old north door of 1689 opens into a porch with two roughly carved windows. Above the south door are three of the most curious faces we have seen, all with eyes very much awake, and one in a high hat and a sort of cravat with a face long drawn-out between them. Above the pulpit is a prim and curious figure of the Madonna looking down on the preacher, with a jester in his cap looking across to her from the chancel arch. Peter with his keys is looking from one of the windows in old glass, and there are other old fragments with heraldic badges and canopies. There is a passage and a squint from the aisle into the chancel, and a Norman font bowl.

Bishopstrow. Here the Romans came and built a house, and here the Saxons built a church. Both have disappeared, and what remains is a church refashioned in the 18th century, with a tower started by the Normans, finished in the 15th century, and crowned with a modern spire. The tower has battlements, gargoyles, narrow windows, and an arch with clustered columns. An armchair in the sanctuary has panels with delicate tracery.

Under a yew on the Salisbury road Cromwell is said to have breakfasted on his way across the Downs after the Battle of Newbury; and in Eastleigh Wood King Alfred is said to have camped after his defeat by the Danes at Wilton about 800 years before.

Blunsdon St Andrew. This tiny place in the hills not far from Swindon has managed to keep part of its 13th century church. We see the old stone pictures in doorways, arches, and corbels, of folk who lived in England 600 years ago, among them a bishop and two women with the fashionable headdresses of their day. The ancient font is here with a 17th century cover, and fragments of medieval glass show the heads of two saints and of the Madonna with golden flowers and stars and crowns round her. In fine modern glass she appears again, with St Peter and St Andrew.

Boscombe. The famous theologian Richard Hooker, and one of the most learned men the Church of England has ever known, was rector here in the 16th century and the vicarage still incorporates part of the old house in which he wrote four volumes of his *Ecclesiastical Polity*.

Here it was, according to Isaac Walton, that two of Hooker's old pupils visited their erstwhile tutor and found him compassed about with "those corroding cares that attend a married clergyman in a country parsonage," having been set by Mrs Hooker to mind the sheep while the servant usually engaged in that employment was taken off for some other domestic function. But Richard Hooker was neglecting his duties, the sheep had wandered abroad and his pupils discovered him seated on the grass translating the Odes of Anacraeon.

The pulpit in the church is a generation too late for Richard Hooker to have preached from it for it is dated 1633. In the nave there are pews of about the same date. In the chancel there are fragments of old glass and there is a Norman font.

Box. It is the last place in Wiltshire on the road to Bath. In the church is a 12th century effigy under a small vaulted roof, sheltered in a recess of the wall.

The 15th century tower has a spire rising in an open arcading, and there are two pleasant windows showing Simeon in the Temple with the Child and Mary carrying doves in a cage; and one showing the Resurrection with the three crosses silhouetted on the skyline and the three Marys arriving at the tomb. The 15th century font is carved with roses.

In the street is a little old lock-up with hundreds of iron studs in its door.

Boyton. In the Wylye valley and the home of the Gifford family who were established here soon after the Norman Conquest. In the 13th century church the chantry chapel for Alexander Gifford was built by his brother Godfrey, Bishop of Worcester and Lord Chancellor of England (1266). Another brother Walter became Archbishop of York. The effigy of Alexander shows him in chain mail and a surcoat. At his feet an otter which is holding the point of his scabbard in its teeth.

A headless skeleton found in a tomb in this church is thought to be that of John Gifford executed in 1322 for his share in a rising led by Thomas Plantagenet who was also executed.

In the centre of the chantry chapel is a table tomb with canopied niches believed to be that of Lady Margaret, the last of the Giffords.

The epitaph on the south wall of the chancel for Samuel Routh, Rector, 1822, was written by his elder brother, Martin Joseph Routh, President of Magdalen College, Oxford, for 63 years, who died in his hundredth year in 1854.

Bradenstoke. It stands on the top of a hill looking over the Avon Valley to the Cotswolds, with Chippenham not far away. It has a modern church, with a broken shaft of an old cross on three tiers of steps. The ruins of the priory are built into the walls of a farmhouse. The remains of the great barn and guesthouse were removed in 1930 to St Donat's Castle in Glamorgan.

A little way off are ancient earthworks on Clack Hill.

Bradford-on-Avon. It has two bridges, the most complete Saxon church in England, one of the finest medieval barns existing anywhere, and one of the noblest Tudor houses.

One approaches the town from the hills and suddenly as into the bottom of a basin, down to one of the most curious bridges in the land, with buildings huddled up in narrow streets all round.

The houses go climbing up the hill so that no horse or car can follow them, and are reached by steps, as in the hilltowns of Italy or in one of the small hamlets behind the French Riviera. Tucked away among these houses on the highest point of the town there is a tiny chapel seeming to be part of the cottages about it. It was dedicated to St Mary centuries ago, but it fell from grace in the passing of time and a hundred years ago it was one of Bradford's 30 factories. Today St Mary's is a chapel again. It has a canopied niche in the east wall and a 15th century window.

Looking down from these terraces in 1858 the Vicar of Bradford noticed what appeared to be a small church hidden among the houses below. He looked into the matter and found that, according to the Chronicler William of Malmesbury, there was a Saxon church at Bradford dedicated to St Lawrence, and in 12 years there was rescued from a mass of buildings the purest Saxon church in England, founded by Aldhelm and standing as it stood nearly 1000 years ago.

With its strong stone walls, the simplicity of its proportions, its elegant pilasters and arcading and the winged angels it was an outstanding example of architecture and sculpture which even the Norman builders must have come to see. Yet on that day in 1858, when the vicar noticed the shape of a cross among the roofs, this Saxon temple was lost among its neighbours. The chancel had been made into a cottage with two storeys, the chimney running up by the arch. The nave was a school, and the schoolmaster lived in a house built up against it. A wool factory butted on to the west wall. For 150 years the church was lost; 100 years before Waterloo it was mentioned in a deed as the Skull House, into which they threw dead men's bones. It was 1870 before the widow in the cottage, the children in the school, the headmaster in his house, and the wool merchant in his factory were all out of the way, and these ancient walls were open again to the light of the sun and the eyes of men; and when they were all revealed Professor Freeman went to see it and declared it to be an almost untouched example of a church of the end of the 7th century. A new interest grew in this old place, which is considered by experts to be 11th and not 7th century.

It is naked and bare, and all the better for that. It is as high as it is long, and twice as high as it is wide. Its chancel arch is the narrowest in England, 3 feet 6. The nave is 25 feet by 13 feet 8; the chancel is 13 feet 4 by 10 feet 2. There is a plinth projecting two inches all round the walls, which are 2 feet 5 inches thick and built of rough and ready stones of all sizes and shapes, laid anyhow with no straight lines, and some of the stones two feet long. The outside walls and the gabled roofs are delightful. Up the walls run dainty pilasters which are part of the structure, and round the walls above the stringcourse run Saxon arches in relief. All this is not decoration added later, but the work of Saxon masons cutting into the face of the finished wall to beautify the temple.

The north porch of this little church is almost as big as the chancel, and the fact that the doorway is not centred suggests that there may have been an altar or a font in the porch. Coming into the nave it is the height of the walls that impresses us. All the doorways are square, and left with their rough stone. Three windows retain their primitive form, and the chancel window is original. High up in the wall above the chancel arch, removed from their original position, are two remarkable figures of angels, sculptured in low relief. They are lying down with great wings outstretched, as if they were flying towards each other, draperies flowing, and hands veiled. It is believed that they may have been part of a Crucifixion scene. When Canon Jones found them in 1858 they were placed over a wooden arch which had been erected as an entrance to the building on the west side, but the canon stated that they had been found embedded in the wall, one on each side of the chancel arch. The figures are in reversed positions and measure about 3 feet 6 in length. They are such figures as are to be found on the ivory covers of the Gospels in early days, or in illuminated Saxon manuscripts.

In the nave are fragments of stones that may, for all we know, have been worked on before England was a nation. It is thought that some of them may have belonged to the shrine in which the bones of the Saxon king Edward were kept, he who was murdered at Corfe Castle and was buried at Shaftesbury, where his coffin may be seen. There is a stone coffin in which a Saxon child was laid.

We pass from Saxon England and cross the road into the church the Normans started and the English builders extended and transformed. It is a church of many fine possessions, with a Norman window over the porch. Through the thick wall of the chancel a peephole to the altar runs for about 20 feet, one of the longest in England, and in it is a fragment of a 13th century gravestone. On the wall below this peephole are three fragments of brass, which are all that is left to remind us of the 15th century merchant Thomas Horton and his wife Mary. They are tiny figures about 12 inches high; on the brass is Thomas Horton's merchant's mark. Above the brass is a fragment smaller still with a picture of the Trinity as the medieval artist conceived it: God with the Crucifixion between His knees, a Dove resting on it—Father, Son, and Spirit. Before the altar is a brass of Anne Lately, her two children with her. She lies between two tombs, a sculptured urn by Rysbrack and a 17th century monument in memory of the son of a Dean of Westminster. Below these are two ancient recesses, in one of which a lady lies in a simple robe, in the other a 14th century knight in armour, lying under an arch adorned with the heads of a king and a bishop and two small ladies in wimples. There is also a 17th century brass of Anne Longe. The chancel has iron gates leading into it and here still is the fine door which once led to the roodloft steps.

On the wall of the nave is one of the loveliest fragments of sculpture in Wiltshire, the portrait of a 13th century lady, with curls in her hair, and her hands clasped.

In the west wall is the tomb of William Baily, who died in the days of Queen Anne. Along the top of the canopy run hourglasses, cross-bones, and skulls. Close by his tomb hangs a panel of painted oak on which it is easy to see, after 400 years, the figures of two monks writing. It was part of the old roodloft and now hangs by the fine oak screen to the tower. The font is 15th century, and a little later is a precious volume preserved in the church, one of the first printed Bibles.

One of the windows to the nave is rich with 28 medallions of old glass, seven of them with enamel figures of 1630, and 21 with Bible scenes of 1760. The Bible scenes show the Flight into Egypt, with Joseph looking back anxiously, and picture stories from the Gospels leading up to the betrayal and Gethsemane; and the charming enamel pictures show St Barbara, St John, and St Mary, Jesus and His Mother, Jael and the Woman of Thebes, both of whom slew tyrants and set their people free.

Outside the church, in the shade of the tower and by his own front door, lies Edward Orpin, known to everybody in Bradford for half of last century, and known to our National Gallery as the Parish Clerk of Gainsborough's favourite picture. He lived at the Jacobean house in front of his grave, and he was parish clerk of this place for 40 years.

The town has a group of fine old houses. The chantry by the church is 15th century with 17th and 18th century additions; the Priory was for 100 years the home of the ancestors of Lord Methuen, pioneers of cloth-making. The house now used as a school, Kingwell Court, is a magnificent structure of 150 years ago. Westbury House, now the civic offices, is a handsome building once threatened by a mob, which gathered outside it in 1791 to protest against machinery being introduced into the mill owned by a man living here; the machinery was given to the mob, who destroyed it by fire on the bridge close by. It was in this house that Richard Bethell was born in 1800. He was Lord Chancellor Westbury. He used to say that from his teens he had supported himself by his own exertions, and long before he was 40 he was making £20,000 a year at the bar. He had a bitter tongue, but his judgments were declared to be perfect as examples of precise statement and lucid reasoning expressed in fine English. But his career was full of incidents which injured his popularity, for he had great power of sarcasm and used it without pity. A judge once appealed to him to remember that a judge was at least a vertebrate animal, and of a sentence passed by Convocation he told the bench of bishops that their judgment was "a well-lubricated set of words—a sentence so oily and saponaceous that no one can grasp it," and he warned them that whenever they were tempted to go beyond their proper limits their best security would be to gather up their garments and flee, and, remembering the Pillar of Salt, not to cast a look behind.

In the marketplace is a building known as the town hall which was never a town hall, a fine stone structure built in the middle of last century.

But the house incomparable is The Hall, a marvellous contrast to the quaint gabled houses and timbered fronts of the narrow streets through which we climb to reach it. It was built by John Hall, a cloth merchant who flourished in the days of Shakespeare, and as we see it from its garden it is a spectacle of wondrous beauty not to be matched for miles round. No more perfect piece of Elizabethan domestic architecture has survived, and it was used as a model for the British pavilion at a Paris Exhibition.

Across the old bridge is another famous place, a barn set up before the Tudors, almost as old as the bridge itself, which is 13th century, with two arches of that time and seven of the 15th century, and with stones added at the widening 300 years ago. The oldest arches are shaped as the Normans may have shaped them in a bridge before this. The curious lock-up on the bridge (once a chapel) is 250 years old and has a domed roof of stone with a copper fish over it known as the Bradford Gudgeon. It is centuries old, and for generations it was said in Bradford of a man who had been in this prison, that he had been under the fish and over the water. Among those who spent an uncomfortable night in one of the two cells was John Wesley.

This old bridge was here in the days when they built the barn to which all travellers come. It was in the first year of our second millennium (the year 1001) that Bradford was given to the Abbey of Shaftesbury, and Bradford grew so rich that early in the 14th century they built its great tithe barn, one of the biggest now existing in England, a magnificent spectacle. The Wiltshire Archaeological Society has given it to the nation. It is 55 yards long and 10 yards wide, with 14 great bays and 4 projecting gabled porches; and gigantic timbers bear up the span of its roof, which spreads itself over 10,000 square feet. This vast roof is built of stone tiles, and there must be 30,000 of them, weighing about a hundred tons. All through these centuries this great weight has been borne by these selfsame timbers, supported on walls strengthened by buttresses. Some of the timber of the great doors has been in its place 600 years, and there are still plainly seen a bow and arrow among the mason's marks; it is near one of the south porches. The way to the barn is across the fields, and close by is a little bridge as old as the barn.

Bratton. On the Downs above this tree-sheltered village is a great white horse 180 feet long, 107 feet high, and with an eye 25 feet round. It was remodelled in 1778, when Lord Abingdon changed it from a heavy horse to one of the lighter kind, but it was first cut out of the turf, it is believed, to celebrate Alfred's victory over the Danes. It is the oldest white horse in Wiltshire, perhaps as old as the white horse of Berkshire. When the Danes retreated after

Bradford-on-Avon: the bridge.

Bradford-on-Avon: the Saxon church.

Bradford-on-Avon: the tithe barn.

this battle they climbed the Downs and took refuge behind the ramparts of Bratton Castle, an ancient camp of 23 acres protected by a double row of earthworks rising in parts 35 feet high. The views of the valley are very fine from the camp.

The church stands on a hillside by itself, with a background of beautiful trees. It is reached by about 180 steps that go steeply down one hill before climbing up; and well worth the climb it is. Seven centuries old, it is one of the most charming small churches in the country.

The 15th century tower has a stair-turret and is embattled like the aisles, and all have big gargoyles. Inside we are delighted by the compactness of the structure and the unity of design. The arcades rest on clustered columns; the tower arches grouped in the centre are plain and dignified and carried on charming piers. The ceiling of the tower is vaulted and has carved floral bosses, and kings and bishops sculptured on the corbels. The chancel is severely true to 13th century tradition; the north transept delights us with its corbel angels, either playing musical instruments or carrying shields; and in the porch and transept are traces of Norman masonry.

Bremhill. Memorable is the home of the parson-poet William Lisle Bowles who was rector for nearly 50 years in the first part of the 19th century. As a poet he is mainly remembered for the encouragement he gave to other poets rather than for his own efforts in verse although his Sonnets, first published in 1788, ran into nine editions.

He was a notable character, rich in eccentricity. Wordsworth, Charles Lamb, Tom Moore and many other literary friends stayed with him at his vicarage which still has the terrace where he set up a few stones from Stanley Abbey, the only Cistercian Monastery in Wiltshire, and as a diversion Bowles provided a few sheep in an ornamental capacity that wandered hither and thither in front of the terrace wearing bells tuned in fourths and fifths.

He was always much in demand at Lord Lansdowne's house at Bowood where he was regarded as a social asset as he could always be relied upon to do or to say something out of the ordinary. Once at a house party at Bowood when hurrying to greet Madame de Staël he fell and severely injured his arm. She expressed a proper concern but Bowles staggered to his feet saying that he would have been happy to endure even greater pain in order to see so great a curiosity!

When, towards the end of his life, he was appointed to a Prebendal stall in Salisbury Cathedral he carefully measured the height of the spire and its distance from his prebendal house to be sure that he would be safe if the spire fell.

The 13th century church is said to have Saxon work in the tower. The chancel arch and the nave arcades have been rebuilt from the 13th century materials; the porch is 15th century and has a vaulted roof with a room over it. One of the buttresses has a scratch dial, one of the early village clocks. The chancel has a barrel roof of oak and plaster. There are carved heads of a king and a bishop on the arches, both 13th century, and round the stringcourse on the outside walls is an extraordinary company of grotesques; a corner buttress has a monster showing a fine set of teeth. The fine font is older than all this carving, for it is Norman, and has six bands of moulding round it.

The windows have some old heraldic glass, figures of St George, St Aldhelm, and King Alfred, and a window with three saints celebrates a vicar's jubilee, 50 years in this pulpit. Many of the carved pews have ancient linenfold panels let into them, and the pulpit is splendidly carved in stone with an elegant arcade.

There is a marble monument to George Hungerford, showing his bust among the cherubs and crossbones and skulls; one cherub has a fiddle, one a harp, and another a skull, and another has its hand on something like an owl.

Many of the epitaphs in the churchyard are the work of William Lisle Bowles and it was for a sundial in this churchyard that the poet-vicar wrote:

So passes silent o'er the dead thy shade,
Brief Time; and hour by hour and day by day
The pleasing pictures of the present fade
And like the summer vapour steal away.

Enough, if we may wait in calm content
The hour that bears us to the silent sod;
Blameless improve the time that Heaven has lent,
And leave the issue to Thy will, O God.

Bremhill is famous not only for William Lisle Bowles, but also for Maud Heath. She was a widow at Langley Burrell 500 years ago and used to tramp each week to Chippenham market selling her butter and eggs. Weary of the terrible road, full of holes and ruts, she saved all her life and left all her worldly goods in 1474 to make a pavement to Chippenham. It is one of the best country pavements in England, still known as Maud Heath's Causeway, and it runs from Wick Hill in this parish through Kellaways hamlet and Langley Burrell village, until it reaches the town. At Kellaways it runs on a bridge of 64 arches, and a stone pillar tells the story of the pavement. A pillar was set up in 1698, and on it are the stern words "Injure me not"; on another side, with a sundial, the passer-by is reminded that the hour is only lent to him. The column with a statue of Maud Heath was set up last century by Parson Bowles and Lord Lansdowne, with the words:

From this Wick Hill begins the praise
Of Maud Heath's gift to these highways.

Brinkworth. It was once the home of the family of William Penn, whose grey stone house is now on a farm and is called Penn Lodge; and its rectory was the home of that good man Tobias Crisp, "harmless of all evil, zealous and fervent of all good." He came here in 1627 and was persecuted for his Puritan principles and driven from his living. He was driven to London, where he caught smallpox and died.

Part of Tobias' rectory remains. It has a brick and timber wing, mainly Tudor, but with parts believed to be 600 years old. The church is 500 years old and has gargoyles on its embattled tower, and an old scratch dial.

Tobias Crisp's pulpit is simply carved with a canopy supported by the lion and the unicorn and the words: Woe unto me if I preach not the Gospel. The brackets supporting the pulpit were old when they were put here, and they are remarkable. In the centre are two roaring lions and at the sides are serpents with wings and heads of birds. Chained to a small desk by the pulpit is a finely bound copy of Foxe's Book of Martyrs, put here in memory of poor Tobias by a member of his family.

In the sanctuary, which has a window of Michael and Elizabeth of Hungary, is a black oak table with ten legs carved with flowers. The roof of the nave is handsome with moulded timbers. There is a 17th century panelled gallery with a traceried screen below it. The tall and beautiful font with a Jacobean cover is 15th century. There is an ancient chest, and in the walls are still the remains of the rood-loft stairs and two peepholes for the altar.

Britford. A tiny place in the Avon valley, it was chosen by the Saxons for a church which has become to us one of their landmarks in architecture. There are still in its walls Roman bricks they used. They made the south doorway and the nave, and the two remarkable Saxon arches at the end of the nave, which opened into chapels that have now disappeared. It would seem that a new Saxon development can be traced to its origin here. The Saxon work was often crude; but at Britford we have the earliest example known of a moulding which might have been done hundreds of years later than it was done. It is a projection running up the north doorway and continuing round the arch, and we can see what it must have looked like over a thousand years ago. Also in this north arch seems to have started the practice of panelling the inside of an arch, the soffit. The ornament on the outer panels is bold and rigid, scrolls enclosing bunches of grapes. The inner row has a complex pattern of interlacing. All this carving was done soon after the death of Alfred, possibly by men who fought under his flag. It is beautiful and elaborate work, a contrast to the Saxon arch opposite, which is of plain though mellow Roman brick.

The fine pulpit is Jacobean, with cherubs in its panels, a dove with an olive branch, quaint trees, and a head with a sword in its teeth. By the pulpit is a great wooden chest about 500 years old, strongly bound with iron. Two old finials are all that remain of the original choir stalls, and one is carved with a barrel. The ancient stone altar is embedded under the altar, and guarded in a glass case is a Bible printed in 1582 and bound up with a 17th century prayer book. By the case are two old tiles dug up in the churchyard. On a windowsill is a pathetic little stone figure carved about 600 years ago. He holds a cup in his hands and wears a long robe; it is a lovely piece of work found embedded in a transept wall.

The chancel has a splendid altar tomb under an elaborate arch carved with fruit and foliage and decorated with small stone figures in niches: St Mary Magdalene with a pot of ointment, St Catherine with her wheel, St George and a tiny dragon, a bishop, and two angels bearing the ducal arms. It was long supposed that this rich tomb was the resting-place of the Duke of Buckingham who lost his head in the marketplace at Salisbury after supporting the blood-stained Richard the Third on his march through murder to the throne. But this is not so. The tomb was brought here from another site about the end of the 18th century, and it is not known whose tomb it is for it contained no body.

The church register mentions a double tragedy of 1653, for a woman buried in the churchyard died from a box on the ear at Salisbury Fair, and the woman who struck the fatal blow was hanged. There are two old houses near the church, one a farmhouse and the other with a moat running round its lawn.

LONGFORD CASTLE, one of the finest houses in Wiltshire, stands beautifully by the Avon in a park of 250 acres. The fronts of the house and two of its five round towers are much as they were when Sir Thomas Gorges completed them in 1591. He had been persuaded by his Danish wife to build the house on the lines of a famous triangular castle in Denmark, but his money ran out, and it seemed as if it would never be finished. Fortunately a galleon of the Spanish Armada was wrecked when Sir Thomas was Governor of Hurst Castle, and his wife begged the hull from Queen Elizabeth, and with the treasure she found in the wreck the castle was completed. It was designed by John Thorpe, architect of Holland House in Kensington, and Sir Philip Sidney introduced it into his Arcadia as the Castle of Amphialeus. The Gorges family was here for half a century and then the castle became the property of Lord Coleraine in whose time it was used as a garrison for the Royalist Cavalry, surrendering to the Parliament men in 1645. Cromwell spared it and early in the 18th century it was bought by Sir Edward Bouverie, ancestor of the Earl of Radnor who now lives here. Longford Castle has been much altered since its early days, but its curious triangular plan can still be seen.

The picture collection is one of the best in the country, with many Old Masters, including famous works by Velasquez, Murillo, Rubens, Van Dyck, Claude, Gainsborough, and Reynolds. One of the most treasured paintings here is the portrait of Erasmus which Holbein brought to England with a letter of introduction to Sir Thomas More. In the long gallery is the Imperial Steel Chair. Made in 1575 in the Bavarian city of Augsburg, and presented by that city to the Emperor Rudolph, it was treasured by him in Prague and lost to that city in the Thirty Years War, when Gustavus Adolphus took it to Sweden, where it was bought for Longford by the Earl of Radnor at the end of the 18th century. The chair is a marvel of the metalworker's art, containing over 130 little scenes, each with a group of figures representing events in the history of Rome and the Holy Roman Empire, from the landing of Aeneas after the destruction of Troy.

The magnificent formal garden is surrounded by a wonderful yew hedge pierced with arches, and beyond is the riverside terrace, where the peaceful Avon winds among lawns and lovely meadows. Hereabouts the Avon and the Ebele meet in a spot where masses of roses bloom among the trees, near a summerhouse built in the year 1745.

Brixton Deverill. In the churchyard propped against the tower is part of a mightly coffin made of Wiltshire stone. It tapers, and is shaped for the head. The church was built 700 years ago. There is a charming chancel arch with a beaded moulding resting on clustered columns. The tower is 15th century, and has a parapet and pinnacles. In the sanctuary is a pair of old armchairs, their backs carved with flowers and foliage.

Broad Chalke. It was given a thousand years ago by a Saxon king to the abbess of a convent, and it would be a noble gift still, watered by the Ebele, graced by willows, and sheltered by smooth downs. Its spacious 13th century church stands on foundations older than itself; its central tower is 15th century and rests on an imposing group of pointed arches; its vaulted roof has stone ribs springing from bosses carved with a dragon, some faces, and a hare and hounds.

The great stone porch, sculptured with strange monsters and sprays of foliage, is 15th century, and the heavy door with an old iron handle-plate has been swinging for many generations. There are two fine roofs, one old and one new. The old one is the trussed rafter roof in the north transept; the other covers the nave, and, though new, rests on beautiful old corbels carved with singing and playing angels. It has handsome wooden bosses from the 15th century roof which covered the nave before it. The old pulpit and reading desk are carved with foliage and beautifully panelled. There are two old chests, and in the sanctuary is a graceful old chair. A lovely piece of 15th century work is the font, its panels vigorously carved with Tudor roses, heraldry, shells, and flowers.

Here was born soon after Quuen Anne died Robert Bateman Wray, a craftsman who became famous in his day for his engraving on jewels. There is a brass to the memory of Maurice Hewlett, a Surrey boy born at Weybridge in 1861, who in his boyhood lived at Farningham in Kent, and went to Sevenoaks Grammar School. The Darent Valley loved by William Blake was familiar to him, and indeed he had much of William Blake's tender delight in the countryside. He was famous at 37, when his first novel, *The Forest*

Lovers, appeared, and he went on writing historical romances such as *Richard Yea-and-Nay* and the *Queen's Quair*. But he felt himself to be chiefly a poet, and in his essays and poems he best showed his deep love of what a friend has called "the English peasantry as the only hope for England." What he would himself like to think his masterpiece is his Song of the Plow, a long poem tracing the story of agricultural labourers in England from the days of the Conqueror. It is to this that the brass in the church refers when it tells us that he sang of the Creation and about mankind.

Broad Hinton. It has one of the six white horses of Wiltshire, 90 feet long and 90 feet high, which has been here since the beginning of the Victorian Era, when it was cut in the turf by the parish clerk; it is a little way out of the village on the Downs between Swindon and Marlborough.

Just inside the door of the church is the tomb of Sir Thomas Wroughton, with effigies of himself, his wife, and their four sons and four daughters. The great stone canopy is decked with death's heads and crossbones and there are curious figures leaning on hourglasses.

One of the two tombs in the chancel is to an earlier William Wroughton who built the manor house and lies under a canopy delicately sculptured with bands of carving and cherubs, two winged cherubs holding a shield above him; but the dominating figure of the chancel is Francis Glanville, who fell fighting for his king at Bridgwater in the Civil War. Above all this hangs the colonel's helmet, his gauntlets, and the sword with which he fought.

The recess in which he stands is decorated with a curious relief. There are two oak trees carved on the wall, and between them is a panel with three people in classic dress, one seated and the others seeming to be crowning him. All down the sides of the recess are other panels, in which classic maidens are running and blowing horns, accompanied by a buck, an eagle, and a dolphin, while below is an extraordinary scene—a struggling, emaciated figure of a woman with gyves on her wrists, her face stricken with anguish. While the colonel was fighting for his king Sir John Glanville was burning down the manor house to save it from the Parliament men; he was Speaker of the Short Parliament and has a tablet here. Hanging near it in an old gilt frame is a square of black silk painted with Wellington's crest, the Iron Duke having held the manor here for the last two years of his life.

The nave has a hammerbeam roof of the 17th century, with pierced drop ornaments, and the chancel roof has a set of neat corbels. Both roodloft doorways remain from the days before the Reformation, and set in a wall is the oldest possession of the church, a collection of fragments of Norman carving. The old font is curious for having been painted, and it appears to have been locked against witches 700 years ago. The chancel screen is made from the ancient choir stalls, and the pulpit has linenfold panels. There is a canopied piscina.

Brokenborough. A quaint little village on different levels in the fine country on the Gloucestershire border. Its small church standing on a hill with the Avon winding through the meadows below. Also a great tithe barn.

The most interesting possession of the church is a medallion with the painted head of a fair-haired young man wearing a coronet, the work of a medieval artist, wonderfully clear in spite of its great age. The Norman arches of the nave are leaning; they have two tiny heads on them. The canopied piscina and the brackets on the chancel arch are 13th century, the font is 15th century, the very neat pulpit is Jacobean. The lectern has old oak panels let into it.

Bromham. A fine village with far horizons, it has attractive cottages, a group of almshouses here in Shakespeare's day, and a church looking down on it all. The almshouses have five gables and three pairs of doors, and gardens gay with summer flowers. Wans House in the park is on the site of a Roman station; and Bromham House Farm, which takes the place of the old Bromham House destroyed in the Civil War, said to have been nearly as big as Whitehall Palace.

The church has an elegant 15th century chapel giving it a captivating exterior, with a marvellous parapet battlemented and pinnacled, a corbel table of flowers, and a mass-dial, and a gallery of huge fierce creatures with wide-open mouths and staring eyes, one biting its foot. At the tops of the windows and at the ends of the hoods are winged angels.

The spire is 100 feet high and there is an embattled porch, with fan-vaulting right across the roof, which has a room reached by steps outside, and there are outside steps on another wall.

The roof of the nave has beams resting on stone angels, kings, bishops, and fine ladies, in striking contrast with the grisly carvings on the wall of the tower of skulls balancing hourglasses on their heads and a skeleton wrapped in a shroud. His shroud is opened to show his bones with the memento mori: As I was so are ye; As I am so shall ye be.

The glory of this 15th century church is the lovely lady chapel built by Richard Beauchamp. It is notable inside and out, for it has an embattled and pinnacled parapet decorated with a frieze of flowers, leaves, and heraldic ornament. Over the five handsome windows, with 25 lights, are winged angels carrying shields—one shield is carried by a bird instead of an angel; and there is a charming canopied doorway. Over its east window is a beautiful niche with two beasts below it, and over another window is an angel crowned and carrying a man. Inside, the timber roof of the chapel is painted red, blue, and gold, with 32 shields in the panels. Helmets hang from the roof, and there are niches with exquisite carved canopies and corbels.

In this place lie the Bayntons, or Beauchamps, who lived at the old Bromham House. Rising in the middle of the floor is the tomb of Sir Roger Tocotes, who married Richard Beauchamp's mother after the death of his father. His alabaster effigy shows him with cleanshaven face, wearing 15th century armour and a small cap, his feet on a queer long-snouted creature, and his helmet with traces of blue and green paint. His wife Elizabeth has a handsomely canopied tomb, and under the canopy her portrait brass. She has a graceful headdress and a flowing gown. On the floor is the brass of John Baynton in armour and with long hair, and on the back of the sculptured tomb of Sir Edward Baynton is his brass with two wives and two children.

Under the east window are five plain niches with the names of Bayntons from 1679 to 1921. One of the windows has glass put here by the Bayntons, some of it 14th century, showing flowers, bishops, angels, lions, the Madonna with Christ crucified, and Christ crowned. The angels in the tracery are gems.

One of the three 15th century arches of this chapel is richly decorated with shafts fluted between with roses, and holds a golden screen with ten bays; it opens into the transept remodelled by Richard Beauchamp, with a fine fan-vaulted roof, beautiful bosses, and a handsome central pendant. The font, which appears to be by the same hand, has eight panels divided by ribs ending in hanging bunches of grapes.

A brass tablet in memory of Elizabeth Eyre of 1637, who died in childbirth, puts her fate in this quaint way:

She, dying, left a little heir behind,
Hard-hearted Death herein was somewhat mild:
He took the mother but he spared the child.

Two windows in the church are in memory of the Irish poet Tom Moore who lived at Sloperton Cottage at Chittoe across the valley for 35 years.

The *Irish Melodies*, which he began to publish in 1807, established his reputation as a poet and many of them such as *The Harp That Once in Tara's Halls* are still popular and his *Lalla Rookh* was translated into many languages. He died in 1852 and is buried in this churchyard.

The poet sleeps under a cross 18 feet high. One of its inscriptions is from Byron, who said of him that he was the poet of all circles and the idol of his own. Below the cross are Moore's own lines:

Dear Harp of my country in darkness I found thee,
The cold chain of silence had hung o'er thee long,
When proudly, my own Island Harp, I unbound thee,
And gave all thy chords to light, freedom, and song.

Broughton Gifford. Round the church porch are four great gargoyles, and in it are two richly carved niches with canopies, and two ancient doorways giving access to a room above, which has now disappeared.

On the wall by the door is an extraordinary 16th century brass for Sir Robert Long. He stands behind a table tomb holding a mace, and facing him stands a skeleton with a long arrow. His short cloak is embroidered with lions and lilies, and below this curious engraving is a rhyme playing on Robert Long's name:

The life of man is a true lottery
Where venturous Death draws forth lots, short and long,
Yet free from fraud and partial flattery
He shuffled shields of several size among,
Drew Long, and so drew longer his short days
The Ancient of All Days beyond all time to praise.

Bulford. It is on a sheltered hollow in the bare hills between Salisbury and Pewsey. There are splendid views from Beacon Hill. Along the path made for the fishermen by the river bank, and near to a sudden rise in the track with bushes about it, can be seen, under the water, and only visible when the weeds are cut away, a stone known to everybody hereabouts, one of the great sarsen stones as at Stonehenge. On the hills beyond is another.

Bulford has two churches, the 12th century church of the parish and the 20th century church of the garrison. The chancel arch is Norman, built about 1130, low and plain. The nave walls date from about 1200. The font is 13th century and there are wall paintings in the nave.

On the chancel wall is a brass inscription of 1633 to John Poore, aged three:

A bud that promised fruit, and before 'twas blown
Death nipped it blooming ere the fruit was grown.

The modern garrison church of St George has a simple hammer-beam roof, and the roof of its central tower rises from ribs resting on winged angels. The east window is the peace memorial, very beautiful with our four patron saints and Our Lord rising from the tomb, all in charming colours of blue, green, and gold. Facing it across this great space is the west window, in which Our Lord is enthroned as the Light of the World, sitting in the centre of a wheel with a sceptre in one hand and a book in the other. At the four corners of the window are the emblems of the four winds, and from the centre the rays of light proceed outwards through all the colours of the spectrum, forming a rainbow round the throne. It is a striking conception, and a dazzling spectacle with the sunlight coming through.

Burbage. It is in the Down country of Savernake. The church was rebuilt in the 19th century but its embattled tower has been here about 500 years, looking down now across the green at a row of black and white houses with thatched roofs. There are two fine stone faces at a window, and a curious old tower stairway in a buttress.

A great barn by a farmhouse called Wulfhall stands on the spot on which stood the home of the Seymours of Savernake, where Henry the Eighth came one day to court Sir John Seymour's daughter Jane. He stayed four days and, it is said, so that the king and his suite might have the house to themselves, the Seymours lived in the barn, of which a few feet of original wall remain.

Burcombe. An old Roman settlement, it is a pretty place by the Nadder, with the great Downs behind. The church, mostly from the

14th century, is rare in having its tower lower than the roof of the nave, but it has a greater distinction still, for the east wall of the chancel has Saxon long-and-short work at the corners. It has good panelling, a carved eagle reading desk, a Chippendale table, an old panelled chest, and a chair carved with a mitred bishop. There is an old cup-shaped font, a scratch dial still marks the hours, and on a windowsill is a little stone crucifix from the wall of an old house. A healthy yew about 20 feet round growing in the churchyard is about 500 years old.

Calne. It has grown up along the Bath road.

Coming from London one enters the broad space called the Strand, with the town hall and its clock tower at one end, on one side of the Lansdowne Arms and the great red bacon factory opposite. The hotel has a huge barometer and 17th century windows; the town hall stands on the site of the ancient water mill. Under the Strand flows the River Marden, and it comes into light again behind the town hall. A corner of the river is known as Doctor's Pond because Joseph Priestley, the discoverer of oxygen, is said to have collected gases from water bubbles here during the eight years he lived at Calne cataloguing and indexing manuscripts and books for the Marquis of Lansdowne at Bowood House.

It is best to walk to Calne's fine church along the little street that leads to it giving a view of its tower which was built in the 17th century, and is attributed to Inigo Jones, to replace the one that fell in 1638. The church has great windows, battlements, and tall pinnacles, and a noble spectacle it is in the centre of the town. It looks down on what is perhaps the loveliest bit of Calne out of doors, the curved narrow street which bends round from the church to the green with a fine row of 17th century almshouses built of stone, their windows having small diamond panes of old glass.

Calne has kept in good repair for 25 generations one of Wiltshire's noblest monuments from Norman days, the impressive nave of its church. It is one of the surprises of this countryside. The great arches are richly decorated and bear up a clerestory raised in the 15th century, its fine timber roof with traceried beams which have been resting on great stone heads for 500 years. The beams have about 100 carved bosses. The huge corbel heads so quaintly dressed are by those master craftsmen who made so many hereabouts; they are all the country round, and here are about 20 in the nave and transepts.

In the chancel are two Stuart chairs, and sedilia with angels in the canopies; the reredos is crowded with painted sculpture of the Nativity and the Crucifixion, and the east window has about 70 figures in its scenes. The pulpit has the Twelve Apostles carved in oak. The font has eight carved panels by a 15th century craftsman. In the north transept is an old Stuart bell that will ring no more. The organ is handsomely cased with trumpeting angels and with splendid carvings of birds and flowers, the work of a Kent guild of craftsmen in our time.

One of the small possessions of the church is a lovely Madonna crowning a screen of a chapel in memory of a vicar of 41 years. The screen has open tracery woodwork, simple and beautiful, and on the top of it, sitting so that she can be seen all round, is the Madonna with angels about her and the Three Wise men adoring the Child. She is seated on a globe of the world.

The most remarkable possession of the church is its primitive chest. Made of oak and almost covered with iron bands, it has three locks which have been working for three centuries, and, as if that were not enough, it is embedded in the roughly-hewn trunk of an oak two feet wide and about two feet deep. Close by this extraordinary chest is another fashioned in the 17th century. They are in the north transept.

The two rectors here who became powerful men in the medieval church were Edmund Rich and Robert Grosseteste. Grosseteste, Bishop of Lincoln in the 13th century brought himself in conflict with the pope, defied him so that he was in perpetual fear of excommunication, and left behind him when he died a remarkable number of writings on all sorts of subjects. Edmund Rich preached the 6th crusade in England in 1227, and as Archbishop of Canterbury threatened Henry the Third with excommunication unless he changed his ways.

Bowood House, two miles away from Calne and which has recently been pulled down, was designed (1761–4) for the Earl of Shelburne by Robert Adam who also built the mausoleum in the grounds. A further wing, 100 yards long, was added at the end of the 18th century in imitation of Diocletian's palace at Spalato.

The chapel was added by S. R. Cockerell in 1824 and in 1834–5 further alterations by Sir Charles Barry who designed the main entrance, called the Golden Gates, decorated with reliefs by Musgrave Lewthwaite Watson.

The park extends over 1000 acres with wooded hills and valleys and contains a lake of 40 acres.

Calstone. A sunken walk leads by the high bank of the rectory garden on one side, the rectory looking across lawns to the church in which is the roodloft doorway, now blocked up but still with one of its 500-year-old hinges in the wall. The old rood beam is across the chancel arch, and there are slender old beams in the barrel roof of the nave. The sanctuary windows have a few fragments of old glass, and one has a stone seat. The altar rails are 17th century. The oak reredos in memory of a rector is carved with the Annunciation, four angels and a saint, and the Madonna with the Child holding a little cross. The modern font has a curiously carved Jacobean cover.

Castle Combe. A most beautiful village set in a hollow. The market cross is set on huge stone steps, the remarkable bridge has three primitive arches of rough stones, the 17th century dower house is in the street, and a lovely row of cottages keep company with the church.

The church was extensively restored in the 19th century, but with much left that is old. Round the top of the tower run 76 arches high and low, and climbing up 85 feet go the pinnacles on the buttresses, reaching the parapet and dominating all. Everywhere the exterior is rich and worthy of its setting. The parapet is carved with arches and the pinnacles have about fifty stone heads. The belfry has a stone lattice. Looking down on the roof of the nave is a little mark put there by the cloth merchants who built the tower, a carving of their shuttle and scissors. Inside they gave the tower a fine vaulted roof.

The aisle roofs have gilded bosses of great beauty and elegance, and the stone corbels are remarkable for their individuality. The pillars of the nave arcade have slender columns round them with neat capitals, and between each pair have been carved extraordinary figures of animals, grotesques, and bearded men, one man apparently holding a bat. There are 24 of these figures, all different. The chancel roof is painted blue with gold stars; the chancel arch has a wealth of decoration with six canopied saints between two lines of foliage. The choir stalls have beautiful poppyheads, and four of them have winged angels at prayer and long-haired faces on the armrests. There is an old oak screen with traceried panels and a fine old panelled pulpit. The one attractive window is rare, a great rose window above the chancel arch.

Walter De Dunstanville (1270), whose family built the castle which gave the Combe its name, has his tomb in the church with effigy showing him in full chain armour with angels at his head and a dog at his feet, and six small figures in the panels of the tomb.

The font is a remarkable piece of 13th century work with a stone book-rest, and an extraordinary stem hollowed out with something like knotted rope work. There are heads round the bowl and eight panels with trefoils. The priest's door is one of the smallest in England, only about five feet high and just over two feet wide. There is a heavy old door in the tower, where we noticed a tribute to a parish clerk who was here from the eve of the Crimean War to the eve of World War I, 62 years. A wall monument pays a tribute to two 18th century parents for bringing up six sons and four daughters "decently educated and formed for the world by their industrious care."

Castle Eaton. Its oldest possessions are a Norman doorway with handsome mouldings, and a Norman font boldly carved with flowers. Also a wall painting of the Madonna wearing a white gold-lined hood and a dark red robe. The sanctus bell still remains in its little bell cote which is built of stone and set on the end of a gable, and is 13th century, 200 years earlier in date than the western tower.

One of the two chapels is a war memorial, the other is 14th century and has a filled-in crypt below, of which the small windows can be seen outside above the grass. In this chapel is a canopied piscina and the battered and contorted figure of a bearded man resting his head on his hand.

The Elizabethan pulpit is richly carved and into it have been worked some of the timbers of the old rood screen; the rest of the screen has been made up into the altar. The chancel has a narrow arch with clustered shafts and a pillared piscina, all about 700 years old.

Charlton. A village of charming gables, in the beautiful wooded country near Malmesbury on the edge of Charlton Park; and its church has been here 700 years, though much restored. It has a turreted tower with pinnacles, a sundial over the porch, a nave arcade with four lofty arches and elegant Norman capitals, and an ancient font encircled by two rows of cable moulding and one of tiny carving with little balls. Above the pulpit is a 17th century oak panel carved with the lion and the unicorn, and there is handsome oak screening round the organ, with ten faces carved on it. There is a black and white roof in the chancel.

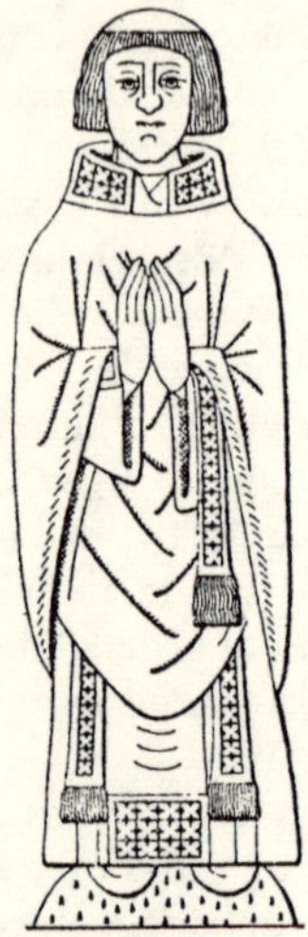

Aldbourne:
Henry Frekylton,
1508

Devizes (St John's): John and Mary Kent, 1630

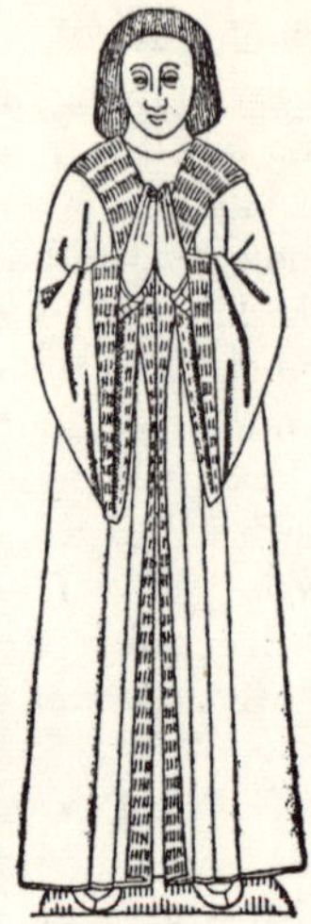

Great Bedwyn:
John Seymour,
1510

Clyffe Pypard:
14th century knight

Charlton St Peter:
William and Mary Chaucey, 1524

Bromham:
John Baynton, 1516

ENGRAVED BRASS PORTRAITS OF WILTSHIRE FOLK

Biddesden House.

Castle Combe.

Above: Westbury. *Top right:* Alton Barnes.
Bottom right: Cherhill

The effigies of Sir Henry Knyvett and his wife lie beneath a canopied tomb with slender white columns. He is in armour, she wears a simple flowing dress with an extraordinary wide ruff, and about them kneel their five children, the son bareheaded with a ruff and the four daughters with hoods over their hair. Their fine Elizabethan house brought into the Earl of Berkshire's family by the marriage of a Knyvett, and thought to have been designed by Inigo Jones, was refashioned in the 18th century. It stands in a park of 600 acres and has a panelled gallery with its original ceiling.

It was in this house that Dryden sought refuge during the year of the Great Plague (1665) and it was here that he met his wife, Lady Elizabeth Howard, and here that his eldest son was born.

It was in this Wiltshire retreat that Dryden wrote *The Maiden Queen*, afterwards performed in London, Nell Gwynne making her name in it as an actress; and while still in Wiltshire he wrote his *Annus Mirabilis*, a description in verse of the Dutch War and the Great Fire of London.

Charlton St Peter. This small place in the Vale of Pewsey was the birthplace of Stephen Duck, the Wiltshire thresher, who became a poet. One of those Peasant Poets of the 18th century like John Clare from Helpstone in Northamptonshire, Robert Bloomfield the Suffolk farmer's boy, Mrs Yearsley the Gloucestershire milkrounds-woman who wrote under the name of "Lactilla," and, the most successful of them all, George Crabbe, whose studied attempts in verse are an interesting by-way in the literary history of England at the period.

But while most of them attracted only a passing notice, making, as it were, but day trips to Parnassus, Stephen Duck got further than most and attracted the patronage of Queen Charlotte who made him Keeper of the Royal Library at Richmond.

But when by their literary efforts the Rural Poets bridged the gap between the bucolic and the genteel it was not always easy to know what to do with them. Under the 18th century system of patronage a berth could sometimes be found for them as "placemen" and some became country parsons which was a success in the case of George Crabbe but not in the case of Stephen Duck.

The Rural Poets owed everything to patronage and while patronage has many faults one of its virtues is that it can discover the George Crabbes and the Stephen Ducks of this world and give them their deserts. Today the State has become the universal patron but even with the vastly greater opportunities for education it is unlikely that Stephen Duck would have got anywhere in a society which requires several passes at "A Level" in the General Certificate of Education.

The Rural Poets had a genuine feeling for the countryside, especially those parts of it they knew best, but one feels they would have made poor examinees. But in those days examinations had not yet been thought of, and when they were some learned men said they would be the ruin of education. We are just beginning to discover that they were right.

The nave and chancel of the small church were restored in the 19th century, but the stringcourse under the east window (carved with Tudor roses and other flowers), the canopied piscina with a stone flower in the bowl, the fine stone angels at the windows and the winged monster above, and the pinnacled tower with a handsome doorway, are all 15th century. There is a peephole cut through the chancel arch. The chancel screen has six panels on each side of the doorway, in two rows, the top one traceried and painted. The chest is Jacobean.

Separated from the nave by a 500-year-old screen, delicately traceried and skilfully carved, is a chapel with the brass of its founder William Chaucey and his wife. The chapel is entered under a panelled arch, and has a canopied piscina with a projecting bowl. There are angels carved on the corbel brackets either side of the window carrying shields emblazoned with the Chaucey cockle-shells, birds, and castles, which also appear on the tower.

The church faces the great thatched roofs of the farm, and there is a mass of red roofs over the high wall close by.

Cherhill. Has a 15th century church with a 14th century tower. An iron gateway in black and gold leads through a stone screen into the chancel, and the altar has elegant oak carving of birds among vines and two Bible scenes, one of the Annunciation, the other of the Nativity with the figure of the Child raising his hand. The east window shows Christ in Majesty. The font has eight pairs of tiny arches. At it may have been baptised Roger Heall, who, according to his epitaph, "desired before he died that his bones may not be moved." There is a gallery fronted with delightful panels of tiny arches, probably 18th century.

The great barn which has kept the church company through the centuries is magnificent. A hundred feet long, it has four huge doorways, a roof rising nearly as high as the church tower, and a nave and aisles like a church. Its tall pillars rise like trees, and one of them is nearly seven feet round. In the floors and walls and roof of this great barn are two miles of timbers, most of which have been here about 500 years.

The white horse, about 130 feet long, was cut out on the slopes of the hillside in 1780 by Dr Christopher Alsop, a Calne physician, who stood a mile away and shouted his instructions through a trumpet to men who outlined the horse in flags. Just over the hill runs Wansdyke.

Chilmark. One of its lanes leads us to the quarries that have supplied beautiful cream stone for many of the old houses, fine bridges, and vanished priories of Wiltshire, for its glorious cathedral at Salisbury, and for Chichester's spire.

The fine church tower has a tapering spire and charming belfry windows; it is upheld by four arches and a vaulted roof. The doorway is 700 years old, and has at its sides two little men wearing pleated collars; one is crowned, and appears to be holding a stick and a drum. Through this doorway may have come for his christening little John de Chilmark, a mathematician and philosopher who in the 14th century was called the Archimedes of his age. In the church is a handsome Jacobean pulpit.

Chilton Foliat. Lies in the Kennet Valley on the Berkshire border.

Its medieval church is worthy of its noble setting. There are two odd faces at the priest's doorway, and indoors are 12 stone angels with painted shields of red and gold. There are more angels on the benches and the choir stalls, and painted angels carved in oak bear up the chancel roof, which has coloured Tudor roses.

The font has two bands of carving and eight sculptured panels, among them Noah in the Ark, the Wise Men at Bethlehem, and the Road to Calvary. In the chancel are two sculptures separated by centuries of time, an unknown knight with his legs crossed, his shield on his arm and his feet on a lion, and close by him, on a cushion in a windowsill, a pathetic figure of a little child six months old, Francis Popham, laid to rest here in 1861.

The home of the Pophams is famous in the story of our countryside, and a beautiful picture it is, set among the trees, with its gabled roofs and its ivied walls seen across the meadow from the road.

The 16th century manor house at Littlecote in this parish was the scene of a famous crime in the 17th century which was described by John Aubrey.

"Sir John Dayrell of Littlecote in Com. Wilts. having gott his ladie's waiting woman with child, when her travell came, sent a servant with a horse for a midwife, whom he was to bring hoodwinked. She was brought and layd the woman, but as soon as the child was borne she sawe the knight take the child and murther it, and burnt it in the fire in the chamber. She having donne her business was extraordinarily rewarded for her paines, and sent blindfold away. This horrid action did much run in her mind, and she had a desire to discover it, but knew not where 'twas. She considered with herself the time she was riding, and how many miles might be rode at that rate in that time, and that it must be some great person's house, for the roome was 12 foot high; and she could know the chamber if she sawe it. She went to a Justice of the Peace and search was made. The knight was brought to his tryall, and to be short this Judge (Sir John Popham) had this whole house, parke and mannor, and (I thinke) more, for a bribe to save his life. Sir John Popham gave sentence according to lawe; but being a great person and a favourite, he procured a *noli prosequi*."

Chippenham. It has grown up on the banks of the Avon with gabled and red-roofed old houses huddled up together, one of that group of country towns of quiet distinction which lie on the road from Bath to London. Its streets are dignified with Georgian frontages keeping company with the timbered fronts of the 16th and 17th centuries. Its High Street carries on as a long stone causeway across the river with a striking bridge if we look along it and see the 20 arches running from the bottom of the winding street.

This little town hall patched up through the centuries has the quaintest bit of frontage in the town, timbered and whitewashed with a wooden turret and two tiny gables, one of the gables filled with a coat-of-arms and the motto Unity and Loyalty, and a date which only deceives the passer-by, for it is 1776. Next-door to it is an old stone lock-up.

The spacious medieval church of Chippenham is a striking place, built in the 15th century and clerestoried in the 19th, with a chancel arch (now built into the chancel wall) which came from the vanished Norman church. With this ancient arch Chippenham has kept a small window 800 years old; it is above the altar. The Norman tower was pulled down and rebuilt again in the 17th century with the old material, including a coat-of-arms of the 15th century. The interior of the church is delightful with windows and screens, and there is brass with portraits of Sir Gilbart Prynne, his wife, and their seven children: it has also a tiny picture showing Sir Gilbart and his Mary with a tree between them and the words:

Man's a plant, and every tree,
Like man, is subject to mortalitie.

A stone in the lady chapel on the east wall by the altar is carved with the unknown figure of a woman at prayer. The lady chapel has an old screen and the chancel has a new one, both fine; it has also the handsome tomb of Andrew Baynton, carved with his heraldic achievements. The old screen is made up from timbers of the old roof and has fine carving; the new screen is a war memorial. The altar rails in the chancel are of Spanish mahogany and are fine 17th century work, and the richly carved organ case is of the same kind of timber and of the same period of craftsmanship. It has a frieze of leaves and cherub faces, and is attributed to Grinling Gibbons. The altar has a painted Calvary group between the figures (painted on wood) of St Peter and St Paul. Above the altar is a Te Deum east window with about 140 figures painted in it.

The east window of the lady chapel is a Jesse window with David in the centre, a Madonna between angels at the top, and kings, prophets, and angels everywhere. The 19th century chancel window, in memory of an MP for the town (a descendant namesake of the Gabriel Goldney who left the six coats), has seven Bible scenes with 50 figures, and among them is Sir Gabriel's portrait, with pictures of Ravenstoke church and Pickwick schools, which the MP befriended.

On the walls of the nave are some old stones with quaint 17th century lettering set in neatly carved borders, and on one of the windowsills when we called was an ancient carving of a skull.

Chirton. In the vale of Pewsey.

The church has a Norman doorway with the rich carving enlivened by a row of 28 men and animals. All round the arch is zigzag, and the capitals are set on slender columns with bead bands.

The font has a remarkable bowl with bands of scrollwork at the top and bottom, and between the bands a set of little arches with one of the Twelve Apostles in each. They are carved with a book in one hand and the other hand raised in blessing.

Above, a Norman roof, almost without parallel in England. It is believed to have been built about 1170, with four cross-beams from wall to wall. The main timbers are barrel-shaped with straight-pitched timbers behind them, all plainly cut except that the great crossbeams have carved billet ornament.

Also a Norman chancel arch and three Norman bays on each side of the nave with finely carved capitals, a magnificent chair carved by an ancient craftsman, a canopied niche six centuries old, a piscina in a window seat with an old Bible box near it, and some old glass in the porch with crowns and angels and a head of Our Lord. Two little windows in the chancel and the nave belong to Jacobean days.

Chisledon. Its little 13th century church has a bodyguard of four stalwart yews, and across the way is a charming group of thatched houses. Gargoyles look down from the tower on the south side. There is a 13th century doorway in a Norman arch; the inner arch is also Norman and the door's great studded timbers and fleur-de-lys strap hinges may be nearly 800 years old.

The door opens on a lovely 13th century arcade with foliage round the capitals and lit through a 15th century clerestory. The roof has fine old timbers and two queer faces among the corbels. The font is 15th century, the richly panelled pulpit is Jacobean. In the nave are some medieval bench-ends and on the choir seats is old panelling with heads, flowers, and pelicans. Two stone coffin lids are preserved with crosses on them, and another with an eight-pointed cross of fleur-de-lys; and there is a relief in marble of a family group very quaintly posed. The men, wearing the curled and flowing wigs of the 18th century, have a swaddled baby on their side of the prayer desk which separates them from the women of the family. By the altar is a handsome old table tomb, and one of the windows has a fine armoured figure of St Hubert with a stag on his helmet and a crossbow in his hand.

Chisledon has a group of seven trees which are the sole survivors of a small copse beloved by Richard Jefferies, who called them "one of his thinking places." He would walk to them almost daily from Coate, where he was born, and pause here watching the clouds move across the dip in the amphitheatre of the Downs. The seven firs remaining have now been scheduled as Trees of Remembrance.

Chitterne. It lies alone among the bare hills of Salisbury Plain, with two ancient burial mounds above it and two churches. A stream which is dry in the summer runs through in the winter, and many are the small bridges linking cottage and farm with the road. One of these bridges leads to a green slope where stands the lonely chancel of the ancient church of St Mary below the manor house. Its windows have lovely tracery and in two of them are pieces of old coloured glass—stars or suns, a crown, and a golden-winged bull under a canopy.

All Saints church was rebuilt in 1861; it has an embattled tower and traceried windows, a handsomely carved Jacobean pulpit and some 18th century wall monuments. One monument has a relief of a tussle between two men-of-war, clouds of smoke making them appear on fire. The monument is to Matthew Michell, who died in 1752. The inscription says he went to sea in 1718 when he was eight, and in 1743 sailed round the world with Anson. A white marble stone on the wall of the tower is to another of his family, Robert Michell, who died in 1779, the tablet telling us that his life was once miraculously preserved, when a stack of ten chimneys fell into his bedroom and on his bed at Lincoln's Inn.

Chittoe. Here is Sloperton Cottage which was the home of the poet Tom Moore who lies buried at Bromham. He died in 1852 and the church here was built after that time. The Wansdyke runs through Chittoe which also contains the 500 acres of Spye Park.

Cholderton. On the Hampshire border. An attractive village beside a stream which sometimes dries up in hot weather and there is a 17th century manor house by the bridge.

The church was entirely rebuilt in the 19th century by the vicar, Thomas Mozley, who was brother-in-law to Cardinal Newman. He discovered an ancient oak roof at Ipswich and re-erected it here over his new church.

The old font, with its sculptured base and big round bowl, lay outside in the churchyard for many years but was restored to its proper use by the descendants of William Noyes who was vicar here in the 17th century.

Christian Malford. The fabric of the church walls has caused much concern over the centuries for the foundations have sunk and the walls have had to be underpinned time and again. But the north wall still leans as does the tower.

The two screens in the church are medieval, the one in the side chapel having beautiful tracery with a carved canopy.

There are some fragments of medieval glass. In the window over the font remains of what was evidently a picture of the Annunciation and in the window near the pulpit the figures of the four doctors of the Latin Church, St Ambrose, St Gregory, St Jerome and St Augustine.

Chute. It is in the Down country on the Hampshire border, with the stumps of five old yews behind its church, and a chestnut 14 feet round near the gate, shading the pump put here for the village folk by Samuel Cosway, a rector of the 19th century. There are thatched barns about the churchyard. The church, which has been restored, has kept its big and boldly carved Norman font, with three bands of carving, and the lovely canopied piscina with the 14th century ball-flower ornament all round and a nine-leaf drain. In a window by the altar is St Nicholas. On the floor, by the stone pulpit, is the handsomely carved heraldic gravestone of Sir Sidney Medows, Knight Marshal of England, who died in 1792, an old man nearly 100. He lived at Conholt Park, the big house not far away, and built its simple front.

Clyffe Pypard. Its high pinnacled tower rises over a church with Norman stones and painted timbers. In the churchyard a yew and a magnificent beech are growing old together. On the walls two old scratch-dials are wearing away.

High up on either side of the church screen are two medieval chalk figures, and in the chancel the effigies of Elizabeth Goddard and her husband.

The screen is one of the treasures of the church and has still its pretty gold cresting and its delicate tracery, all gaily painted as in medieval days, in spiral bands and with black and gold uprights. The chancel roof is painted like the screen and in the sanctuary are blue and white stars.

The nave has lofty arches and a fine barrel roof with oak bosses. The canopied pulpit is 17th century and is richly carved with birds, flowers, and fruit, and in the spandrels of its arches are queer figures with hands in the mouths of fishes or dragons. The brass of an armoured knight of the 14th century is on the floor.

Under a canopy is a stone figure of a young man with curly hair, a crested helmet for a pillow, and a shield on his arm; he was a lord of the manor long ago. Much nearer our own time is the white marble statue of a handsome man leaning forward with outstretched hand. He was a carpenter, and at his feet are his tools, with a boy and girl on each side holding books and quills. He was Thomas Spackman, a good friend of the village, who lived to be 76.

There is also lovely old glass in the north aisle windows, with crowns, roses, flowers, and six small scenes. One scene is the Crucifixion, with angels hovering round the cross with golden chalices. There is a Madonna with long hair enthroned in front of trees, and another scene shows Christ lifted from the cross. There is Abraham bidding farewell to Hagar, who walks sternly past him, her bread wrapped in her apron, a bundle on her back, her hand holding her little son; in the background is Sarah playing with two children. Another scene shows a man kneeling at the foot of a man with a book; and still another shows two women disposing of the head of a tyrant.

Codford St Mary. It has fine views of the valley from the Downs, and a low bridge of three arches over the Wylye river. Its 13th century chancel has a pointed arch decorated with scrollwork on the handsome mouldings and beautiful capitals. The font is Norman. The pulpit is Jacobean and the altar is made from the old pulpit at St Mary's, Oxford, the University church.

One of the treasures of the church is a chalice with a stem and base fashioned in the Middle Ages. The base has a quaint engraving of the Crucifixion. Under a beautiful canopy carved with flowers and foliage, and supported on columns, lie the battered remains of the statues of Sir Richard Mompesson and his wife.

From this small place came James Ingram, one of the most learned men of the 19th century and the most distinguished Saxon scholar of his day. He was a Fellow of Trinity College, Oxford, and in 1824 was its president, and he was one of our forerunners in touring England, for he described Oxford and Winchester cathedrals in John Britton's great work on the Beauties of England.

Codford St Peter. It is on a slope of the Downs just above the River Wylye. The tower of the church was built 600 years ago. The font is Norman, sculptured on the sides and the base. The panelled baptistry has two old chairs with a lamb carved on the back, and there are two more ancient chairs in the chancel, which has a good modern screen. But the finest possession of the village is in the sanctuary, a remarkable piece of Saxon sculpture, probably part of a stone cross whose sculptor lived 1000 years ago. It shows a man with a mallet in his hand standing by a tree and reaching for the fruit. A striking piece of craftsmanship, it remains almost as clear as the day it was done.

Colerne. Its tower is raised high above the landscape round about, its buttresses rising to the top, its open parapet crowned with pinnacles, and a turret rising over all. Three statues look down from this tower so richly adorned, modern figures of Samuel, Joseph, and Elisha. One attractive gargoyle has two angels holding open the mouth of a lion. The cross on the green is in memory of Richard Walmesley who has a white marble effigy in the church and whose wife is remembered by a handsome cross in the churchyard.

It is hard to believe that this nave has been here 800 years, for the Norman arcades have been cut to look like new. Their capitals are richly carved. In one of the aisles are 14 splendid carved stone corbels, among which is a curly headed young man, a jovial monk, an old man looking sadly worried, and a beautiful lady in a veiled headdress.

Perhaps the most beautiful piece of the whole of this fine church is the canopied sedilia. The chancel has been rebuilt and these stone seats with it, but they incorporate much of the old work in them. The seats have vaultings above them, with delicate bosses, in one an enchanting little face.

The oak reredos is the work of ten craftsmen of the village, almost entirely voluntary; it represents the Crucifixion, with saints under canopies and a prophet at each side.

The clerestory is on one side only and the narrow rood stairway passes through a pillar. The font is 15th century, and there are some fragments of Saxon carving placed on the windowsills.

Euridge Farm, a mile or so away, was once the home of Sir Walter Raleigh, and the village was also the birthplace of William Grocyn, one of the greatest scholars in the Renaissance period. He became the first public teacher of Greek at Oxford, and he had Sir Thomas More as his pupil and Erasmus living in his house. Erasmus said of him that he was the most upright and best of all Britons.

Collingbourne Ducis. Domesday Book describes the church here as a ruin but it was rebuilt about 700 years ago, and has a 15th century tower. The chancel was rebuilt in 1856.

Near the top of the tower, battlemented and with fragile looking gargoyles, is an opening with a projecting ledge which was the entrance to a dovecot. No bird comes into it now, for the door is filled with glass, but here are the hundreds of holes as neat as when the doves flew in and out.

The nave has simple arcades carried on round 12th century pillars, with finely carved capitals, one of which has two carved faces. By the pulpit is another face worn with many centuries.

In the chancel is the brass, a few inches high, of Edward Saintmaur, a fat boy in voluminous clothes, a distinguished ruff, and big sleeves from which his small hands emerge to fold in prayer. His hair curls round his tight-fitting cap; his tiny feet just show below his skirts. He was the Earl of Hertford's son, just 11 months old when he died in 1631. Below is a rhymed epitaph mourning his early death, so unexpected, for

Such frame of body, such a lively soule,
Argued him written in the long-lived roll.

On the vestry wall is an engraving of Adoniram Byfield the Puritan, who held the living after the Royalist rector had been ejected. He is shown as being bidden to do the Devil's bidding, the "gentleman in black" appearing out of the clouds behind. In the registers is an entry in Byfield's beautiful handwriting, with his signature. Born about 1615, third son of Nicholas Byfield, a Puritan preacher and grandson of Richard Byfield who became vicar of Stratford a year after Shakespeare's return, Adoniram served as chaplain to a Parliamentary regiment in 1642 and became one of the two scribes who kept the records of the Westminster Assembly of Divines. Appointed in 1643 by the Long Parliament to reform the English church.

Collingbourne Kingston. It is sheltered by great Downs and the little Bourne river runs past. The church is set amid thatched roofs and walls by the old manor house now a farm. A rise in the village is called King's Hill because it is said that, in the days when the farmhouse was still a manor house, a certain Dame Pile met Charles Stuart on the hill and gave him a lapful of gold.

In the church is the huge canopied tomb of Gabriel Pile, who died in 1626. He lies by his wife Anne and is dressed in wonderful armour of white and gold, with patterned knee-pieces and scarlet trappings. She is in a severely simple black gown. The canopy is piled high with heraldry, topped by a helmet, a cannon ball beside it, and has a double arch in the centre studded with Tudor roses and other flowers. It has two such compartments, under one of which kneels a bearded man in simple armour with his wife in black wearing an embroidered bodice. On the side of the tomb kneel two smaller armoured and bearded men, probably the sons of Gabriel.

On the opposite wall under a canopy, gay with gilded flowers on a scarlet ground, is the small figure of Gertrude Pile kneeling at prayer. She was the wife of another Gabriel, and is wrapped in a full white garment covering her head as well. "A goodly flower soon fading," she was only 22 when they laid her here in 1630. Near her is the white marble monument of Edward Richards, who died in 1728, his handsome bust having a curly wig falling to the shoulder. In the chancel is the gravestone of Constantine Darell, with the brass of him and his wife.

The oldest possession of the church is the group of round Norman pillars in the nave, each with a different capital, some daintily moulded and one with a lady facing the doorway, a delightful but rather sad woman with wavy hair, plain cap, and a brooch fastening her gown. The 13th and 15th centuries gave the church a beautiful chancel arch, with four depths of moulding, on foliage capitals, the fine tower with its carved pinnacles and strange gargoyles; the clerestory windows of varied star-like shapes date from 1861.

Compton Bassett. Was the home of the Heneage family for many generations who lived at the manor house hard by the church.

The nave of the church is mainly 15th century but the chancel was entirely rebuilt in the 19th. It is divided from the nave by a magnificent 15th century screen standing on four pilasters in which are stone figures of the 12 Apostles under canopies. The arches bearing up the canopy on the west side are crested and embattled and the ceiling is panelled.

The Heneage family pew facing the pulpit (in which the hour glass still remains) are both of the same period. The pew being panelled and divided into 22 sections each with arcading. The roof is panelled in black and white with 21 oak bosses carved with foliage and is upheld from 14 oak corbels.

Compton Chamberlayne. A lovely village on the Nadder River. Compton House, standing with its battlements just below the church, with a lake in front and a park mounting up the hill, was for four centuries the home of the Penruddocks, who come into history because Colonel John Penruddock rebelled against Cromwell and was executed by the Commonwealth. There is an account book still preserved at Compton House with items of £7 9*s* for bringing home John Penruddock's body from Exeter, and it is recorded that in 1855, when repairs were being made to the floor of the Penruddock pew, the remains were seen, first in a shell of elm, then in a mahogany coffin, and next in oak with thick pieces of wood screwed on the outside as if for a packing case.

The tower, with its gargoyles and belfry windows, rises above a wide porch, and pointed arcades lead into the transepts and the chancel, where is a tablet with the names of all the Penruddocks buried here since 1598. Edward heads the list; the last name when we called was Charles, who died in 1929. The altar table has a carved rail and is 300 years old. The oldest possession of the church is the font bowl, fashioned by the Normans.

In the pulpit, which has beautifully carved linenfold panels, John Marten preached for 48 years; he must have preached often with John Penruddock in the pew. He wrote the entry of the burial which we can still see in the register; and the memory of that bitter tragedy would be with him through nearly the whole of the second half of the 17th century.

Two of John Penruddock's brothers died for the king in the Civil War, and John himself, who came into the estate on his father's death in 1648, made this entry in an account book preserved with the letters: "My own debts contracted during six years sequestration, £1,500." Yet he spent himself unwearyingly to set Charles the Second on the throne.

The rising in the West was planned for March 12, 1655; and it was still dark on that morning when a little band of 200 men marched into Salisbury led by Sir Joseph Wagstaffe, John Penruddock, Colonel Grove, and Colonel Jones. They broke open the gates of the gaol and found there many willing recruits, but they did not pillage; they did not burn. Their leaders had them well in hand. The only things they commandeered were horses, and the only prisoners they made were two judges on circuit and the high sheriff, all three dragged shivering from their beds. There was some talk of hanging them, but Penruddock would not permit it. The sheriff was kept as hostage, and the two judges he set free, to meet them again in a week's time, himself a prisoner before them.

Charles the Second was proclaimed in Salisbury marketplace, but the townspeople were cautious and apathetic, and remained only spectators. Disappointed in the support of Dorset men, the Cavaliers turned their faces to the West. They got no farther than South

Molton, for their reduced army had barely settled down there for the night when Captain Croke, with his troop of horse from Exeter, fell on them. Many fled in the dark, but the rest, with Penruddock, Grove, and Jones still at their head, fought on till surrender was the only way. He was found guilty at Exeter and at the trial based his defence on the fact that Cromwell was no king, and therefore the Act of Treason could not apply. He had fought for his lawful king, and Cromwell it was who had committed treason. It was in vain; the death warrant was signed and sent post haste to Exeter.

Like his sovereign he faced death with dignity and courage and on the eve of his execution he wrote to his wife Arundel:

Look not towards my grave where my body lies, but toward heaven, where I hope my soul shall gain a mansion in my Father's house. The greatest conflict I have had in this extremity was my parting with thee; the next encounter is to be with Death, and my Saviour hath so pulled out the sting thereof that I hope to assault it without fear.

Coombe Bissett. The 13th century church was refashioned in the 15th, when the transepts were built, but there are two Norman arches with beautiful capitals. The nave, chancel, and font are 13th century. The curious font rises on five pillars and has several rows of moulding. Parts of the graceful chancel screen may have been here since the 15th century. The village has many old cottages, and a three-arched stone bridge.

Corsham. It lies unspoiled a little way off the road from Bath to Chippenham, with a long street of old houses and Dame Hungerford's 17th century almshouse looking down a green way to the church and the Elizabethan seat of the Methuens, Corsham Court. The great house stands in 400 acres and the chief glory of the park is the avenue seen from the London road.

Dame Hungerford lies in the ruins of Farleigh Castle, her figure sculptured in white marble, but her almshouses keep green her name in Corsham, and it was from one of them that they bore old Edward Hasted, who died here three years before Waterloo after giving 40 years of his life to struggling along the terrible roads of Kent for his famous History. They made him Warden of Dame Hungerford's Charity as his reward, and here in Corsham church they laid him, a brass tablet reminding us of his long and faithful industry. On the tablet is a lovely enamel crest kept bright in memory of this old man who did so much for Kent.

Among the old buildings in the town is a chapel, built in the year of the Great Plague (1665). It has its old pulpit and gallery, old box pews and hat pegs, and is still used for services, having belonged to Presbyterians and Quakers and being now in the possession of the Congregationalists.

The clerestoried church, with something of nearly all our great building centuries, is a fine spectacle with its three western windows and its southern tower; and it has a Norman doorway recessed in the south wall. The tower was formerly central but was rebuilt in its present position in 1874. The nave has Norman piers, and the roofs are 15th century. By the south porch is a scratch-dial and the porch has a vaulted roof holding up a room above it, the vaulting resting on stone corbels carved with heads of a king, a queen, a bishop, and an angel.

There are screens at the eastern end of the aisles, a modern one at the south and a 15th century stone screen in the north. Fan-vaulted and with delicate cresting, the old screen divides the aisle from the richly decorated lady chapel in which is the fine tomb of Thomas Tropenell, who built the screen. His tomb is handsome with red, blue, and gold fading away in the heraldic panels. His screen has a figure of St Thomas in a niche, and the screen balancing it in the south aisle has one figure with a sword and one with a lily.

In the Methuen chapel (forming a north transept) is an effigy of Constance Methuen, a child of two, and in the chancel by the altar are two white marble angels modelled on another lady of the Methuens who sleeps in the churchyard and will not be forgotten; the panelled reredos is in her memory. Also in the Methuen chapel lies the figure of Alice Cobb on her 17th century tomb. She was a maid 19 years, a wife 26, and a widow 13, and she buried 13 out of 16 children in the days before the Civil War. Her tomb was at Adderbury in Oxfordshire, but Lord Methuen, to whose family she belonged, collected its fragments and brought them here. They were kept at Corsham Court and at last set up in this place—six kneeling figures in alabaster and some richly coloured heraldry.

In the chancel (which has a modern arch) lie two brothers John and Thomas Hulbert:

John was the eldest, a man discreet and stout,
Faithful and Just in all he went about.
By seniority he first obtained
The blessed Port that Thomas since hath gained.

Scarce two such brothers hath the world again, we are told, and of Thomas, a clothier whose portrait is here in brass, we read that "he finished his course in powerful prayer to God." It is probably his son James Hulbert who looks down on the altar—like a cherub, for he has a golden face with wings, and we are led to believe that he was so famous that merely to mention his name is enough.

Reached by an old door in the chancel, with fragments of a remarkable wooden screen round it, is a curious little upstairs room.

The windows have a little old glass showing the wheatsheaf and sickles of the Hungerfords, and the lady chapel, which is much as it was in the 15th century, has a window of the Last Supper beautifully copied from a Flemish window in the Cathedral at Lichfield. There is a modern window with Bible scenes in blue and white and gold.

The church has a charming canopied piscina, a 15th century font panelled with Tudor roses, stone corbels carved with fine faces holding up the 15th century roofs, a 17th century oak chest with six planks four inches thick, and two stone altars used in the bottom panels of the ancient screen. The chancel has a marble floor inlaid with shields, carved stone panelling and richly decorated oak pews, and there are three old bench-ends still left in one of the aisles. In a windowsill in the south aisle are the remains of a piscina belonging to a vanished chapel, and in this aisle are striking corbels carved with the heads of a man with a turban, a queen and a demon, and a prince with his mouth open.

In the churchyard is a gravestone which tells us of Sarah Jarvis who died at 107 in 1753, and is said to have had another set of teeth just before she died. She may have known John Smith, whose stone has these lines:

Short was my life, yet live I ever
Death hath her due, yet die I never.

Outside the porch are modern figures of Peter with the key, Paul with his sword and book, and St Batholomew.

Corsham Court stands close by the church and a little way off is a small bath-house built by the Adam brothers, with a pinnacled roof, some old glass in the windows, and a curious decoration of moss and cones in a passage. The cones have been here since the days of the Adams.

Corsley. Four miles west of Warminster, this tiny village has a beautiful house built about 1545. It is approached through a stone

Edington Church.

Edington Church: the interior, facing west.

Great Chalfield Manor. (*National T*

Great Chalfield Manor: the great hall.

gateway by a path running between neat lawns with cedars and flowers. Its lower stage is of grey stone, its upper floors of russet brick, its roof is gabled. All round it are big farm buildings, and above it is the church.

It was from this house that the widow of Sir John Thynne married the brother of Sir Walter Raleigh.

The church was refashioned in 1833, but has Jacobean work in its oak pulpit.

Corston. It has a small church with a tiny bell turret above the west window. The east window, which is a war memorial, contains two roundels of Flemish glass. There is an old screen with a lovely cornice and delicate arcading, and on the wall near the door is a small enamel in rich colours of Our Lord bearing the cross, with two women kneeling as He passes, and Simon of Cyrene helping him.

Cricklade. Not far from the source of the Thames. There are two churches.

The magnificent Tudor tower of St Sampson's is a landmark which dominates the town. It has almost every kind of adornment—rich panels, fine windows, and great turrets crowned by spirelets. Thought to have been built by John Dudley a few years before Elizabeth the First came to the throne, it is a remarkable work for that time. Within the church is a vaulted roof with 64 bosses, no two alike, and its walls adorned with heraldry including the bear and ragged staff of the Earls of Warwick. Its four pillars are oddly carved with symbols we have seldom come across in a church: a heart, a diamond, a club, and a spade; and in vivid contrast with all this old stonework is the scarlet colouring of the modern choir-stalls and screens.

But St Sampson's has much that is far older than its tower; most ancient of all are two stones over the richly moulded doorway in the porch. They are carved with knotwork and may have belonged to a Saxon cross a thousand years ago. From the 12th century come two nave arches decorated with foliage, and from the 13th another arch. From the 14th part of the north aisle, with two fine windows and a worn stone figure lying in a rich recess. From the 15th the transepts and the south chapel.

There is an ancient chest with four locks, an Elizabethan altar table, a fine brass candelabra 200 years old, a modern stone pulpit, and a case containing a Breeches Bible. The Calvinist "Geneva" version of the Scriptures so called because Genesis 3 verse 7 is translated "And (Adam and Eve) sewed fig leaves together and made themselves *breeches*." Also some coins and glass, a charter with a great seal and a drawing of King James, and part of a machine broken in the street riots of 1841.

The roofs of this lofty and impressive interior are supported by angels and quaint grotesques, and all about the church there are medieval windows and arches. A fine 13th century window of three lancets is aglow with modern glass showing Christ with St Peter and St Paul, as well as other figures including St Sampson and Bishop Dubricius who ordained him in the 6th century. Also in these windows we see a St Christopher in memory of a vicar's little boy who was drowned, and a picture of a ship in full sail breasting the waves, with the wind blowing it along while a gigantic St Nicholas stands by the mast.

On the wall is the black marble monument of a goldsmith who worked in London a few years before the Great Fire. He was Robert Jennor, the founder of Marston Meysey church, of Malmesbury almshouses, and of the old school here by the churchyard, a grey stone building with gables and mullioned windows.

Between the school and the church stands one of the two fine 15th century crosses in Cricklade, still with its carved base, tapering shaft, and canopied head. The other cross stands by the other church, St Mary's, a little building tucked away in a garden by the wayside, and has at the top of its tall shaft a lantern head with angels at the corners. The head is carved with little scenes and figures showing Mary and John by the Cross, the Assumption of the Madonna, a knight and a queen, and a bishop. It is among the most beautiful churchyard crosses we have seen there is a modern copy of it at Stanton Fitzwarren.

St Mary's has a Norman chancel arch, fine with chevron decoration, the font and a lancet window are 13th century, the aisles are 15th, and the altar plate includes a fine Elizabethan cup. There is a handsomely carved Jacobean pulpit, a chained Bible as old, and an 18th century brass candelabra. Much timber of 500 years ago is still in the black and white roofs, which have a fine border adorned with rich tracery.

Crudwell. Its little stream flowing through the village and widening into a pool above its two-arched bridge is one of the early sources of the Thames.

The church contains some Norman work but belongs mainly to the 13th and 15th centuries. The nave arcades are curious for being of different heights, the piers of one being round Norman and the other piers octagonal.

The roof of the nave is borne on a series of carved heads, among them a bearded king, a lady, and an angel. The 13th century chancel has an arch older than itself with the roodloft doorway in it and an old oak screen across it. There is a plain old font, a canopied piscina, and an old carved chair. But the chief treasures of the church are in its old glass and its bench-ends. The carvings on the benches are early 16th century. There are roses and thistles and fruit; a bird, a stag, and a winged dragon; a man with a rough beard, long hair, and three feathers; and a laughing man in a rakish hat.

The old glass has brightly blazoned shields in its tracery, and in the centre of the window is Christ raising His hands to show the marks of the nails; He is in white and gold under a gilded canopy. There are canopies massed with angels, and under them scenes which apparently have once shown the Seven Sacraments; now they show only Baptism, Confirmation, Marriage, and Extreme Unction. In Marriage the priest sits in a gold chair, the bride and bridegroom in blue. In Extreme Unction a man in a blue-quilted bed is being anointed by the priest; and kneeling by the bed is a man holding the chrism, or holy oil.

By the church is a buttressed stone barn, and in the porch wall is a stone with the words (1673):

Received of Philip Herd, his borrowed earth.

Dauntsey. Was the home of Henry Danvers who founded the school here (now an Almshouse) and who had been a page to Sir Philip Sidney and who was with Sir Philip when he died upon the battlefield of Zutphen. His sister Jane married George Herbert from Bemerton and it was Herbert who wrote the epitaph on the tomb to Henry Danvers in the church here, in a chapel enclosed with iron gates.

Sacred marble safely keep
His dust who under thee must sleep
Until the graves again restore
Their dead, and time shall be no more.
Meanwhile, if he (which all things wears)
Do ruin thee, or if the tears

Are shed for him dissolve thy frame,
Thou art requited; for his fame,
His virtues, and his worth shall be
Another monument to thee.

The church has Norman north and south doorways and Norman carving is incorporated in its 13th century walls. The tower was rebuilt in the 17th century. Inside there are tower and chancel screens with 14th century tracery and the box pews are Jacobean.

On either side of the chancel are two 16th century altar tombs with brasses for Sir John Danvers and his wife Anne. She gave the choir stalls, some of which remain, and glazed the window above her husband's tomb, which shows the Virgin Mary in the centre with her mother St Anne, below members of the Danvers family and in the top lights shields of arms. The glass in the window above her tomb has figures of St John the Evangelist (with Chalice) and St Margaret, the Shepherdess of Antioch, with a dragon under her feet.

But the most remarkable possession of the church is the Doom picture which was originally fitted into the chancel arch above the rood screen and formed a kind of painted scenery behind the rood beam with its central figure of the Crucified. At the top of the picture is Our Lord in Majesty with the blessed going up one side, towards St Peter bearing the keys, and the damned going down on the other into hell's mouth; and at the bottom of the picture figures rising from their graves in shrouds.

Devizes. An excellent centre from which to make a tour of the most impressive prehistoric remains in Wiltshire. It is close to the Wansdyke, Stonehenge, and Woodhenge, to Old Sarum, Savernake, and Bath, to Avebury and Silbury Hill.

There are three churches and a museum, and a fine market square. The town still has timbered houses of the 16th century clustering about the old Norman church of St John's and, as at Bradford-on-Avon, a town hall that never was a town hall, a stone building of Queen Anne's day which was built as a cheese market but was used for civic meetings while the actual town hall was building. In the real town hall, built in 1806–8 by Thomas Baldwin of Bath, is a list of mayors from 1302 and the royal charters granted to the town, pictures of old Devizes, some fine oil portraits, and three marble busts, one of Prime Minister Addington, one of Mr Sotheron Estcourt, and one of Henry Merrewether, Recorder of Devizes for 30 years. The portraits on the walls are those of George the Third and his queen in their coronation robes, and Queen Victoria. The finest civic building in the town is the Assize Court, with a central portico built on four columns; it has a muniment room with documents of much interest concerning the life of the town, including about 200 autographed letters from interesting people; among them are letters from Cromwell, John Bradshaw, Archbishop Laud, General Fairfax, and Sir Walter Raleigh.

As one of the oldest towns in Wiltshire, Devizes had a wooden castle soon after the Norman Conquest. It was rebuilt in 1120 after a fire. It was said long ago "that such a piece of castlework, so costly and strong, was never afore nor since set up by a bishop of England" as the Bishop of Salisbury built for himself here. But by 1538 it had fallen into ruin. Its stones were used as a quarry for the building of houses; it passed into private hands, and windmills were worked on the site. The castle as it stands was built in 1842 to the designs of H. E. Goodridge, who did much work in the Greek revival manner at Bath, but later abandoned the classical tradition for the Gothic. Devizes Castle with its round towers, oriel windows, and battlement walls belongs to the later period of Goodridge's work but it had the old moat encircling it.

On each side of the great market square is an interesting old house. One is a doctor's house of the 17th and 18th centuries with columns in front and a carved figure of Aesculapius sitting in an alcove with a scroll and a serpent. The other house is a famous inn of Queen Elizabeth's day. It is next to the Corn Exchange, which has dignified columns and an open parapet with a huge pedestal behind it on which is perched the figure of Ceres, Goddess of the Fields, holding the Horn of Plenty. Behind the old coaching house (now the Bear Hotel) is the castle, and the ruins of the Norman Castle were still on the mound when a parson's son became landlord of the Tudor inn in 1773. He was Thomas Lawrence, and he is remembered because he set up white posts across Salisbury Plain, with S on one side for Salisbury and D on the other side for Devizes. The posts were 12 feet high and half a mile apart, and were a sure guide for travellers.

Thomas Lawrence the innkeeper was the father of Thomas Lawrence the portrait painter. He was born in Bristol but came here as a child, and it was here that he showed his genius. He would recite passages from Milton and Pope, and astonished visitors to the inn by his sketches. He was only five when he drew a portrait of a Lord Chief Justice.

On one of the windows of the inn is scratched the words:

John Blome, merchant, on his way from London to Bath and Bristol for execution, February, 1760.

The market cross, which was built by Benjamin Wyatt for Lord Sidmouth in 1814, has four open arches, many pinnacled columns, and an ornamental spire, and on a panel inside is set out the story of Ruth Pierce, a local Sapphira who told a lie in the marketplace in 1753 and instantly fell dead. Three women agreed to buy a sack of corn and that at the settlement the money was threepence short. All three declared that they had paid their share and a quarrel arose in which Ruth Pierce "wished she might drop dead if she had not paid." She dropped dead, and at the inquest the jury declared that she was struck dead with a lie in her mouth from the visitation of the Great and Almighty God.

St John's church has an impressive tower, its stringcourse of stone heads, and a wealth of sculpture. The exterior of its Beauchamp chapel has rich pinnacles rising from the battlements, a canopied niche with a bracket of open stonework, and pinnacled buttresses.

Inside, the chapel is equally beautiful, with its elegant timber roof cut out in 288 small squares of tracery, set in finely moulded beams. Everywhere it is richly sculptured, and looking down from its northern wall is a gallery of stone faces on which the wind was blowing and the rain was falling for centuries before Richard Beauchamp's chapel was built to shelter them. Three of them have double faces. Across the chancel is another small chapel, with the same beautiful roof but only half the size.

But it is the chancel which is most magnificent, with a central tower adding depth to it all, so that one enters the sanctuary through three great arches. The arches, all made by the Normans and splendidly carved, bear up a vaulted roof with massive round ribs in keeping with the strength of the piers, and all round the sanctuary are interlaced arches with zigzag moulding, the walls above being filled with fish-scale work. The rounded east window has two blind arches to match it, with charming ornamental columns.

There is also much Norman work in St Mary's church. It has a small Norman window high up in the east gable, Norman arches and roof vaulting, with an interlacing reredos to match and finely carved capitals. The 15th century nave, with its lofty clerestory, has a handsome roof borne on 12 corbels with gilded bosses, carving in the tracery, and tracery over the beams. There are sculptured canopies by the chancel arch and a door which led to the rood-loft. The old studded door still swings on its hinges in the finely carved south porch.

Outside, in a niche over the gable, is a statue of the Madonna; inside are two wooden carvings—a pelican feeding its young over the south door and the old weathercock on the wall of the tower; and in the 15th century nave the corbel brackets are carved with figures of men and women in quaint attitudes, women holding their hair, a man with his chin in his hands, and a man with a wig. Contrasting with these are the sculptures of a hundred years ago, two mourning figures by E. H. Baily, and two by Westmacott, one of a mother weeping for her three children.

The third church, St James's, has nothing old except its 15th century tower, but it is the best tower in the town and is one of a group of five in Wiltshire which have the top stage panelled and the centre of the panelling pierced to let out the sound of the bells. It rises nobly by the great pond on the green, known as the Crammer.

The Kennet and Avon Canal passes through the town, carried up Caen Hill by means of 29 locks; and there is a pleasant walk in Roundway Park, through a long avenue of fine elms which brings us up to the top of the hill where the battle of Roundway Hill was fought in 1643. Hereabouts is an old earthwork from the Iron Age which is known as Oliver's Camp.

The museum was established by an 18th century antiquary, William Cunnington. Most of the exhibits come from the round barrows of the Bronze Age, of which Wiltshire boasts something like 2000, about 300 being in the neighbourhood of Stonehenge.

Though the museum has but few remains of the Celtic race which succeeded the Bronze Age men, it has one priceless object, the Marlborough Bucket, a sepulchral vessel two feet wide. Originally of firwood, which has perished, its three bronze bands are now fixed in new wood, and they reveal a craftsmanship of high order, decorated with human faces and grotesques.

There is also a Saxon coffin of wood found at Roundway Hall by the Wansdyke. Also a model of Woodhenge, with another model of the more familiar Stonehenge close by. In this first of all Woodhenge models, the modeller has fixed 156 sticks of concrete to show where the wooden posts rose from their holes in the chalk.

Dinton. It has a dark little lane which brings us to Dinton Beeches, and an ancient British fort. It has a cottage in which a friend of Milton is said to have been born, and a house which was the home of a great historic figure. Its church, reached by a path arched over by tall yews, has been here 700 years, with a central tower and a pointed doorway with carved capitals. An old scratch-dial is on the walls. The doorway opens into a lofty nave linked with the chancel by an impressive group of tower arches, with a vaulted roof resting on corbels carved with the symbols of the Four Evangelists. The chancel has seven windows with beautiful 14th century tracery, and the square grey font with little arches round it is as old as the church.

The ancient house at one end of the village was the home of Edward Hyde, first Lord Clarendon, who was born here in 1609. The author of *The History of the Great Rebellion*, who became Lord Chancellor under Charles the Second and whose daughter Anne married the Duke of York, afterwards James the Second, and was the mother of two queens, Mary the Second, wife of William of Orange, and Queen Anne.

Dinton was also the birthplace, in 1596, of the musician Henry Lawes who invited Milton to write the masque *Comus*, for which he himself composed the music, and in which he played the part of the Attendant Spirit when it was first performed at Ludlow Castle, and Milton honoured him with the lines:

Harry, whose tuneful and well measured song
First taught our English music how to span
Words with just note and accent—not to scan
With Midas ears, committing short and long.

Ditteridge. Here the Romans built a villa and the Normans a church. The work of the Romans has vanished, something of the Normans remains in the splendid doorway which for generations stood in the wind and the rain and for 600 years has been sheltered by a porch. From the capitals of the Norman shafts two crowned heads look across the doorway to each other, while two queer creatures, a dragon and a horse, watch our approach as we come up the little lavender path from the gate. Above it all is a beautiful arch with delicate carving.

The church has a crude and leaning chancel arch leading into the chancel up two steps, where there is a canopied piscina with a flower carved in its bowl by a 15th century mason. On the walls are tablets to 17th and 18th century folk, one with an odd winged angel above the stone of Hannah Clement who died on a summer's day when she was 21, "Now in the blossom of my years."

The stone pulpit has a band of foliage round it and a carved cornice of oak leaves. The neatly carved tub font was made by the Normans. One curiously shaped window has the iron hinge with which it used to be shuttered before it was glazed. Facing this window is another curious little one, high in the wall, splayed about three feet deep.

Donhead St Andrew. It is watered by the River Nadder and sheltered in a hollow of the Downs in the delightful country near Shaftesbury. Its church has lost some of its ancient interest, but it has kept the tower which has been looking out from its cosy churchyard for 500 years, embattled and pinnacled. The nave arcades have clustered columns, and one arch has a shield on its capital crudely carved with the emblems of the Passion, and underneath it the head of Our Lord. At the top of the tracery in the east window is a piece of old stained glass with the arms of the Abbey of St Edward at Shaftesbury. The old roodloft doorway has been filled in, but the outline may still be seen.

Donhead St Mary. It is on the hills above the Nadder river, with the old camp of Castle Rings up Sticklepath Hill, and has a fine Norman church. The tower is 15th century, tall, embattled, and pinnacled; the stone porch is a hundred years older, with an unusual vaulted roof. The nave is high and beautiful with clerestory windows and two arcades of pointed arches. At the end of each aisle are 12th century arches leading into 14th century chapels. The chancel has a noble arch, one capital sculptured with odd little figures, and there is a handsome Jacobean altar richly carved, showing strange creatures writhing among foliage. The pulpit is also Jacobean and has carved panels. The font is Norman, its bowl having a band of strapwork on the rim and arches on twin columns.

Downton. On the Hampshire border with the Avon running through.

In the street facing an old cross is an inn with two ancient wooden busts of King John and his Queen Isabella. They are set in niches, and as John was at Downton three times to see the Bishop of Winchester, who had a palace by the river, it is believed they may be copies of busts placed here to celebrate his visits. The graceful and slender shaft of another cross is in the churchyard, and may have been here when King John came.

In the church three of the western bays are Norman. An ancient scratch-dial is on the walls and there is a door which has been on its hinges 600 years, now protected by a 17th century gable. Everywhere the arches are impressive, some with beautifully sculptured capitals. The tower arches rest on clustered columns, and over them springs a noble 15th century tower of grey flint and brown stone. The spacious chancel is 14th century, and may have been built under the eye of William of Wykeham, for when he became bishop and founded Winchester school he applied the rectorial tithes of this church towards its endowment. The chancel, with its neat flint walls, has lovely tracery in its windows, and handsome corbels with quaint faces supporting a modern roof. In one of the windows is exquisite glass of the 14th and 15th centuries, with St Christopher fording the river, St Barbara, and odd fragments.

There is an imposing 18th century wall monument of Lady Feversham, leaning on an urn with a book in her hand, and two lofty wall monuments by Scheemakers to members of her family. In a transept is the carved canopy of a recessed tomb. There are modern stalls set here in memory of the owner of old Downton House, who preserved the Moot in his lovely garden. It was probably built by the Britons as a defence against the Saxons, and was later used by the Saxons as a meeting-place. The outer ring of it is easily seen from the road, a big earthwork nearly hidden by trees. There is an inner ring in the form of a double horseshoe and an outer ditch which can be traced for 600 yards from the river and back to it.

The old manor was once the home of the Raleighs, Walter Raleigh's brother Carew representing Downton in Parliament. His son Walter was born here, becoming Dean of Wells and finding himself captured by the Parliament men, who placed him in the custody of a shoemaker. The cobbler quarrelled with his captive and is said to have given him a mortal wound.

Here was born Sir Roger Curtis, who was in charge of the gunboats when the Spaniards were besieging Gibraltar in 1782. By his energy the strong floating batteries from which the Spaniards were bombarding the Rock were destroyed. Curtis was knighted, and lived to fight more battles, and to see George the Third come out to his ship and throw a golden chain round his neck, telling him to keep it as an heirloom. He became an admiral in the year before Trafalgar, and died the year after Waterloo.

There were only three vicars of this parish between 1661 and 1824, two having held the appointment for more than half a century.

A little way off is Cleobury Ring, a prehistoric earthwork of five acres, crowned with trees and having a 40-foot rampart.

Draycot Cerne. Entered by its original doorway, the church is mainly 700 years old, but has a 15th century tower with a plain parapet; a 15th century stone porch with lovely windows, and three sundials. At the top of one of the buttresses are two heads which the sculptor has carved turning away from each other. The nave is full of richly carved box pews.

The chancel is lower than the nave and has the simple beauty of the 13th century; it has a priest's door and a twin piscina under a canopy, as well as two Jacobean stalls. On the wall hang two helmets, a pair of gauntlets, and a short sword. The plain goblet-shaped font is about 600 years old.

There are portrait brasses for Sir Edward Cerne and his wife (1393). A stone effigy of a knight drawing his sword, his feet crossed and resting on a lion, his shield on his arm, lies under a canopy. He is thought to be the founder of the church, Sir Philip de Cerne. Sir Thomas Long, who married into the Cerne family in Tudor times, has a handsomely panelled altar tomb painted and decorated with emblazoned shields.

There is a fireplace in the chapel with the tablets of 17th and 18th century monuments to the Long family including a bust of Sir Robert Long.

Durnford. In the Avon valley, it lies below the downs with the entrenched earthwork of Ogbury Camp. Two Norman doorways lead into its ancient church, still with the doors that have been on their hinges for centuries. The variety and ingenuity of the carving are striking, one of the arches with three orders of carving, having a row of something like shuttlecocks, of which six are wonderfully preserved. The tower is 13th century.

The chancel arch is finely moulded, and has on its capitals a dove and an owl. The Norman font has a splendid array of interlaced arches, and an old wooden cover carved with flowers. The Jacobean pulpit is decorated with arches and heraldry, and a blue velvet cloth embroidered in the days of Cromwell hangs over the top. It is said to be made of goat's hair. There are curious old altar-rails of lattice work, old pews with carved ends, an ancient chest, and a dignified Jacobean reading desk containing an old chair, its high back carved with flowers. Chained to this desk is a copy of Bishop Jewel's *Defence of the Apology of the Church of England* (1562), a book which was ordered to be provided in all churches in 1568. The nave windows are 15th century, and in one of them is some old glass showing part of a Crucifixion, fragments of the portrait of a bishop, and little fiery suns. Over the chancel arch are the remains of a wall painting of what appears to have been a Crucifixion.

There are two tomb recesses of the 13th and 14th centuries, one containing a stone beautifully carved with a cross. In a recessed altar tomb are brasses of Edward Young and his wife, with their six sons and eight daughters. They lived at Durnford House, the home of the uncle of John Evelyn, who thus mentioned a visit here in his diary:

Dined at a farme of my uncle Hungerford's called Darneford Magna, situate in a valley under ye plaine, most sweetly watered, abounding in trouts catched by speare in the night, when they came attracted by a light set in ye extreme of a boate.

Durrington. Not far away from Stonehenge, and here was what is known as Woodhenge, one of the most remarkable of all our ancient monuments.

By this small place the Avon flows, shaded by willows. The village has charming thatched cottages, rich groups of elms, and a small church built 700 years ago and refashioned in our time. The church stands on a mound above the water meadows, and has a 15th century tower with parapet, pinnacles, and a fine arch with lofty panelled piers. There is a simple Norman arcade and a Norman aisle, a Norman doorway with carving on the pillars and their capitals, a 13th century chancel with a canopied piscina, a little priest's doorway, a scratch-dial, and much fine 17th century wood-work. The chancel arch springs from the walls, without pillars.

The pews and choir stalls are carved at the back, at the front, and at the ends; the fine Jacobean pulpit has panels with the Four Evangelists wearing quaint little hats, and with a lion, an eagle, and two saints. The altar has a carved front rail, and a chair in the sanctuary has on it two angels bearing a crown. On the reading desk is a group of Faith, Hope, and Charity with her children. A splendid screen has a coat-of-arms painted in 1634. There are heraldic gravestones of the 18th century.

In 1925 an airman flying over Durrington noticed white chalk marks in a circle on a bare wheatfield below. He took a photograph of it, and in the summer, when the wheat had fully grown, he took another which showed the wheat higher in patches, forming six distinct circles. The inference was that a greater depth of fertilising soil lay below these patches of tall wheat.

Two archaeologists (Captain Cunnington and his wife) resolved to excavate the field, and found in the chalk 160 holes into which piles of wood had been inserted, bearing a striking resemblance in plan to Stonehenge. Charcoal was found round about which proved to have come from the wood of oak, birch, and pine.

The number of holes in each ring (from the innermost outwards) was 12, 18, 18, 16, 32, and 60. There were larger holes for the ring of 16, indicating the insertion of larger poles, ten inches in diameter, while the poles of the three inner rings were three inches in diameter. Beyond the outer ring are traces of a ditch and rampart as at Stonehenge, broken (as there) by a causeway through which the circles were entered. There are four other holes which are so placed beyond the circles that their poles would serve as sighting posts for the Sunrise at the Summer Solstice (like the Friar's Heel at Stonehenge), Sunrise at the Winter Solstice, the South point of the compass, and some other purpose not clearly understood. Within the inner ring (the position where the flat altar stone lies at Stonehenge) was a shallow grave cut a foot deep in the chalk. In it was found the skeleton of a murdered child. The position of this grave in relation to the holes of the sighting-posts give these rings exactly the same orientation as Stonehenge, and there is little doubt that the elaborate monument in wood which stood on this site was the prototype of its great stone neighbour, as the wooden Saxon churches were forerunners of the great Norman churches of stone.

Woodhenge, as this place has been called, served as a centre for fixing the calendar in 2000 BC, but what other purposes it was used for are unknown. The excavators bought the site and handed it over to the Office of Works, and the holes have now been filled with concrete so that we can easily grasp the plan. We can study it more closely at Devizes, where Woodhenge has a fine exhibition in the museum. There are timbers left of Woodhenge, but those who would study these wooden circles of prehistoric days will find the actual timbers of one in the museum at Preston in Lancashire, brought there for preservation from the Bronze Age burial place at Bleasdale.

East Coulston. The birthplace of Mary Delaney, one of the most remarkable women of her time, a close friend of John Wesley's and George the Third's "dearest Mrs Delaney" often mentioned by Fanny Burney.

Born in 1700, the daughter of Bernard Granville, brother of Lord Lansdowne, she was first married to a Mr Pendarves and after his death she married again, in 1743, Dr Patrick Delaney, Dean of Down.

Mrs Delaney was well known to the most outstanding people of the period and her salon was the rendezvous for many of the artists and men of letters of the time. She herself was a talented exponent in oils and water colour and after the death of Dr Delaney in 1768 spent much of her time in making a ten volume collection of flower mosaics in paper, now in the British Museum.

In the church there is a built up Norman doorway and a 17th century brass to "the most virtuous, most loving, and most beloved wife of Francis Godolphin."

Outside in the churchyard, to the east of the church, is a flat gravestone with the following inscription:

Mary Anne Saville Kent who died May 5, 1852 aged 44 and Francis Saville Kent, who was cruelly murdered at Rode, June 30th, 1860, aged three years and ten months. Shall not God search this out, for He knoweth the secrets of the heart.

It was not until 1865 that the perpetration of the crime was discovered and then on the voluntary confession of Constance Kent, Francis Saville Kent's half sister. She made the confession to a clergyman at the time she was being prepared for Confirmation and said that she wished to make it public.

Accordingly she was tried and sentenced to death but the sentence was commuted to penal servitude for life and during the 20 years she was in prison at Portland she became a talented artist in mosaic, and examples of her work in this medium can be seen in the prison chapel at Portland, the Bishop's Chapel at Chichester, and in the convent chapel at East Grinstead.

East Grafton. The village green, with its group of elms and limes, is surrounded with thatched cottages. The church was rebuilt in the 19th century in imitation of the Norman style and on one of the pillars is a brass recording a tragedy when the church was building, when George Montgomery, rector of Bishopstone, was killed by the falling of an unfinished pillar.

East Kennett. It is on the main highway to Bath, a mile or two south of Avebury. Near the neighbouring hamlet of West Kennett, below Silbury Hill, is a famous long barrow 336 feet long, and close to East Kennett is another Woodhenge similar to the famous rings at Durrington. Here are two circles of holes for stone and six for wooden posts. As a skeleton of a Stone Age youth was found together with pottery of the Early Bronze Age, this Woodhenge was probably set up about 1800 BC. The barrow here is one of the longest known.

The church is 13th century with a tower and spire, and in the sanctuary is a curious bust of Charles Tooker wearing a turban, and with two cherubs. He is described as de Kennet Orientali, and facing him is a wall monument to his mother, with her medallion portrait.

East Knoyle. Christopher Wren was born in this village where his father was rector. His birthplace was a small house called Haslam's which stood on the site at present occupied by Knoyle House, Mr Wren and his family having moved into lodgings at Haslam's after a fire at the rectory. The rectory itself has been rebuilt. The church has a fine tower (15th century) with crocketed pinnacles and battlements, with queer gargoyles looking down, and charming belfry windows. There are Tudor roses and marigolds, scrolls and cherubs, and Bible scenes, the angels of Jacob's dream ascending on one side of the altar and descending on the other; the Ascension; and Elijah being fed by the ravens, all in plaster-work on the chancel walls. The east window has lovely glass by Sir Ninian Comper.

One of the rectors who followed Wren's father seems to have been an artist, for he carved the panelled pulpit from which he preached. He was Canon Wake, rector here for 51 years till 1746.

The village has two fine houses: Clouds on one of the hills and Knoyle House below it. Clouds was burned down in 1889 but the present house is an exact copy of the old one by Philip Webb.

Easton. Lies in the shadow of the downs by Savernake Forest. On Easton Hill, 700 feet high, crowned by trees, is what is left of a

British camp. In a meadow by the church are the remains of the priory.

The church itself is late 16th century much renewed. It is raised on a mound with a flagged path between six small trimmed yews, and what we remember of it is a tablet in memory of a brave young man whose father was vicar here. He was David Llewellyn, surgeon on the Confederate steamer Alabama, the ship made in England and sent out to the Confederate Forces in the American Civil War. An act for which the British Government paid three millions sterling after a court of arbitration.

Easton Grey. In a valley near Malmesbury, with a stream meandering past under five old stone arches. The shade of a giant elm falls on the drive from the garden of the great house. Preserved in this house is a rough sculpture of human figures found in a quarry, and inscribed Civilis fecit.

The sturdy tower has stood 600 years, but the church itself is 19th century. The old tower is filled with pews, looking along the quaint white nave through lines of box pews, past the canopied pulpit, to a tiny sanctuary with painted angels and flowers on its walls. They are to the Parry family, who held the manor three centuries ago. There are more painted angels in blue and white on the walls at the west end of the nave, where two sculptured tablets face us. One is to a young wife of 1730; the other is half a century earlier, to Arthur Adye and his Mary. There is a winged cherub above and the words:

Full of all loves, and free from discords here,
Lived and died this very happy pair.

It was Mary who died first, and

Like a turtle, being left alone,
He never ceased to sigh or ever ceased to moan
The loss of his dear comfort, dead and gone.

Ebbesborne Wake. It lies in a hollow of that group of Downs of which White Sheet is a noble member. The 15th century church stands on a hill, its tower about 400 years old, with beautiful pierced stone windows. The chancel has a canopied stone seat with elaborate pinnacled canopies, and along the wall of the sanctuary is a band of heraldic carving from the tomb of an ancient family. The Norman font is carved with arches and flowers.

Edington. It was William of Edington, Lord Chancellor of England and Bishop of Winchester, who began the great work of rebuilding the Norman Cathedral at Winchester in the Gothic style. Here in his native place he founded a priory of the Bonhommes (an Order almost indistinguishable from the Augustinian Canons Regular) in 1362.

The priory is now the parish church which stands by a green hill clothed with trees and has a magnificent exterior. Across the graveyard and a meadow is an old grey house with a turreted garden wall which is all that remains of the conventual buildings.

The lofty porch, with two rooms over it, has a vaulted ceiling, and its great door, studded with nails, and with splendid iron hinges and a big wooden lock, swings ponderously back to reveal the wonder of this place. Lofty clustered columns line the clerestoried nave 75 feet long, its plaster ceilings still with the pink and white colourings of the 17th century. In one of the arches is an elegant stone screen of a 14th century tomb, and across the end of the nave is an altar which completes the nave as the parish church, separate from the chancel and transepts which were the conventual church of the Priory. The central tower has fan-vaulting over the crossing. On the back of the new nave screen, looking into the transepts, are eight portraits painted by Miss E. Warre; they are the Black Prince, John of Aylesbury, William of Wykeham, and William of Edington, with four saints.

Famous for its beauty indoors and out, this fine church is famous also for its series of consecration crosses. There are 12 inside and 10 on the outside walls, only two missing of the complete 24. No old church in England has a complete set left. Here some of these crosses, marking the spots on which the bishop laid his hand on Consecration Day, have been used for memorials, but the new metal crosses are still in the ancient places.

The chancel roof is painted white, patterned with a series of pointed arches with mitred bishops looking down from the spring of each arch. The chancel is rich in small sculptures, lovely heads at the windows of nuns, dainty ladies, and men with chain mail, an angel resting on an elbow, and most beautiful work in six remarkable niches running up the wall. The niches rest on brackets with charming figures of women and angels, and on each bracket rests a great niche for a lifesize figure (two headless ones still in them). The niches are crowned with fan-vaulted canopies which flow into pinnacles, with a charming bracket at the top for another statue.

By the altar is a broken sedilia with three stone seats, one canopy being still complete with the Tudor roses in its vaulting. There is a pillar piscina, Jacobean altar-rails with spikes and balls, and in one corner of the chancel is the only original bench-end still here.

At each end of this magnificent chancel, once the choir of the canons, is a piece of oak carving—a small Jacobean reredos and the great screen, the screen a remarkable possession, for it is one of the few roodlofts still left in England, though its roodbeam has gone. It is a mass of intricate and delicate carving of the 15th century, with a noble canopy. It has very deep cresting and is about five feet wide, and we can stand inside it and look up to the barrel roof, with scores of little bosses. The arch over the doorway is dainty with lovely spandrels.

In the chancel is a great 17th century monument. It is a fascinating piece of work with its superb detail and its fine procession of children. Lady Anne Beauchamp lies a little above her husband, Sir Edward Lewis, to show that she belonged to higher rank than he, but he is more richly clothed. They lie on a bed of plaited straw, with their feet on lions, and a cherub descending from the roof offers them a starry crown.

Lady Anne is robed from head to foot in a long white gown, her hands folded in prayer, with beautifully chiselled features. Sir Edward is in armour with a small moustache and beard, his lace collar falling low on his shoulders. He was a member of the Privy Council of Prince Henry, elder brother of Charles the First. Below their parents kneel five children with praying angels; two of the boys are in armour and one in priest's robes, and the girls are in caps and dainty dresses with pretty shoes.

Across the chancel on the left of the altar is a fine monument by Chantrey, who was paid £2000 for it by a devoted sister. It shows Sir Simon Taylor, who died in Waterloo year, a handsome man on his deathbed with two women mourning. At the west end of the nave is a wall monument to the Taylors with a procession of six kneeling figures, unusual for the 19th century; three old ladies in long gowns and frilled caps tied under their chins, and three old men with stocks, big-buttoned coats, and gaiters.

There is a monument of great beauty under an arch in the nave, a lovely canopied altar tomb in which lies the young friend of William of Edington, his ward Joan, who married Sir Ralph Cheney and died in 1401. She lies here with her lord, their arms and shields along the canopy, borne by angels. There are charming niches and panels of rich heraldic carving round the tomb, and at one end is a doorway with carved panels and crocketed finials. The brasses are gone, but here is still the little fan-vaulted ceiling. In the south transept is a richly canopied 15th century tomb on which lies John of Baynton. It has many niches and a lovely vaulted roof with traces of its medieval colour, and in the sculptured panels is his rebus; a spray of bay leaves and a tun.

In the windows is still much of the original glass. The 14th century Madonna is still bright in her blue robe and golden hair, and St John in a white and gold cloak over his blue gown. There is some 14th century glass in the clerestory.

The old stone font has a 17th century oak cover and the pulpit, with its simple panelling and its carved canopy, is of the same period. On the back of one of the pews near the font is a fine piece of ancient linenfold, and in one of the transepts is a huge oak chest. Perhaps the oldest timbers here are the fine cross-beams still below the plastered roof of the nave; the oldest visible stone is the base of a column from the Norman church at the west end.

In the middle of the 15th century William Ayscough, the venerable Bishop of Salisbury, was rudely dragged from the high altar here, taken to the top of the hill rising so abruptly by the church, and stoned to death. He had been a great favourite with Henry the Sixth and was for many years his confessor, but it is not known for what reason this mob of Jack Cade's followers were incensed against him. "It happened [says old Thomas Fuller] that Jack Cade with his cursed crew fell foul of this prelate; I conceive it was because he was learned, pious, and rich, three capital crimes in a clergyman. They plundered his carriage, taking 10,000 marks from him, then dragged him from the high altar into a hill hard by, barbarously murdered him, tore his shirt in pieces, and left his body naked in the place."

Enford. The church belongs to the 12th and 13th centuries with a 15th century tower. The long and narrow nave has plain round arches set on square pillars, each having a slender round column at each corner carved with delicate capitals. The chancel is remarkable for a series of panelled arches rising from stone seats along its north wall; the arches have delicate mouldings round them, of varying shapes and sizes, and in the midst of them is a passage leading us into a small octagonal chamber. The reredos has paintings of the Annunciation and the Crucifixion. The pulpit has the old hourglass stand. The old font has an elaborate wooden cover. On a pillar of the tower arch there still remains one of the consecration crosses.

There is also a tiny 16th century effigy for Jenifer Baskerville. In the churchyard is the stem of the old cross, and along the bottom runs one of the fine thatched walls which are everywhere in this part of Wiltshire.

In the grounds of Chisenbury, a handsome house about a mile away, is a deep wide tunnel with trees growing on its banks. It is of great age and is called the Gladiator's Walk.

Erlestoke. Many of the cottages have sculptured panels or quaint statues over their doors.

The church, rebuilt in 1880 by G. E. Street, stands at the foot of the hill crowned by a big grey house in a park of 260 acres, a river flowing past. The capitals and bosses of the old Norman piers which carried the old arcades are turned into tables for prayer books. The fine modern font has graceful panels. The 17th century pulpit is richly carved with leaves, flowers, and strapwork. On a wall are some lovely heraldic stone carvings, showing squirrels and a stag's head with a cross between its antlers and an arrow in its mouth.

Etchilhampton. On entering the church one is faced with a figure of the archangel Gabriel set in the wall facing the door, a quaint but splendid figure with a pinnacled canopy to shelter him, and a row of flowers down one side of the panel. There are flowers also round the capitals of the chancel arch, and more on the 17th century wall monument to Gertrude Ernle. The font is Norman, but most of the church is 13th century. The graceful tracery of the west window is 14th century.

There is a 15th century tomb in a chancel recess of an unknown knight and his lady. He is a fine figure in armour, a sword and dagger at his belt, at his head a shield, and at his feet a lion. His lady has a long cloak over her dress, an embroidered bodice, and an elegant headdress. Round the tomb are 12 small weepers, their sons and daughters, all wearing long gowns. One of the weepers holds a sword, another a shield, a third a wreath, a fourth a small disc; the rest are folding their hands in prayer.

Everleigh. There are British camps about the village, which is set in the fine open country near Pewsey.

The church is early 19th century but contains the Norman font from the old church. In the nave a striking monument—with cannon ball—for Francis Dugdale Astley.

The fine timbers of the roof rest on 16 stone corbels, with carved heads curiously varied in their expressions.

On a mound by the inn is a fine group of trees named Alma Clump, planted by Sir John Astley on his return from the Crimea.

Farley. Sir Stephen Fox, who told Charles the Second of Cromwell's death, built this handsome church about the time Christopher Wren was building St Paul's. It has simple panelling and pews, a 17th century font, and three dignified screens. The handsome pulpit is carved with arches and festoons of fruit. There is a marble wall monument by Westmacott to the second Earl of Ilchester and his wife, whose busts are shown in relief. Sir Stephen Fox, who died in 1696, has a wall monument with an excellent portrait bust of his wife, her hair falling over her shoulders, and the words:

A patriot's even course he steered
Mid faction's wildest storms unmoved,
By all who marked his mind revered,
By all who knew his heart beloved.

A great builder of his time, Sir Stephen Fox gave Farley the fine group of almshouses facing the church in which his portrait hangs, said to be by Peter Lely. Sir Stephen has monuments in many churches, but is buried here, where he was born in 1627, a yeoman farmer's son. Entering the Percy household as a page, he was taught soldiering and at the Battle of Worcester was second in command of the ordnance of Charles the Second.

Accompanying Charles in his flight to the Continent, he was appointed manager and financier of the royal household. Throughout those poverty-stricken years, when Charles's followers starved in rags and Charles's own belongings had to be pawned, Fox contrived to raise money and to avert disaster.

Sir Stephen set up churches and almshouses, founded the Chelsea Hospital for disabled soldiers, Evelyn working out the plans with him, and Fox gave £13,000 towards the work.

By his first wife he had ten children, and, hale and hearty at 76, he married again and had four more, of whom one became Earl of Ilchester, and another Lord Holland, father of Charles James Fox.

Fifield Bavant. A pretty village in the Chalk valley, it has one of the smallest churches in England, 35 feet long and 15 wide, perched alone in a field on a grassy hill. The roof beams are dark with age. The font is Norman, and has a round bowl standing on a single pillar. The cover is solid and of great weight, probably 15th century.

Figheldean. In the prehistoric world round Amesbury, it is made charming by elms, orchards, and thatched roofs.

In the church, on raised stone benches on either side of the door, are effigies of two armoured knights, their shields broken. It is said that they were found in a field. The angels at the head of one are nearly gone, but have escaped sufficiently for us to admire their beautifully draped coats, the lions at their feet; and the way they are drawing their swords. The lofty 13th century nave has a 14th century clerestory with cusped windows set in pairs, simple columns and arches, 14th century aisles; and under the charming modern balustrade of the bellringers' gallery is a lovely little Norman arch with sculptured capitals. From the chancel steps this arch and gallery, set within the high arch of the tower, are seen to great advantage.

The chancel is raised up five steps, and in it is a canopied piscina. There are delightful traceried windows and an old roodloft doorway, and eight stone heads supporting the fine roof of the nave.

Fisherton-de-la-Mere. A charming hamlet in the Wylye valley, reached by rough but pretty lanes, it has a 13th century church rebuilt in the 19th, keeping its old pinnacled tower, and its ancient scratch-dial and font, and an old pulpit with carved panels. Also a wall monument of 1624, with two small figures stretched on beds. There is a beautiful modern rood screen and loft by F. C. Eden.

Fittleton. A beautiful corner of the Avon valley near Amesbury, it has a church which takes us back to the Conqueror's day. Its medieval tower has a turret and a miniature spire, and round the walls are toy-like buttresses. The lofty tower arch looks through the clerestoried nave to a very small pointed chancel arch leading up steps to the altar. By the altar is the tomb with two brass inscriptions by Thomas Kaye, one to his father who was rector here in Elizabethan days, and one to his wife Anne, who left 11 children motherless. She was Miss Joy, and the epitaph, which comes from the days when puns were regarded as the very soul of wit and says that, though the Joy of Heaven is gone, she left some joys her dearest joy to cheer.

Under the altar, his tomb hidden by the embroidered hangings, lies Lord St Aldwyn, familiar as Sir Michael Hicks Beach, Chancellor of the Exchequer in the years before World War I.

Bromham: Sir Edward Baynton with his two wives and two children, 1578

Dauntsey: Lady Anne Danvers, kneeling before the Trinity, 1539

Fovant: George Rede and the Scene of the Annunciation, 1492

THREE NOTABLE WILTSHIRE BRASSES

Round the walls of the nave, bearing up the roof and decorating the clerestory windows, is a fine gallery of sculptured heads. In one window is a figure of the Good Shepherd, a tribute by seven children in memory of their parents.

Fonthill Gifford. Only a tiny portion remains—one of the small towers and one of the rooms—of the immense house built by the millionaire eccentric William Beckford to the designs of James Wyatt. It was built in the "pasteboard gothic" style, a vast house with a dining-room 40 ft long, a picture gallery 45 yards in length, and a central tower about the same height as St Paul's dome.

Beckford, who commenced this house in 1790, was so impatient to get it built that 500 men were employed night and day and all through a bitter winter, fires being kept burning all round the site to prevent the cement and mortar from freezing. There were two disasters with the central tower in the course of its erection but it was eventually completed in time for Christmas 1800 when Beckford entertained Lord Nelson. But even so the upper stages of the tower were little more than lath and plaster, its foundations were hopelessly inadequate and it collapsed—and demolished much of the house—quite suddenly on a still summer day in 1807.

But by that time Beckford had lost much of his fortune, had left Fonthill and had gone to live on Lansdowne Hill at Bath where the local architect, W. E. Goodridge, built another, and a more secure, tower for him in 1825–6.

Fonthill Abbey has vanished, but Beckford's most abiding memorial is in the hundreds of trees he planted and still growing in the park, around which there was a wall seven miles long and 12 feet high.

Some of the treasures Beckford collected to furnish his great mansion are preserved in the modern house which has been built on its site.

The church at Fonthill was rebuilt in the 19th century. The apse in memory of a rector for 46 years.

Fovant. It has a little river running by the village street and reflecting bright gardens, and cut on the downs above it is an inescapable reminder of World War I, the badges of the regiments encamped here.

The church is 15th century, and its splendid turreted tower has a beautiful pierced and embattled parapet, niches with canopies, angels with spread wings, stone lattice windows in the belfry, fierce-looking gargoyles, a scratch-dial, and a pointed doorway with angels. A wall brass in the chancel records the building of the tower. It is in memory of George Rede who was rector at the time, and shows the Annunciation; the rector with his rosary over his arm is kneeling behind the Madonna, rays of light pouring down on her, the paraclete in a form of a bird (which looks astonishingly like a duck!) flying towards her. The angel is kneeling at her feet, and the background is patterned with flowers. There is a small and unusual Norman doorway in the chancel, with an arch decorated with interlaced strapwork. It has four pillars with carved capitals. Grotesques grin down from the old windows, and many of the roof brackets have deeply carved foliage.

On a gable at the east end of the church is a Norman cross with a horseshoe carved on it in relief; it was found during restoration.

Froxfield. The small flint church was built 800 years ago. There are two simple 12th century doorways with solid pieces of timber wedged across the lintels, deeply splayed windows, a scratch-dial, and a font that was here when the church was new. The north, south, and west walls are from the 13th, 14th, and 15th centuries. In the chancel are two richly carved chairs.

The charm of Froxfield, a village of thatched cottages and half-timbered houses, is in the spacious green quadrangle of the Duchess of Somerset's almshouses. The Duchess was buried in Westminster Abbey in 1692, and her portrait hangs in the dining-room of an Oxford college, but her chief monument is here. Her arms are on the gatehouse leading from the Bath Road into the great square of simple red brick houses in which widows have lived for generation after generation. A small chapel in the middle of the lawn has been rebuilt, and the almshouses were added to in 1775, when the architect put his name in black bricks under seven blank windows (Thogale).

Near Froxfield is Rudge, famous for the Rudge Cup found in 1725 in a well filled with rubbish, bones, skeletons, and Roman coins. The cup is bronze, and remarkable because it has round it the names of stations on or near Hadrian's Wall. It is now preserved at Alnwick Castle in Northumberland.

Fyfield. It is on the Marlborough road, with a striking ruin from the prehistoric past and a small church of the 13th century. The tower was added in the 15th century and has gargoyles and pinnacles. Its arch has panelled sides, and an ancient little screen across it has four oak carvings showing the Road to Calvary, the Madonna, the Ascension, and Christ with a disciple. On the pulpit are three figures of Our Lord with Peter and Paul. The fine Norman font has elegant arcades resting on 20 slender columns. The roof has ancient timbers.

Up a lane across the Marlborough road and passing through the fields to Clatford Bottom, is a low arch made of four great stones. They are all that remain of a long barrow, the surrounding earth having been taken away. Thousands of these monster sarsen stones are scattered about this neighbourhood, resting in disorder as if a giant had thrown them down. The ruined monument is known as the Devil's Den.

Garsdon. A village set in the hills round Malmesbury.

The church is reached by a long path between yew hedges. The bells in the tower were given by Richard Moody, a servant of Henry the Eighth, who was given the manor of Garsdon because, it is said, he helped his majesty up one day after he had fallen in the mud, such deep mud that he was unable to extricate himself from it on account of his mighty bulk.

Richard Moody sold the manor to the Washingtons. Their gabled house stands on a hill with noble views, with its gables and its groups of square chimneys, but a manor house no more. Here lived Washingtons for generations, and in due course came Laurence Washington, whom they brought here in 1640 when he died, setting on the wall a heraldic monument with a shield painted with gold stars and red stripes. Centuries before they came on to the American flag the stars and stripes were on this wall, with a winged cherub guarding them below and above a pair of the most extraordinary figures we have seen, loosely draped and lounging on cushions over the top of this odd sculpture. The memorial was found broken long ago and was restored this century (twisted columns, wreath of flowers, weird figures, and all) by the Bishop of New York and American friends, Laurence Washington having been the cousin of the great-great-great grandfather of the President. It was Laurence Washington's wife who gave the plate for the altar; she is buried here.

Great Bedwyn. A richly timbered place, with a canal threading its way under little bridges. In the church is the tomb of Sir John Seymour, father of the third wife of Henry the Eighth, and of the Thomas Seymour who married the king's widow.

In a window of the church, near the tomb of Sir John Seymour, is some heraldic glass brought from Wulfhall, the vanished home of the Seymours, of which the ruins of a barn remain at Burbage close by.

Sir John Seymour was the father of Lord Protector Somerset, Queen Jane Seymour, and the admiral who married Catherine Parr. Two of his sons lost their heads in rebellions and one lies with him here, his portrait in brass on the wall showing him in a long robe with furred cuffs and collars. Sir John himself is a noble figure in his long black hair, wearing gilded mail, white armour with gold studs, and black straps with gold buckles. His head rests on a stone helmet with wings springing from a wreath, the wings made of wood. At his feet is a lion with crossed paws, and at his side is a dagger in a black sheath.

On the wall close by Sir John is the monument of Lady Frances Devereux, an 18th century Duchess of Somerset, wearing a bodice with elaborate clasps and pearls in her hair, which is piled on her head.

Under simple arches in a transept lies the builder of this impressive place, Sir Roger de Stokke; he built the church in memory of his father, who died in 1313. Sir Roger's tomb has lost its brass cross, but Sir Adam's has his statue in chain mail, his crossed feet on a lion, and his hands on a sword. Near their tombs are part of the lovely canopy and a piscina with an ape's face carved on it, its brow crowned with oak leaves and its mouth holding an oak spray.

The great arcades of the nave have on their capitals some of the best carving of our early sculptors. The capitals are all different, and there seem to be hundreds of leaves on them, one having also a group of three heads looking like portraits, very natural faces. The transepts and the chancel roofs are rich with stone corbels carved with faces, among whom we noticed a lady in an extraordinary wimple, drawn about her throat. The stone pulpit is modern, buttressed and canopied with panels of rich carving round it.

The ancient rood screen and 13th century chest are both at South Kensington.

There are two magnificent cedars and a noble beech in the churchyard and the tower has a splendid parapet of open arches, looking a little odd without their pinnacles. There is a fine old cross in the churchyard with a tiny figure of a bishop standing on a lamb, much worn by 500 winters, and in this village of raised pavements and dormered houses is a thatched cottage with a high-pitched roof in which Thomas Willis, Charles the Second's doctor, was born in 1621.

His father was a Royalist farmer who was killed during the siege of Oxford. Thomas entered the household of a canon of Christ Church, but the Civil War called him to Charles's army. He managed, however, to study surgery, to take his medical degree, and to build up a practice at Oxford.

He obtained a professorship of natural philosophy, published the results of his exploration of the brain and nervous system, and had his friend Sir Christopher Wren as an illustrator of some of his work. At Oxford he was the friend of the group of scientists who formed the Royal Society. Combining research with a practice and unwearied authorship, he made the first important discovery as to the cause and treatment of diabetes, whose complete cure remained for our own age to achieve.

He took no part in the controversy aroused by Harvey's discovery as to the circulation of the blood, but his own work on the course of the blood through the brain was fundamental, and a portion of the brain is still called Willis's Circle. His observations on hysteria and other nervous disorders, recorded from his own cases, were important to his own and succeeding generations. He died at his house in St Martin's Lane, London, in 1675, only 54, and he is buried in Westminster Abbey.

Great Chalfield. A beautiful group of buildings reflected in the still water of a moat. Standing in green fields watered by a stream, it is like a picture of England's country life in the days when manor, farm, and church were the centre of a small community. For ever we must be thankful to Thomas Tropenell, the benefactor of this place in early Tudor days. He added the charming bell turret with its graceful spire to the 13th century church; he built the chapel and made it a miracle of colour; and he built the lovely manor house with the farm buildings still largely Elizabethan, brought up to date in later days, and once surrounded by a towered wall of which battered remains still show along the brink of the moat. The house has been described as one of the most interesting and perfect examples of domestic Gothic architecture in England. Fierce heads of griffins top the gables, figures of men and women rise at the roof-ends. The porch roof has carved bosses, and the front has lovely oriels, one with delicately carved cresting.

The church has a shallow-hooded porch, panelled underneath, sheltering an ancient studded door. There are two consecration crosses painted on the nave wall in the 15th century, bright fragments of ancient glass in the windows, an old bench with poppyheads, and two old chairs by the altar. The old font is plain, the old two-decker pulpit is panelled, and there is a modern reredos. The modern chancel screen has carving of a vine, birds in branches, and a climbing lizard; over its arch are two smiling cherubs, while on the side posts are the Twelve Apostles, one above the other under tiny canopies. Between the chancel and the vestry is another screen with much of its 15th century oak.

The 18th century vestry houses a handsome old chest as well as a little modern organ gay with painted panels.

Thomas Tropenell's chapel has a finely panelled stone altar, a lovely stone screen emblazoned with heraldry, and a squint into the chancel; and there are traces of paintings on the walls to suggest the glory of this chapel when every inch of wall space was covered by paintings. His arms are in the roof and on the screen, but his pictures, which survived 400 years and were covered last century with a thick preserving coat, have lost their glory, and we can trace them now only with the help of an old description that has been in existence since 1760. They have been cleaned and treated in our time.

We know the story of the six panels on the west wall of the chapel; it is the story of St Catherine, and the first and second scenes are the best preserved. In the first Catherine is disputing with the emperor, she in a red cloak and a coronet, the emperor in scarlet with a drawn sword. In the second scene she is disputing with the pagan doctors, who wear green robes and red caps, and the emperor is striking one of them in the face with his sceptre. The third picture shows the scourging of Catherine, the fourth shows her in prison with the empress and the captain of the guard kneeling before her, the fifth shows the executioners being struck down by a miracle, and the sixth shows Catherine beheaded, with the emperor looking on.

Thomas Tropenell's manor house has been restored after a long period of neglect, and is now in the keeping of the National Trust.

Great Cheverell. It lies in the hilly country on the northern borders of the Great Plain. Its manor house and church are next-door neighbours, the manor garden lining the churchyard with a lovely yew hedge. In the garden is an ancient brick court house with tall windows and a flight of stone steps to the door. A pretty little doorway leads to the cells below.

The church has a 13th century chancel; the rest is mainly 15th century. Note the lofty porch, 17th century colouring on the nave wagon-roof, and a chapel with a delightful roof of moulded beams and charming floral bosses. On the walls is a handsome heraldic monument, with the painted shield still bright, to James Townsend and his wife who died in the 18th century. By the new font is the carved bowl of the old one.

In the chancel is a canopied recess in which the founder probably lies, and in the nave is a stone with the name of Sir James Stonehouse, who died in 1795. He is remembered because he appeared as Mr Johnson in one of Hannah More's tracts.

Great Somerford. It is a village of charming old houses. West Street Farm has in its walls some chevron moulding, a shield with a lion, and some floral medallions, all from the ancient church. Near the vicarage is a little timbered house, and Brook Farm on the banks of the Avon is Georgian, with an old sundial on the lawn and a remarkable summerhouse made out of a flourishing yew. On one side of the church is the 17th century vicarage. A circular mound with a group of ash and chestnut trees is thought to have been the site of an old castle.

The church has been here 500 years and has fragments of Norman carving. The font is 15th century, carved by the men who set the arches of the nave on their clustered columns and gave them their fine capitals of leaves and faces; on one of them they put a queer cherub and a heart, and on another, peeping from among the leaves, an odd creature like a flying monkey, next to a woman with curls. On a smaller capital are the emblems of the Passion. The modern pulpit has a Jacobean canopy, and in a narrow lancet window above it is old glass with angels leaning out of the pinnacled top of a canopy. On the sanctuary wall is a tablet in memory of Stephen Demainbray, Chaplain to George the Third, who is remembered here as the poor man's friend because he let his glebe in small allotments and obtained portions of land for the people. On the right of the altar is a window with the Madonna and her mother and St Catherine with her wheel. On the north aisle wall is an 18th century sculpture of the Good Samaritan; his neighing horse is tied to a tree, and the callous passers-by are walking up the hill, caring nothing.

Great Wishford. An old low bridge with poplars and silvery willows to keep it company crosses the Wylye flowing on to Salisbury, and leads us to this quiet place.

Above it on the Downs is Grovely Wood, with trees so great and so old that their branches sweep the ground. The wood was once one of the biggest in Wiltshire, and had a British camp shaped like a crescent, a mile long.

Facing the church is a row of almshouses founded in 1628 by Sir Richard Grobham for four poor people. They have tiny dormer windows and railed steps up from the street.

A pierced cornice with battlements and pinnacles crowns the 15th century tower of the church. It has traceried belfry windows and gargoyles. A splendid possession is the font, fashioned by the Norman masons. Its sides are decorated with ten columns, carved with capitals of which no two are alike, and the spaces between are also carved. The chancel is 700 years old. Here is a canopied tomb counted as one of the finest of Wiltshire's 17th century monuments. Under the canopy lie Sir Richard Grobham in gold and white armour with scarlet strappings, his feet on a gilded boar's head carved in wood, and his wife in sober black, resting her feet against a wooden dove on a tree stump. The lower side of the canopy has small panels, each holding a cherub with golden wings. At each end, in a niche, stands a gold and white angel, one weeping and one praying. Opposite hangs Sir Richard's white banner with a lion on a crimson ground, and on a bracket is his helmet, with a golden board's head crest. Sir Richard is said to have been the last man to kill a wild boar in Groveley Forest. By the pulpit is a great chest with a coved lid, three big locks, iron handles, and round feet.

Under a heavy stone canopy lies Sir Thomas Bonham as he was in 1473, in a long gown with a bag hanging from his girdle and his sword beside him. His head, showing much character, rests on a pillow, and near it kneels the tiny figure of his wife dressed like a nun. Not far away in the floor are four worn little figures in brass, all that remain of the brasses of their nine children. An unknown stone lady in a simple headdress and a long gown, her feet on a lion, lies under a plain canopy close by.

Let into the churchyard wall are stones giving the price of bread per gallon in 1800, 1801, 1904, and 1920 (3s 4d, 3s 10d, 10d, 2s 8d).

Ham. Among the chalk hills and lovely woods of the Berkshire border; with thatched cottages. The church is small and ancient with a low embattled tower, a simple old font, panelled box-pews and altar rails of the 18th century, a canopied piscina, a gallery and dormer windows, and roof posts like deer antlers. There is a handsome heraldic wall monument to Richard Gillingham, a rector of 200 years ago.

Set on a wall, in a wood imitation of the marble monuments of the period, are two excellent brasses of John Hunt, yeoman, and his wife Christian, both kneeling. John was born in 1500 and died at 90. They were generous friends of the village, John leaving dowries for the marriage of poor maidens, and endowing an almshouse in Berkshire, "moved thereto by Christian."

Hankerton. It has a row of grinning apes and men looking down on it from the battlements of its 15th century tower. In the buttresses of the tower are graceful canopied niches, and on top of these are curled up two big dragons. One is a splendid specimen practically as its sculptor left it; the other has suffered sadly from the hands of Time. The doorway has a single band of moulding ending with still more dragons, sculptured in the 13th century, and on the gable is a three-faced sundial.

On the wall of this small church is a dignified monument of Giles Earle (1746) by Nollekens, the sculptor, miser, and collector, who left behind him more than 300 busts, statues, and monuments. The great arch of the tower climbs to the roof, looking like a chancel arch; the new chancel arch is one of the smallest we have seen, like a doorway. Between the two are four little round columns with Norman arches on them.

In the chancel is a neat piscina with a trefoiled arch and a projecting bowl. The 15th century font is carved with flowers. The wagon roof has its old timbers. Outside are two charming little heads at a Tudor window, and in the churchyard is a fragment of an ancient cross.

Hannington. In a hollow among the trees round Cricklade, it has a fine elm avenue with its big house at one end and its little church at the other. Hannington Hall is a beautiful Elizabethan house with a pierced parapet. The church has 17th century walls and a 15th century tower. The lid of a stone coffin is in a south buttress, and on the simple 14th century porch is one of the old scratch-dials which were the first village clocks, with a hole for the pointer. Above a lovely Norman doorway, rich in mouldings, is a small head.

In the tower an elaborate wall monument portrays an engaging couple who died over 200 years ago, Thomas Pile and his daughter Elizabeth Freke. Their busts are borne by cherubs. Probably from the 13th century is the ancient woman in a wimple and long gown, who lies on the floor with two heads by her stone pillow, one of a bishop.

Hardenhuish (pronounced Harnish). Has a most beautiful little church built by John Wood of Bath in 1781. The stones of the old Norman church, which stood at the foot of the hill, were used in its building. There are balustrades round the parapet, an octagonal tower with open arches and bands of foliage on the altar with bunches of grapes.

Near the altar is a monument to the famous 19th century radical and political economist, David Ricardo, who has an elaborate tomb in the churchyard by William Pitts who was responsible for many of the carved reliefs at Buckingham Palace. Besides being a sculptor Pitts was also a talented painter and designer of china and was ambidextrous, using both hands at the same time.

Heddington. On the Marlborough Downs, it lies with burial mounds about it, in sight of Cherhill's white horse, and Wansdyke passing by.

The church has been here 700 years, and has a 15th century tower with a turret looking across the Downs, a pinnacled porch with a canopied niche, a roof like a barn with beams bleached by centuries, an old mass dial, an ancient font with 25 little arches round the bowl and a Jacobean cover with a charming dove, a new chancel arch of Norman shape on fanlike corbels, small and dainty, and one of the rare organs that are elegant and pleasing. It has been giving out its music since the 18th century and is made of lovely wood and decorated with musical instruments.

It is one of those churches which are also museums and preserve whatever is of interest to the village, and in a case are kept fragments of medieval tiles and Roman bricks, and a Bible older than the Authorised Version, still with its chain; it is the edition of Miles Coverdale; that Bible known as "The Treacle Bible," as the phrase There is no balm in Gilead, is rendered "There is no treacle in Gilead."

Heytesbury. It has a fine park with an early 19th century house in it, a charming group of 18th century almshouses, a 700-year-old church, and one of the finest views in Wiltshire, across fold upon fold of hills.

In the village street is an old stone lock-up with a door, and here are the almshouses, founded by the Hungerfords in the 15th century and made new in the 18th, when they were rebuilt round three sides of a square. They are for 12 old men and one old lady, with a chaplain. The men wear a blue coat with a red cross on the breast, and on Sundays a red coat and top hat.

The church has a 13th century tower with a medieval bell, a chancel with three Norman pillars, and a 15th century aisled nave with clerestory windows. The beautiful vaulted ceiling of the Hungerford chapel is a ruin, with broken fragments of stone ribs springing from corbels carved with an angel and a winged bull. The stone screen of the chapel has happily survived; it is an exquisite piece of work with lovely fan-vaulting and the three sickles of the Hungerfords over the archway. Near the screen kneel three alabaster figures from the 17th century tomb of Thomas More and his wife Rachel who has a pretty gown with flowers on her bodice, and their little one is in a long frock. The arcades in the chancel were remade last century from the stones of the old arches; the nave arcades are original, and round their wallplates run little flowers.

Wiltshire antiquarians should make this churchyard a place of pilgrimage, for here lies that William Cunnington who was the Father of Wiltshire Archaeology. His stone, we read, has been renewed by his grandson, his great-grandson, and his great-great-grandson.

Near the church is Parsonage Farm, its house having a 17th century plaster ceiling from which bearded heads rise out of crowns, birds, fruit, and flowers, with pendants, and the coat-of-arms of the Mores.

Highway. Far from the highway, it lies in a wooded valley north of Calne, a new church with an old farm for its neighbour. The church, with a shingled turret, was built last century, incorporating a Norman doorway. The old font, with leaves curling gracefully round its shallow bowl has been taken to the restored Church of St. Nicholas at Great Yarmouth in Norfolk. There is also an old stone screen pierced by a simple arch and six panels. On the top of it is a painted beam beautifully carved, once part of the rood screen.

Highworth. On one of the hills of this old town one can see three counties.

The handsome 15th century church was fortified and held for the king but was stormed by the conquering Fairfax. The fallen soldiers were buried in a field near by, and we can see the mark of the battle on the tower, which was hit by a cannon ball near the doorway, and in the south chapel of the church is a cannon ball which struck the tower. By the west door are three headless angels, perhaps yet another sign of those tragic years.

The church has a parapeted porch with pinnacles, a splendid triple niche over its doorway with vaulted canopies, and an upper room reached by a turret. The ceiling of the tower has beautiful fan-vaulting, and over the south aisle door is a rare piece of Norman carving, the tympanum of some lost doorway. It has a man gripping a lion by its jaws under an arch of twining flowers, and is thought to represent David fighting the king of beasts. The richly carved pulpit is Elizabethan; the font, carved with shields and flowers, is 15th century; the chancel has a few 15th century misereres showing angel, man, and mermaid; and the altar has a silver cross in memory of a vicar killed by falling from his horse in 1932. It has a lovely chalice 400 years older, engraved with the figure of Our Lord holding a palm leaf.

A splendid transept window has figures of King Alfred, Richard Lionheart, and St Michael, shining warriors standing here in tribute to those of Highworth's warrior sons who never came back.

One of the odd possessions of the church is in a glass case on a transept wall, a small tattered tunic with a lion across the breast, such as medieval knights wore over their armour; above it is a helmet.

Hill Deverill. It lies among the Downs and is watered by the Deverill stream. The lovely manor house has a parapet and round-headed windows set in groups, a huge gabled barn with timbers five centuries old, and thatched stables that set us wondering, for they have queer windows and peepholes in unexpected places, charming low doorways, and traces of colour on the plaster walls. A big letter C suggests that the stables were once the home of the Cokers, whose monuments are in the church by the reed-covered banks of the River Wylye. The church was poorly rebuilt in 1843. There are two curious wood tablets and a brass. Sir Henry Coker, who died in 1661 a faithful servant of the Stuarts, has painted on his tablet his arms and a sleeping figure in a shroud. On the brass is engraved a skull, a pickaxe, a winged hourglass, a cherub, a shovel, and crossbones, in memory of Henry Croker who died in the reign of George the Second.

Also the tomb of John Ludlow, which has been here about 400 years. Its traceried sides are sculptured with heraldry and the shields are borne by angels.

Hilmarton. The church has a handsome pinnacled tower but its finest possession is the stone chancel screen, with fine tracery picked out in gold. It is about five centuries old, and superbly guards the chancel as we see it from the tower. The oldest thing it has is the arcade of pointed arches in the nave; they are from the end of the 12th century, the work of our earliest English builders. The fine barrel roof of the nave is about 500 years old, and its oak is carved with gilded bosses. There is a modern font, a canopied recess for a tomb, and the remains of the rood stairs. From the aisle to the chancel we pass through a passage in a buttress.

Also a fine copy of the Authorised Version of the Bible (1611) chained to the lectern.

A hamlet a mile and a half away is called New Zealand.

Hilperton. It has grey stone houses and colour-washed cottages, an old stone lock-up with a dome and no windows, and a 14th century church tower with a small stone spire. Most interesting of all, the Norman font with arches and leaves sculptured round it.

Hindon. This village was entirely destroyed by fire in 1765. The church was rebuilt in 1871.

But beyond the Downs is a fine company of trees called Great Ridge Wood marching along the hilltops 700 feet up, where W. H. Hudson used to come and where he stood and watched with joy a stray roebuck flashing through the trunks of trees.

Holt. A wide village green and a modern church, built to match its 15th century tower. Beneath the pinnacles and gargoyles of the old tower are the remains of two canopied niches, an angel spreading its wings under one. Below the angel, and carved also on the embattled parapet, are spiked wheels for St Catherine, Holt's patron saint.

She appears with her wheel in a niche of the porch, and again in the gallery of fine modern glass in the chancel windows. With her are Dorothy carrying a basket of roses, Lucy with her palm and a lamp, Edith holding a crucifix, and Agnes with a lamb. Other pictures in this gallery show Jesus with the two disciples in the room at Emmaus, St Nicholas and his ship, St George in his armour, and two delightful portraits of Aldhelm and Birinus, with their churches of Sherborne and Dorchester in the background.

Also a small Norman font.

Horningsham. It is a village with a great house and a little chapel a mile apart but belonging to each other, and in between them, at the inn, one of the most remarkable groups of trees in England. It is a company of knotted limes, four rows of three with hundreds of arms and literally countless heads, their tops all meeting so that they stand like a living group and we walk in and out among them as in a cathedral crypt. They are called the Twelve Apostles, and four companions a little way off are called the Four Disciples.

The church was rebuilt except the tower in 1844. In the chancel are 15th century glass medallions showing events in the life of Christ.

The windows are not all the church has of interest. It has a noble tower with seats all round the bottom and traceried windows at the top. All over the walls a sculptor has left us something to captivate the eye—queer animals on the stringcourse, one climbing up, one creeping down, one afraid to do either; horned gargoyles, little heads on windows and doorways, canopied niches on buttresses, and winged angels. There are four stone angels in the chancel roof and oak angels looking down with the lamps for the altar hanging from them; and there are more angels and winged creatures on the choir stalls.

The tower looks out on a magnificent countryside with a splendid clump of beeches on the skyline.

The little chapel is older than the Spanish Armada, the oldest Nonconformist chapel in the kingdom. In those days it belonged to the great house, and they rose together. It happened that Sir John Thynne, who married the heiress of Sir Richard Gresham, one of London's richest merchants, was not satisfied to have merely a great house but must have a veritable palace, and he brought down a company of artisans from Scotland to build Longleat. It was in 1566, and as there was nowhere for the Scottish Presbyterians to go on Sunday, Sir John set his builders to work on a little chapel with white walls and a deeply thatched roof, where his men could meet and hold their service. They lived at a place still called Little Scotland, and they started the first regular nonconformist chapel within these walls.

White, square, with thatched eaves about two feet all round, it is likely to stand as long as Longleat. Its neat pulpit rests on a pillar and has an oak back; its gallery stands on eight black columns with a gold band round; its windows have small leaded panes.

In this little place Nonconformists have been meeting for nearly 400 years. Its first minister walked here from Warminster and so cleared the Five Mile Act by which no Nonconformist could hold a service within five miles of a town.

It is to LONGLEAT HOUSE, at the end of a straight walk of three-quarters of a mile between two splendid avenues, that the village owes its beauty and all its great possessions.

It was perhaps the most magnificent house in England 250 years ago, said Macaulay, and we may say so still. Whether it is approached down the straight drive from Warminster or from this village it is thrilling to come upon this noble place. It is one of the rarest gifts of the 16th century to the domestic architecture of England, a stately place inside and out with a front which is majestic. It is 800 feet round, crowned with domes and cupolas and with sculptured figures standing on the parapets. Everywhere is the relief of ornaments, and busts set in medallions. There are hundreds of windows and over a thousand stone mullioned lights.

Its walls are rich with tapestry, some of it priceless. Its ceilings are superb and all different, crammed with wondrous carving or lovely painting; hundreds of paintings and thousands of carved and gilded fragments there must be. The pictures on the walls would furnish any gallery and make it rich, the marvellous cabinets with their loveliness and ingenuity of construction must be the envy of museums. Here is Sir Joshua Reynolds's portrait of Lord Chancellor Thurlow, Holbein's portrait of Protector Somerset; a portrait of the Countess of Nottingham who kept the ring of Essex from Queen Elizabeth the First; and there are portraits by Kneller, Peter Lely, and Raphael.

There is a 14th century marriage chest. There are hangings of 16th century velvet, Gobelin tapestries, astonishing mantelpieces sculptured in marble, borne on the backs of colossal figures and crowned with sculpture. We do not wonder that Queen Elizabeth came to see this house building, and that Charles the Second delighted to be here, but the man who is always identified with Longleat is Bishop Ken who was one of the seven Bishops who went to the Tower rather than conform to the wishes of James the Second. They were acquitted at their trial but in after years a few among them went into exile rather than take the oath of allegiance to King William the Third who they did not regard as their lawful sovereign.

Bishop Ken is one of the most famous of these Non-Jurors and after his resignation of the See of Bath and Wells he came to Longleat as the guest of Lord Weymouth.

He brought his library with him and his books are still on the shelves. Here it was that he wrote his famous morning and evening hymns—"Awake my soul, and with the sun" and "Glory to Thee, my God, this night."

It was George Herbert of Bemerton who gave in prose an account of the ideal country parson in *The Priest to the Temple* and it was Bishop Ken who gave it again in verse:

Give me the Priest these Graces shall possess:
Of an Ambassador the just Address,
A Father's Tenderness, a Shepherd's Care,
A Leader's Courage, which the Cross can bear,
A Ruler's Arm, a Watchman's wakeful Eye,
A Pilot's Skill the Helm in storms to ply,
A Fisher's Patience and a Lab'rer's Toil,
A Guide's Dexterity to disembroil,
A Prophet's Inspiration from Above,
A Teacher's Knowledge, and a Saviour's Love.

Huish. At the foot of the Marlborough Hills a little track climbs up to a church and a farm. The church was rebuilt last century after 700 years, and has little to show except an old scratch-dial and a small portable font with a domed cover. The farm is said to be that of the John Reed who lies in the big table tomb in the graveyard at the west end of the church. His was a sad story, a bit of real life which interested Dickens, who told it in *Household Words*.

It is the story of a thriving young bachelor farmer, respected and liked by all, and a young lady brought to his house after an accident on the Downs. John Reed fell deeply in love with her, but she felt no love for him, and when she was better she rode away, and John went into one of his barns and took his life.

On Huish Hill are the remains of a prehistoric village, and there are many ancient camps and earthworks hereabout; the ancient Wansdyke runs this way.

Hullavington. In a farmhouse of this village between Malmesbury and Chippenham lived the man who wrote two lines that rang through England and have never been forgotten, and who was hanged for writing them:

The Cat, the Rat, and Lovel the Dog
Rule all England under the Hog.

The hog, of course, was Richard the Third, and he executed William Collingbourne who wrote the lines in the farmhouse here, which was then the manor house and stands a mile away under fine trees and among old barns. Refashioned in the 17th century, the house still has William Collingbourne's dining-room with two traceried windows.

We found grapes growing here on a cottage wall, but the surprise of the village is its church extraordinary. It is a remarkable medley of good and bad, old and new, for the 19th century took this 13th century place and mixed it up incredibly. Its arcades are 700 years old, its windows are recessed on slender columns, its roofs have old timbers as well as new. There are charming old bench-ends, old glass with black and white flowers, and two curious ancient possessions facing each other across the wide nave.

One is a piece of old wood carving by a Flemish craftsman, showing with remarkable vividness the appearance of the angel in the nick of time to save Abraham from slaying his son Isaac, the ram caught in the thicket, and at the top corners are two most fearful-looking creatures. The other possession is a piece of tapestry three or four feet square, worked in delicate gold and silver threads and coloured silks which four centuries have faded into a harmony of blues and yellows and greys. In the centre is Our Lord on the Cross with angels about Him. At the corners are four saints looking like oldfashioned country folk, and there is a figure of the Madonna embroidered on the shaft of the cross, wearing a yellow shawl.

In the chapel by the chancel is an old chalk monument to Simon Jame, gentleman, who died two days after Shakespeare and whose epitaph begs us all in this way to prepare to follow him:

Serve God, therefore, while thou hast time
That thou to bliss at length may climb,
Every estate, lord, duke, and king,
Rich man and poor man, mark this thing.

Also a stone set up by her sister Katherine to Lydia Fuye, with the lines:

Deservèd praise might perhaps have missed her
Had not these lines been fixt here by her sister.

Idmiston. It is in the Bourne Valley with hills all round. The small church has Norman work in its tower. The 14th century porch has an upper storey reached by a steep flight of stone stairs.

Two of the three arches in the tower are from the same time; the third arch is 15th century, but rests on two Norman heads. The fine roofs of the nave and the aisles are 500 years old. The moulded timbers have carved bosses, their angles are traceried, and they rise from wonderful corbels carved with faces of charming women and handsome men, and angels playing instruments or carrying shields.

The arcades rise on clustered columns and have pointed arches with clerestory windows over them. The chancel is 700 years old. The font is 14th century. There are tablets to John Bowle and his family. He died as vicar here in 1788; he was called Don Bowle because he edited an edition of *Don Quixote*. On a 17th century wall monument with pillars and much heraldry kneels Giles Rowbach wearing a black cloak, full breeches, and a ruff.

Imber. Seven miles from any town, and is now swallowed up in "battlefields" and still not released from military occupation.

The 13th century church contains the tombs of two members of the Rous family. One wears chain mail, a long coat, and a helmet with raised vizor. His mailed hand is drawing his sword, and a small lion crouches at his feet, a 14th century canopy covering all. The other knight, who has a moustache, wears plain mail from head to foot, his shield is blazoned with three rampant lions, and two battered angels support his head, while a huge lion lies at his feet. Some time in Queen Anne's reign they laid to rest below these huge figures Grace Chambers, and the mason, cutting the stone above her grave, misspelt her name Greas and corrected his mistake just above it.

It is an attractive church. Its tower, like the porch and its charming doorway, is 500 years old. On its walls inside are the fading figures of the table of changes for the ringers, painted by a 17th century hand. A Jacobean screen shuts the ringers off from the nave. The great bowl of the Norman font, greeting us as we come in, has a band of herringbone round the top and a wooden cover of the 17th century. From the same time come most of the carved pews, the simply decorated pulpit, the charmingly carved stalls in the chancel, and three chairs by the altar. Most of these fittings have now been removed elsewhere. The nave has ancient frescoes fading on the walls and an old wagon roof in which we noticed a boss carved with a mitred bishop. There are some fragments of old glass, one piece with a small head of Christ.

Inglesham. For 700 years this small church has stood a long way from the village, reached by a lane leading to a farm. It has a wide stone porch, which has two stone seats and two old doors, one of them set in a Norman doorway. There is a third old door studded with nails in one of the aisles. The little Norman nave is filled with old box pews and has a small Jacobean pulpit with a canopy. The roof has ancient beams, and the aisles, each with its canopied piscina, are enclosed by 15th century screens carved with flowers.

The 13th century chancel, only 21 feet square, has tall and slender altar rails, box stalls with carved tops, and a canopied piscina. On the east wall are the remains of a stone reredos, and a block of carved stone with four small worn figures touched with red and green. In one of the windows is a black and white flower painted 700 years ago, and another window has a little old glass with more flowers, some crowns, and what is left of a bishop carrying his crozier. The font is partly the work of a medieval mason and has a 17th century cover.

Among the most interesting possessions of Inglesham are the traces of patterns on the walls and a bold sculptured relief of the Madonna with the Hand of God reaching down to bless the Child. This Norman carving must have stood for ages in the wind and rain, for it is much weatherworn, and a sundial has been cut in one corner. On a wall is an inscription set up in 1823 to Stanhope Bruce, rector for nearly 60 years.

In the churchyard are the steps and shaft of an ancient cross.

Keevil. It has many charming corners and beautiful old timbered houses, a particularly handsome one called Talboy near the church.

The 15th century church has a stone tower, an ancient scratch-dial, a splendid old door with a great wooden lock, a fine nave roof with painted timbers and carved and coloured bosses, 12 sculptured faces looking down on the nave.

Two 18th century monuments face across the nave. One of Jane Talbot is a pretty little figure with a wreath by an urn; and on James Richard's is an excellent portrait of him in relief, showing us a man with humorous eyes and mouth and crisp, curling hair. He died in 1782. There is a great and splendid font, with flowers in its eight panels and bands of carving above and below, and in the tower is a stone to George Williams:

Who on this spot for 40 winters trod
To call the people to the House of God.

A sad story is told of Keevil Manor, the beautiful 16th century house in the park by the church, with the initials of its architect formed by clipped trees planted in a double L in front. The story is that the house was long ago sold to William Beach of Fittleton, and that Anne Beach fell in love with the curate William Winahouse. Disapproving of the match, her father locked her in her room over the porch for two years, and she watched her lover from her window as he went about the parish. When her captivity was over she was given the choice of marrying the curate and losing her fortune or giving him up and being rich. She married him, but in three months she sickened and died.

Kilmington. This village on the Somerset border has a manor house rich in old woodcarving, and a church with a handsome tower and a fine modern pulpit. The tower has a pierced parapet, pinnacles, two lovely image niches, and traceried windows; the pulpit is in memory of Josephine Paynter, who lived in the manor house by the church. Little gilded cherubs with many wings smile from below the cornice; the panels, separated by figures and grotesque heads, are filled with painted heraldry.

Kingston Deverill. Here the River Deverill, after travelling underground for miles, comes to the surface again.

Kingston Deverill has on a patch of green a heap of sarsen stones brought down from one of the hills and believed to have been placed on the Down to mark the place where Alfred met the forces from Somerset, Hampshire, and Wiltshire on his march against the Danes. Such stones, scattered in thousands on the Wiltshire Downs, are of the kind of which Stonehenge is mostly built, remnants of the rocks which covered the whole chalk downs millions of years ago.

In a window of the church is a 16th century glass medallion in delicate greys and gold, showing Christ seated among the Twelve Apostles. On the chancel floor is a statue of a 14th century man with long hair and beard, wearing a robe and laced-up sandals. An odd lion crouches with raised head at his feet. On the floor by the ornate modern font is the simple font bowl carved by the Normans, whose place the new font usurps. Though the church was rebuilt in 1847 it has two 14th century arches in the nave, and a chair of 1682.

The tower is 500 years old, rising in the middle of the church on pointed arches. It has graceful windows and fine gargoyles.

Kington St Michael. It is on the Gloucestershire border and near the Roman way, and has in its main street the beautiful almshouses set up by Isaac Lyte, who lived through the Civil War, became a London alderman, and gave to the old folk of his birthplace these fine stone houses with six gables.

The church in which Isaac Lyte was christened has been refashioned, but the 13th century arches are in the nave, and the fine old door still hangs between two Norman pillars with sculptured capitals, a Tudor arch above it. There is a pretty canopied piscina in the chancel, and the chancel itself has great beauty, its wide arch set on slender columns and adorned with lovely diamond shapes, having at one end a comical face.

There is a fine heraldic tombstone to Isaac Lyte, a tablet to a schoolmaster for 48 years, and one to a vicar whose wife felt herself "obliged to erect this stone to him," a stout Norman font, two stone heads looking out from an arch, and a window with St George in memory of John Aubrey.

John Aubrey was Isaac Lyte's grandson and was born at a house called Easton Pierce in this parish in 1626. From his very earliest years he was interested in history and his grandfather was old enough to tell him about some of the famous Elizabethans he had known; old enough also to have known people who had seen Malmesbury Abbey and what it was like there before the dissolution of the monasteries.

He became one of the first of the Wiltshire antiquaries (he was one of the first to investigate Avebury) but like many scholars he was not a very good man of business and lost most of his money over a series of law suits concerning the mortgaging of his property, and he had to sell Easton Pierce and lived for a time at Broad Chalke.

He was made a Fellow of the Royal Society at the same time as Dryden and Wren and obtained a Patent from the Crown for making antiquarian surveys. In 1667 he got to know the Oxford historian Anthony Wood, to whom he gave great assistance in the collection of biographical essays known as the *Athenae Oxonienses*. Aubrey was keenly interested in biography. He was a shrewd observer of men and events and in addition to his antiquarian writings is remembered for his *Brief Lives* in which he gives admirable pen portraits. Can one, for instance, ever forget his description of William Prynne sitting reading and wearing "a long quilt cap, which came, two or three, at least, inches below his eies, which served him as an umbrella to defend his eies from the light. About every three hours his man was to bring him a roll and a pott of ale to refocillate his wasted spirits: and so he studied and dranke and munched his bread."

Aubrey gave a description of the convent that stood on the site of the Priory Farm in this parish and how the girls educated by the nuns there learned needlework, confectionery, surgery, physics, writing, and drawing. "A fine way," he says, "of breeding up young women."

Kington St Michael was also the birthplace (in 1771) of another Wiltshire antiquary, John Britton, who travelled 3500 miles at the time he was editing *The Beauties of England and Wales.* His book on *Christian Architecture* was described as "the most beautiful work of its kind that had ever appeared."

Britton is commemorated with John Aubrey in the same window in the church.

Knook. It lies among hills strewn with the ruins of prehistoric camps. Its beautiful old manor house, all that is left of a monastery, stands on the brink of the River Wylye near the church. Very small and with no tower, the church has a gabled porch of 1623 with a bell in the upper storey. There is a blocked Norman doorway with a fine tympanum, on which is carved elaborate interlacing with the heads of two strange beasts. The little pillars have charming capitals, and by one pillar is part of an ancient scratch-dial said to be Saxon. There are those who believe the chancel is Saxon though it is probably early Norman. It has round-headed windows. The corbels of the lost Norman chancel arch are carved with great skill, flowers and foliage beautifully blending. There is an old carved chair, and an ancient gravestone with a raised cross.

Lacock. It is one of the most beautiful villages in this county, with winding streets of medieval houses, gabled roofs, timbered fronts, charming porches; a medieval abbey, a house with a medieval hall, and a great barn with 14th century timbers still intact; and a golden cockerel rather like a wriggling serpent looking down on it all from a church of great possessions. It looks down, too, on a cosy hollow with an old bridge over a stream, a group of handsome houses, and a square.

Outside the church, which has stood about 500 years, queer

creatures are creeping up the pinnacles, some holding their faces with mouths open, one a curious face of a man in a crescent moon. The roof above the chancel arch has an elegant open parapet, and the outside of the lady chapel is worthy of its marvellous interior; it has a battlemented parapet with delicate carving of leaves and flowers, little heads, a canopied niche, and decorated pinnacles.

The church is full of interest, but it is the lady chapel that is most notable. It is crowned with tiny beautiful things and painted carvings. Its arches and the ribs of the vaulted roof are decorated with foliage, one part of the roof having floral wreath-work in colour, with winged angels wearing hats. The piers of the arches have flutings and slender columns round, the columns with elegant capitals and the flutings with tiny sculptured fragments tucked away in them. We noticed a pug dog crawling down, a tiny lady with a wimple, and an old woman in a skirt. There is a big mournful head of a man with long hair, and at the entrance of the chapel is a queer creature resting its head on its paws. The chapel is full of charming fragments, and one of its canopies has a tiny cap of vaulting painted red like a fan, ending in a comical face with its tongue out.

In the chapel's east window are fragments of old glass rich in pale gold medallions, and there is a tomb with remarkable heraldic carving of painted angels and odd lizard-like creatures. In it lies Sir William Sharington, a great man brought low by fraud who managed to rise again and came to live at Lacock Abbey.

In the south transept are four tributes of unusual interest. Two are on old wooden tablets painted and gilded, in memory of Edward Baynard of 1575 and Lady Baynard of 1623, both rather extraordinary sort of people. Of him we read:

Let envy say what it can
This was an honest man;

and of her we read that she had all she wanted:

Earth could not yield more pleasing earthly bliss
Blessed by two babes, though death brought her to this.

On the floor is a brass to Robert Baynard and the wife who gave him 18 children in the 15th century. They are a strange procession, and above them, under their father's feet, are two little dogs.

Facing the old wooden tablets is a stone to Frederick Augustus Courtenay Montagu. He was born with the choicest gifts of

Heaven. Nature had wreathed an olive branch which flourished so conspicuously on his brow as emblematic of a noble and affectionate mind. Patriotism and Loyalty roused him to seek martial glory at 16, and after displaying undaunted courage in Holland and in Martinique he fell at 26 while leading his men at Albuera.

On one of the walls is a memorial to an old couple who died in the middle of the 18th century at 84 and 87, having been married 60 years, and the stone says:

We are gone to our fathers in peace,
and we are buried in a good old age.

There is a very neat stone to Robert Hellier, one of King Charles's criers to the Court of Common Pleas, and a window in the tower is in memory of a schoolmaster's 38 years with the children of Lacock.

High up in the nave, looking down from the west end, is a roaring lion on one side and a crowned beast with a man's head on the other, and at the east end is a sculpture on each side of the altar in memory of the wife and daughter of Admiral Charles Feilding, who was descended from the Hapsburgs and lies here in oak from a warship. One of the sculptures shows a woman reaching out her arms to a child, with an angel attending.

Lacock has one of the rare windows above the chancel arch, a fine tracery window with winged angels carved in the soffit of the arch. We feel that there is carving everywhere in this rich place, from the porch with its vaulted roof, ending in a face made out of a sun and moon, to the farthest recesses of the church.

At Lacock Bishop Jewel preached his last sermon and then, worn out, rode on to Monkton Farleigh to die. "A Bishop had best die preaching," he said to a friend who had warned him against undertaking this strenuous tour of visitation, and die preaching he did.

The beautiful Lacock Abbey, standing in the spacious meadow by the Avon, has come down the centuries from the days when men were still talking of the victory of the barons in forcing King John to seal Magna Carta. Its story is woven into the life of a beautiful woman whose husband was on Runnymede when the king sealed the charter. She was Ela, Countess of Salisbury, and he was William Longsword; he was the first man to be buried in the new Salisbury cathedral. She lies here, in the shadow of the abbey she founded.

Ela was only seven when her father, second Earl of Salisbury, died, and as a rich heiress she was the king's ward, and Richard Lionheart chose for her husband his own stepbrother William Longsword who so became Earl of Salisbury. They lived at Canford Magna in Dorset. He served three kings and was often away at the wars, but he was a devoted and faithful husband, and when, on his long absence in France, everyone assumed his death his wife waited for him to come home. Nothing could persuade her that she would not see his ship come into the harbour of Poole with her husband standing on the deck watching for her to bid him welcome. Her dream came true, but the earl came home worn by shipwreck and privation, and they laid him to rest in the finest tomb of its kind in England, in the nave of Salisbury cathedral. His sorrowful countess waited for their son to come of age and then founded the Abbey of Lacock. She became its abbess, died here, and here was laid to rest, having carried on her work for 35 years after William Longsword died. The sacristy, the chapels where she prayed, the chapter house where she zealously governed her nuns, the cloisters where she walked, are still here, and have an enchanting vista of vaulting.

From the river the abbey presents one long windowed front with sloping roof and twisted chimneys, and, at right angles to it, separated by an octagonal and balustraded tower, is a front of a later day with oriel windows and sumptuous decoration in stone. It was through the smallest oriel window on this front that Fox Talbot made his first negative, taking a photograph that has become historic.

If we seek other aspects of this lovely place we find tiled and gabled roofs, some so plain as to be domestic, some heraldically ornamented but glorified by their chimneys. Below them are fronts as diversified as the roof, and if we seek an explanation it will be to find the simple one that though the building began as a convent its later owners made it into a mansion, and more than one desired to bring it into line with the architectural fashion of his day. The result is a blend of styles hardly to be found outside England, so well do they fit one another.

They are so happily preserved because centuries afterwards, when Lacock fell with other places under the despoiling hand of Henry the Eighth, Sir William Sharington determined to preserve what was useful to him in the nunnery and build about it a mansion. He surrounded the convent walls with buildings typical of the new Italian influence then making its way in England. He kept the sacristy and the chapel, pulled down the convent church, and built stables. But they were good stables, and the excellent octagonal

Lacock Abbey. (*National Trust*)

Lacock Abbey: the hall.

Lacock Abbey: the courtyard.

Lacock village.

tower, the square and decorated doorways, put us in his debt. The refectory with the finely moulded roof and the dormitory were both preserved, and they cover the long stone gallery with the magnificent chimney-piece which is another of Sharington's gifts. In the library Queen Elizabeth knighted her host. In the three-storeyed tower is a charter of Henry the Third. In a vaulted chamber is the tremendous medieval cauldron known as the Mechlin Pot.

Later owners were less inspired than Sir William, and much of the abbey became Palladian in style during the 18th century; but, taken all in all, this ancient place, with its entrancing 13th century sacristy and chapter house, its 15th century cloisters, its fascinating hall rebuilt in the reign of George the Third, and the miraculous way in which all are blended, make it a remarkable example of the evolution of architecture in England and at the same time one of the most beautiful of our historic houses.

It was at Lacock Abbey that William Fox Talbot carried out some of the earliest experiments in photography and published in serial form between 1844 and 1846 the first book illustrated entirely by photographs.

Langley Burrell. The church is 13th century, the tower 14th; but there are some 12th century walls with an old mass dial. The arches of the nave are from the days when Norman was passing into English, and they have beautifully carved capitals. The nave roof of open timber is held up on angel corbels, with two big faces at the west end, where there is a window of Fortitude crowned by an angel, in memory of one who was faithful unto death in the last few days of World War I.

There are ten splendid stone heads in the south chapel, women with curls, a woman with a remarkable headdress, a very fierce fellow at a window, showing his teeth.

There is a room over the porch, and crowning the roof outside, high on the gable above the chancel arch, is a cross with statues of St John and the Madonna.

Langley Burrell is associated with the diarist Francis Kilvert who was born at Hardenhuish in 1840 and was curate to his father here before going as curate at Clyro in Radnorshire in 1865. He came back to Langley Burrell to help his father again in 1872 but soon after accepted the living of St Harmon's, Radnor, and shortly afterwards that of Bredwardine in Herefordshire.

Though the diary covers only nine years, 1870–79—and Kilvert died of peritonitis on 23rd September 1879 only five weeks after his marriage—it gives a most beautiful, and in some places very moving, poetic account of country life in the Victorian age which is not so very long ago in time but now seems so very far distant.

Latton. In this open country, on the willow banks of the river Churn, a little Norman church keeps company with a group of charming cottages. Near by is part of an old cross standing on a patch of grass sheltered by elms.

The squat Norman tower, surmounted by 15th century battlements and gargoyles, has a sundial on a buttress. The Norman doorway has a handsome arch on shafts with chevrons. Below the fine roof timbers of the nave is an interesting company of stone figures, a demon, an ape, a jester with some quaint creature on his head, a queen, two bishops, an old man wearing a hood, and a fox disguised in a cassock. Two fine Norman arches face each other, one in the chancel and one in the tower. The chancel arch has crude carvings, the sturdy tower arch has a simple moulding. The panels and carved bosses of the tower ceiling are in memory of a vicar here for 53 years, Hyde Wyndham Beadon.

Leigh. The young River Thames waters its meadows. Its old church being out of reach in the winter, it was taken down in the 19th century and rebuilt on another site, with the exception of the chancel.

All its ancient treasures were taken with it: the old door with its handmade nails and the rude carving at the top, the fine roof with its bosses and pierced spandrels and the delicate little carvings of men and women on the beams, the belfry carried on mighty timbers, the simple font at which many generations have been christened, and the precious fragments of glass from the dim and distant days of the past in which are still recognisable faces and the golden tip of an angel's wing.

Leigh Delamere. It puts on the map the name of its lords of the manor 600 years ago.

It is an attractive group, its church set between a farm and a row of almshouses looking like a manor. The church has a handsome bell turret with weird winged creatures on it and a Madonna over the doorway. If we can forget its terrible west window we find it a handsome place, the gift of Joseph Neeld, who lived last century at Grittleton House. He spared no cost to restore the church.

The south arcade of the nave has open round arches; on the north side the arches are filled in with smaller ones; and on both sides are heads of men in queer hats and long beards and moustaches. The roofs are handsome, barrel-shaped in both nave and chancel, all resting on painted angels and all having carved and painted bosses. The chancel roof is daintily gilded. On the armrests of the choir stalls are six oak angels kneeling, and in wood and stone there are about a hundred faces, bosses, and angels in the roofs and on the walls. Even the organ is charmingly housed in this well thought out little place, for it has an effective gallery with painted and gilded screenwork.

But most remarkable of all the unusual things we come upon here is the little stone chancel screen with a pair of stone gates. The stone is arcaded, and at the gates (which have ten little arches) is held in a metal band.

On three monuments are the following inscriptions:

Stand, look down,
And behold the stone under which was laid
the body of Elizabeth, the eldest daughter of
Secole Chiver, lord of the manor, the miracle
of her age for reason, language, and religion.

Elizabeth died young in the 17th century, but here is a tablet to a Darby and Joan, Joseph Browning and his Alice:

Death in a very good old age
Ended our weary pilgrimage;
It was to we an end of pain
In hope another life to gain.

One other little one there is, to a child of fifteen weeks:

This little babe like a harmless lamb
Is here laid down to sleep.

Liddington. A tiny village on a hill near Swindon, it has an Elizabethan manor house which keeps part of its old moat, the ancient earthworks of Liddington Castle, and a 13th century church with a Norman font.

In the church are two proud possessions. One is the memory of two abbesses of Shaftesbury; it is believed that two stones with crosses cover their graves, and that one of these women founded the church. The other proud possession is a superb little organ which used to lead the music here, a barrel organ with ten golden pipes and only two stops. The oldest possession of all at Liddington is the Norman font with beading and vandyking round the rim. Above an Elizabethan altar is a window of Christ in Glory, in which is the portrait of a young man who was the son of a rector here. He died of sunstroke and is shown in armour in front of a tree, thrusting out its branches to keep off the rays of the fiery sun. Two little heads look out from the south doorway, and in the churchyard when we called a rose tree was embracing all that is left of the ancient cross.

Liddington Hill was a favourite haunt of Wiltshire's famous naturalist Richard Jefferies, and was a place beloved by the Wiltshire poet, Alfred Williams:

Ofttimes on Liddington's bare peak I love to think and lie,
And muse upon the former days and ancient things gone by,
To pace the old castellum walls and peer into the past,
To learn the secret of the hills, and know myself at last,
To woo Dick Jefferies from his dreams on Sorrow's pillow tossed,
And walk with him upon the ridge, and pacify his ghost.

At the highest point, on a concrete pyramid, fixed to the ramparts of the Iron Age Camp, 900 feet high, is a plaque bearing the inscription:

Liddington Hill
The hill beloved of Richard Jefferies and Alfred Williams

From this pillar is a wide and noble landscape of the country round Alfred Williams's birthplace at South Marston, with the remnant of the copse of firs which Richard Jefferies loved at Chisledon, and with Coate Water, near which Jefferies was born, just below.

Limpley Stoke. It hangs on one of the precipitous hillsides above the Avon near the Somerset border, a cluster of stone houses with a church above them.

For nearly a thousand years a little throng of worshippers has found its way to this place. Set in the turf is a group of medieval coffin lids on one of which the figure of a lady is fading away.

There is a simple Norman doorway leading into the nave with an open timber roof, a small gallery with a Jacobean front, and three clerestory windows. But what draws the eye as one enters is a Saxon doorway, a doorway no longer but standing here like a great stone horseshoe set in a modern arcade. It has been said by a great expert that this horseshoe is almost unique among our Saxon relics. It is one of the two remarkable features this small church has, looking across its nave to one another.

On the north wall is a recess reached by three steps and used for the pulpit, with a charming panelled stone front of the 15th century; facing it is this Saxon arch, standing where it stood 1000 years ago, perhaps nine feet high and just wide enough to pass through, built almost entirely of huge blocks of stone, with small capitals. It has the marks of winds and rains of centuries, with the old hinges and what appears to be the old bolt-hole. Above it is a high window through which the light still pours from a well left in the roof, looking a little odd outside.

Close by is the great stone viaduct between Limpley Stoke and Bath, nearly a hundred yards long and with 11 spans. It carries the Bath–Warminster road over the Midford Brook.

Little Bedwyn. It lies in a deep hollow of the hills on the Berkshire border, with high banks and bright gardens, and a canal running by.

The great stone spire is a fine landmark in the countryside, and one of the nave arcades is a landmark of Norman art in Wiltshire, for its capitals are superbly carved by the Norman masons who fashioned those at Great Bedwyn. One has four faces round it, all pleasant and one smiling and showing teeth. There are charming clerestory windows, arches 700 years old into the chancel and the tower, a 14th century font, old glass in the window over the vestry door, and a pewter flagon of 1682. One of the aisles has a delightful old roof resting on small wooden pillars standing on stone corbels, its timbers moulded and its frieze richly carved.

A very old place is this; it had a Roman camp and a Saxon mint, and was the scene of a battle 1250 years ago. On the hills are the remains of a great British earthwork and a dry moat, an area of 15 acres known as Chisbury Camp, with a farm in which is a deserted chapel, now a barn. The east window has still its beautiful 14th century stone tracery, and little stone heads still glancing across the window to each other.

Little Hinton. The church stands between the vicar's garden and an old thatched barn, under a fine old yew which spreads its branches from the door to the gate, making a shade 50 yards round.

It has what is no doubt a surprising thing to most who come, an arcade built of chalk which has survived from Norman times. More remarkable still is its font, probably Saxon, a masterpiece with something of a story, for the mason who made it was apparently not sure of his plan. Round the top is a row of delicate arcading in which we counted 37 pairs of tiny columns, and below is a broad band of carving which goes nearly all the way round and then breaks off, a curiously coiled up snake with two birds perched on it and two fishes near it taking its place. Next comes a hand holding a plant, the other end of the plant being in the mouth of a dog standing with its tail between its legs. Below the dog is a duck.

The old door is still swinging in the Norman doorway. It brings us into a lofty clerestoried nave with a very fine roof of 24 oak panels. There is an old chest, and a lovely pulpit with the inscription "Miss Martha Hinton gave this pulpit 1637."

Little Langford. The fine Norman doorway of the small church has a rare tympanum carved with a bishop raising his hand in blessing; and at his side is a curious kind of tree with three birds sitting on its three branches. Below is a boar hunt. Three dogs with spotted collars are attacking a boar; the eager huntsman, his spear in his hand, watching the fray as he winds his horn. The arch above has wavy mouldings and the capitals have much-worn figures. One is a sort of mermaid, a rare figure in a church, and perhaps the only one in Wiltshire. In the south transept on a handsome tomb lies an Elizabethan gentleman. He has a ruff, a short cloak, padded breeches, and a small cap. In the floor near him are some old tiles, one with a stag on it. In the sanctuary is a table of old traceried panels, and in the wall of the transept is a delightful little tombstone with a raised wheel cross.

Little Somerford. Near Malmesbury with so much history is this small church with so much beauty. It has stood about 700 years and has a 15th century porch with a scratch sundial on the gable. The old door is still on its hinges, there are pews with ancient bench-ends, a two-decker Jacobean pulpit with beautiful carved panels divided by tall thistles, and on the door of the desk is a little graceful tree and the date 1629. The fine moulded panels of the choir stalls and the reredos are copied from the pulpit. The font has a 17th century cover.

Of rare beauty is the pierced chancel screen with crocketed

pinnacles on each side of the doorway. It is about six centuries old and is believed to have come from Malmesbury Abbey. On the windowsill near the pulpit is the round top of an old cross, found embedded under the pulpit; it has the Madonna crowned on one side and the Crucifixion on the other, the delicate work of an artist of about 1300. There is a charming window in the nave of a mother bringing her little ones to the Master, one of the children standing by with a small shepherd's crook and a lamp. Above the chancel arch hangs a painted board with the Royal Arms of Elizabeth the First, showing the dragon instead of the unicorn.

Littleton Drew. Opposite the Manor Farm is a mound supposed to contain four stone cells which can only be entered by removing a stone in the roof. The farm itself has much stone carving and an interesting relic of medieval days. In the garden stone gargoyles and an eagle, a lion's face and a woman's head, and an old pointed doorway in the wall; and in an orchard an old dovecot. Its walls are full of square nests to which the doves came through a charming stone lantern on the roof.

The church has been rebuilt but contains the old font. Under a canopy is an effigy of a woman in a wimple.

There are two blocks of stone in the porch, both richly decorated with foliage and arcading. It is thought they may be Saxon, possibly part of one of those crosses set up hereabouts to mark the resting-place of Aldhelm's funeral procession on its way to Malmesbury.

Longbridge Deverill. Today the village has a group of charming almshouses built in 1665 by the lord of Longleat, one of the noblest Tudor houses in Wiltshire. He was one of the three John Thynnes we come upon here, and his little gabled houses of charity are rare places with shelters over the doorways.

It was the John Thynne of Henry the Eighth's day who started Longleat, and we were brought close to him in the medieval tower of the church above the little River Wylye. Still growing in the churchyard is a yew he may have known and hanging on the wall of the tower is his funeral helm. By it hang two others about three centuries old, with a sword of the same age and a pair of gauntlets.

There is an old font with a band of sculpture round the bowl, and one of the nave arcades is Norman too, while both are made of great chalk blocks.

One of the aisle roofs is 450 years old, and there are two ancient chests. In modern windows are scenes in the history of Glastonbury. On the wall is a clever profile portrait of the second Marquis of Bath, and in memory of his wife is the figure of a weeping woman. A tablet on the wall tells us that Mary Cole and her husband were housekeeper and steward in Lord Bath's family at Longleat for over 60 years.

The bronze and alabaster memorial to a John Thynne who was killed at 19 in an accident, was designed by Sir Alfred Gilbert, the sculptor who made the statue of Eros in Piccadilly Circus. The monument stands on the floor of the tower, bronze columns supporting an alabaster bowl under a bronze canopy.

Colour is given to this old church by the three modern screens and the 18th century panelling behind the font. All this timber is gilded and painted, and the screens have been designed in the 18th century manner, a green and gold screen under the tower and a white one bright with flowers.

One approaches Longleat through Horningsham, though it is also reached from here. Its great park covers 2000 acres through which we may wander with the deer, and it has magnificent views, Scots firs 100 feet high, a yew 30 feet round, and a lake of about 40 acres.

Luckington. It is the birthplace of the Bristol Avon. The church (dedicated to Our Lady and Ethelbert of Kent), which had stood about 700 years, was much renewed in the 19th century. A great house which is a golden spectacle is seen over the churchyard wall. A stone lion sits on the edge of the roof, the ivy creeps up the golden walls, and in the shelter of the trees rise the old stone roofs.

The nave arcades rest on Norman columns with crudely carved capitals; its massive font, 27 inches across the bowl, is Norman and was once locked against witches; and its two roodloft doorways remain, the top one with an old lady at each side, one with a remarkable headdress and a frilled collar and a cross on her forehead, the other with a rather distressing face. By the chancel arch are the heads of Mary and Ethelbert, and both appear again in the east window. In one of the chancel windows is William of Malmesbury holding a church.

The Avon, here so small but soon to grow big, passes Malmesbury and Chippenham and begins to work westward at Melksham through pleasant country to the historic little town of Bradford-on-

Avon, with its old bridge running over it and its houses perched high above a Saxon church. At Freshford the Avon receives the Frome and enters the beautiful wooded Warleigh Valley leading round to Bath.

Between Bath and Bristol the scenery opens out after pretty country to Saltford. At Keynsham the River Chew pours into it, and at Bristol it receives the River Frome. From the Clifton part of Bristol the Avon passes out through the gorge known by pictures all the world over, bridged by that magnificent bridge which came from Charing Cross; and on it flows to join the Severn at Avonmouth. It has come 75 miles and drained a basin of 900 square miles.

Ludgershall. In the Norman wall of the church is a tiny fragment of what is believed to have been a Saxon Crucifixion.

Down a lane is the ruined keep of the castle the Normans built on the site of a Saxon stronghold; it is said that Queen Maud sought shelter here when flying from King Stephen, and the seal of a mounted knight belonging to one of her helpers has been found. A little way out of the village stands Biddesden House, with a lovely Queen Anne front and a fine red dovecot. Standing within railings made by the village blacksmith, fine rails with crowns at the corners, is the broken shaft of the ancient cross. It has four weatherworn sculptured panels showing the Command of St Peter, the three Marys, the Ascension, and a beautiful Descent from the Cross.

A remarkable possession is a canopied tomb of Sir Richard Brydges and his wife, resplendent with gilded lions' heads, cherubs, birds, and dolphins, the work of 16th century men. It is the glory of the church. In the centre of the painted canopy, among the heads of 16 golden lions, is an angel carrying the souls of Sir Richard and his wife to Heaven. Their five children kneel below, one of the oddest collections of young folk we have seen. By one of the sons sits a brown dog, begging as if he, too, would kneel in respectful memory of his master and mistress. Hanging from his collar is a tasselled lead.

Sir Richard, whose feet are on a merry-looking animal like a lion's cub, wears gold and white armour and his wife is in black. Their portraits are carved on medallions in the frieze running round the top of the tomb, where are two cherubs riding on very queer creatures. Knighted at the coronation of Mary Tudor, he was sheriff of Berkshire at the trial of a martyr at Newbury and made a gentle offer to the prisoner of meat, drink, books, and £10 a year if he would live with him and renounce his error. The brave man thanked Sir Richard for his offer and went into the fire.

There are seven lancets in the chancel, a fine canopied piscina, and a font 700 years old.

Lydiard Millicent. Its churchyard has the elegant shaft of an ancient cross, set on high steps. Its tower is 14th century and the porch has something older still, what seems to be part of a Norman pillar piscina, probably made by the craftsmen of the Norman font, which has a fine bowl carved with 19 little pillars and linked-up arches. The pulpit is modern but covered with rich carving. In the top lights of some of the windows are jewel-like fragments of old red, blue, and gold glass. The neat barrel roof of the chancel has gilded and painted bosses. There is a low stone chancel screen. Gargoyles look down from the tower and six small stone faces from the south wall, where a sundial marks the sunny hours. It marked them for one of its rectors, Robert Jenner, for nearly 60 years from 1665 to 1724.

Lydiard Tregoze. It was the home of an ancient family which has lived in this lovely hill country, with their house and the church together in a beautiful park, for four centuries.

This course of time by God's almighty power
Hath kept this land of Lydiard in one race.

The monuments are captivating, and as we look round them we remember that it is the proud boast of this family of St John that one of them in 1440 married John Beaufort, Duke of Somerset, and so became the grandmother of the Tudor dynasty, for their daughter was the famous Margaret, Countess of Richmond, mother of Henry the Seventh. On each side of the chancel is a striking monument, one of the Tudor John St John lying with his two wives, and one of Edward St John of the following generation, who fought for the king in the Civil War. He is a marvellous figure shining in gold and looking very like Cromwell. He stands lifesize in gilded armour, a dazzling statue which draws all eyes to it. He is under a canopy with two boys holding back the curtain, a bird at the top, and at the bottom a small relief of Sir Edward at the head of a troop of cavalry, his men slowly trotting behind, and a bugler jogging before him on a cob.

Across the small chancel lies the great Sir John St John, he and his two wives superb in white marble. He lies raised above them, and they are a lovely spectacle, with a canopy over them raised on four pillars with a central arch, a brilliant painted shield at each side, and a little host of enchanting children about them.

The two wives lie in beautiful gowns with big sleeves and lovely lace, and one of them holds in her arm a pathetic child, gaily dressed in lace and swaddling bands. In all there are 13 children, a pretty study for an artist, the boys in short coats and jackets tied with bows, the girls in pretty caps. Along the front lie two boys, their heads resting on their elbows and both with skulls, and at each end is an enchanting child with a skull and a palm leaf, both with lovely gauntlets, one with a laurel wreath round her hair and one with curls. Five sons kneel at the head of the tomb, and three daughters at the foot. At the four corners of the canopy are sculptured groups of women, one with two fanciful children, and the whole is crowned with pinnacles, shields, and birds. A helmet with a bird on it is hanging from the roof. Next to this entrancing monument is a sculptured tomb of Viscount St John of 1478, rich with heraldry, crowned with eagles and glowing shields. Sitting reading a book to his wife, one of the daughters of the house, is Sir Giles Mompesson; she sits listening with a finger against her cheek and a skull on her knee.

But perhaps it is the tomb which stands a little apart that we remember most in this fine place. It is a canopied tomb with a multitude of badges, one badge having a black monkey. There are birds on the ceiling and an extraordinary coat-of-arms, and enshrined in all this richness is a superb little couple in black and gold kneeling on tasselled cushions. The arch above them is charmingly painted and gilded, resting on clustered and fluted columns, and they kneel with great dignity and beauty, Nicholas and Elizabeth St John, with all the graciousness of Tudor days.

Rich in sculpture, this treasure house is rich in colour too, with much of its medieval painting fading on its walls but with windows all aglow with scenes through which the sunlight has been falling for many generations. These walls are 13th century, and on them are little patches of frescoes in which we may recognise Our Lord rising from the tomb, and a fragment in which a small figure is carrying a lantern to light the way for Christopher across the stream. The chancel roof is painted with the sun and moon and stars floating in a clouded sky, and on the left of the altar is a great screen with painted doors and the family tree of the St Johns.

But it is the windows that glow with colour. Those in the aisles are full of precious 15th century glass, with gold winged angels and many vivid fragments in which we may discover saints and kings and prelates, croziers and canopies. The east window has some 17th century glass by Bernard Van Lange. The top and bottom lights have angels and emblazoned shields, and in the centre of the window is a sombre olive tree growing out of a tangle of grass and fern and hung with the bright shields of the heiresses who married St Johns. In the background is the familiar countryside picture of a man with a gun and his dogs walking in wooded country, the eaves of barns showing through the trees, cows grazing, and boats sailing on a river. One of the shields has a portrait of Oliver St John, and on either side are the tall figures of John the Baptist in a deep blue cloak with a lamb in his arms, and the Evangelist St John in red and gold.

The 18th century home of the St Johns is now the property of Swindon Corporation and is open to the public.

Lyneham. It is in the hilly country of Braden Forest round Chippenham, its houses scattered about a wide green. All through the centuries a noble yew has been throwing its shadow on the church doors, watching a smaller one grow up close by; the big one has an extraordinary trunk about 25 feet round. The church, which gives us a glimpse of what all our churches were in medieval days, has painted its font and its screens; the great font is painted all over, the bowl red and green with gold stars. The chancel screen has a dainty cornice, red, white, green, and gold, over its two tiers of panels, traceried and panelled. The painted tower screen faces it.

Maiden Bradley. The great hills about it are buried in deep woods, the houses lining its streets are mostly old and charming—even the general stores are housed behind ancient walls and mullioned windows. In the village street is a wayside fountain with water laid on by the Duke of Somerset in 1891, bearing the words:

Drink, travellers, drink of Bradley's purest rill
Which, strange to say, runs quite a mile up hill;
Then to your panting steeds let all attend,
An honest horse is surely man's best friend.

Bradley House, home of the Dukes of Somerset, stands behind the village, with crested gates. Beyond is an avenue leading to New

Mead, where was born General Ludlow, a courageous and clever soldier and an honest politician. At Priory Farm, lying below the road on a green hillside, are the remains of a hospital founded for leper maidens in the 12th century by Margaret Bissett, who endowed it with all she had on condition she might live there. It is probable that Bradley took its Christian name from Maiden Bissett. Two buildings remain of this once famous hospital; they house horses and stores, but have their deeply splayed windows.

The 14th century church, in a churchyard with two yews, has a tall tower, its turret with a graceful pierced parapet. The ancient nail-studded door has fleur-de-lys hinges. The Norman font is on five pillars. The old pulpit is carved, and the lovely old pews have a shell on the top of each bench-end. Some of the loveliest possessions of the church are the fragments of old glass from Burton Hall in Leicestershire, from the 14th century to the 17th, set in a window in memory of the men who did not come back. There is a queer little dog, fine heads of saints, and a Descent from the Cross. The most charming piece is part of a picture showing 14th century harvesters binding sheaves, a castle keeping guard on the hill behind.

The east window has a striking picture of the conversion of Paul, who lies on the ground by his frightened horse, another rider struggling with his rearing steed, and men-at-arms crowding about. Another window shows harvesters, but they are protected by watching angels instead of a castle. We see the husbandmen sowing and reaping, part of a glorious sheet of colour forming a fine window from the workshops of Christopher Whall, who has done so much to raise the standard of our modern windows.

There is a fine marble monument to Sir Edward Seymour, Speaker of the Commons in the reign of Charles the Second. It was he who, when his carriage broke down at Charing Cross, stopped the next carriage behind him and took it, telling the ejected owner that he could hardly expect to ride while the Speaker of the House of Commons was walking. He is shown on his tomb as a handsome man in fine clothes and a splendid wig, and lies on his side below two little boys sitting on the top of the monument, one putting out his torch, the other holding a snake.

Pepys found Sir Edward Seymour "very high proud and saucy" and he is known to have compromised himself by his acceptance of bribes for political services. "It was strange," says Macaulay, "that the haughtiest of human beings should be the meanest, that one who seemed to reverence nothing but himself should abase himself for the sake of quarter day."

Maiden Bradley is also the birthplace of Edmund Ludlow, the Parliamentarian General who was a member of the Court that tried King Charles the First. After his campaign in Ireland Cromwell sent Ludlow there as second in command to General Ireton and after Ireton's death Ludlow became Commander-in-Chief, but when Cromwell became Lord Protector Ludlow's republicanism made him refuse to recognise such an office. He was allowed to live in retirement unmolested but at the Restoration he left the country. He died in 1693 in exile and is buried in St Martin's Church at Vevay, near Geneva, along with four other Regicides who had signed Charles the First's death warrant.

Malmesbury. It has been famous for a thousand years. Not only is there a monument that men will never tire of going to see, but here in this place lies the first King of All England. In the great Norman abbey, with the marvellous nave borne on pillars five yards round, stone dragons have been looking down for about 800 years, but it is a thousand years since King Athelstan, who is also buried here, made the English nation into one. His tomb is in the north aisle, but his dust is in a grave that no man knows.

He was Alfred's grandson. Hordes of pirates had come across the sea and Athelstan caught them at Brunanburgh in 937, and there fought a battle which settled for ever who was to be ruler of all Britain. Athelstan won; the Saxon poet tells us how blood flowed on that fateful day from the rise of the sun till the sun sank to its setting, when it was found that five Viking kings and seven strong earls had been put to sleep never to wake again. Athelstan survived this victory for three years and made England a country to be reckoned with abroad, but it was his welding of the nation into one, his conquest over all his enemies, that made him powerful. They buried him in Malmesbury Abbey, where we see him lying on a tomb by the altar. His figure, with a canopy over his head and a marvellous looking creature at his feet, has been fashioned since his day and the tomb is empty, but it is known that he lies in this famous place, one of the most impressive Norman monuments remaining in the land. Here Athelstan's name has always been famous, and the Common is called King's Heath after him. Here is a little hospital he established, and the 500 acres he gave to the people, every freeman of Athelstan's borough being entitled to one allotment.

But even farther back than Athelstan we must go to the early days of Malmesbury, back to the year 640 when there came one Maeldub from Ireland or Iona, setting up a school and starting a church. He was lucky with one of his pupils, the brilliant scholar Aldhelm, who grew so wise that under him Malmesbury became second only to Canterbury for learning. He became a bishop and wandered into Dorset, where he built up the great school and abbey of Sherborne, but when he died in 709 it was here they brought him, and they laid him by his old church walls. He lies with Athelstan.

Here came monks on pilgrimage. Both the Confessor and the Conqueror showered good gifts on Malmesbury, and they set up this abbey when the 12th century was half way through. It was almost the last monastery in the country, but fell into the hands of Henry the Eighth and his destroying Thomas Cromwell. One William Stumpe, a rich cloth merchant, bought the abbey for fifteen hundred pounds and handed over the nave of the church to the towns-people in place of their own church, St Paul's, which was in a ruinous condition. The noble pile that survives is far less than half of what was there originally. A western tower collapsed at some period after the departure of the monks and wrecked the west end, All east of the nave, except fragments of the crossing and transepts, has perished completely.

This famous abbey, with its flowing parapet crowning a noble clerestory, which crowns a great triforium, is as superb a monument as our Norman masters left us.

The outer doorway has eight depths of carving, three of them with figures in medallions, each figure typical of Creation. The whole doorway has hundreds of figures, among which we recognise Eve taking the apple from the serpent, a man turning a somersault, an angel and a peacock, and the Tree of Knowledge. The inner doorway has three orders of carving with Christ and angels over it. Inside the porch are two massive sculptures cut in the wall by the Normans; they are crude but remarkable figures of the Twelve Apostles with angels descending on them, and are perhaps the most precious single possession of Malmesbury. They are cut out in the stone after building, resting on four beautifully carved arches below each group.

The columns, rising to the Norman ceiling in the aisles and up past the triforium to the 14th century clerestory in the nave. The great bays rise in three tiers, beginning with short Norman pillars with Norman pointed arches (fashioned at the end of Norman days), continuing up to the triforium in which one big arch holds four small ones, and rising to the clerestory added 200 years later, when the roof was vaulted with magnificent bosses and the flying buttresses were built to hold it up. The two west bays of the roof are new, the rest are 14th century. Looking down from the arch of each bay are three striking dragons. High up above the triforium is a curious stone compartment which may have held the first cathedral organ or may have been a watching loft; it is 500 years old. Along the east end, across the aisles and above the altar, runs the old stone screenwork, complete in the aisles but with only the top seen in the choir, where an oak screen and stalls match a charming panelled pulpit decorated with eagles and angels. In the north aisle stands the empty tomb of Athelstan; he has lain here since 941, but not beneath this monument, on which he looks a stately figure under his rich canopy, with a melancholy creature at his feet.

On one side of the walls hangs a picture of Our Lord healing the sick which is said to be by a pupil of Michelangelo and once hung over the altar. The east end of the church is draped; the west end has a six-light window with deep and beautiful tracery, the old organ is still awaiting restoration. It was built in 1714 by Alexander Jordan for a church in London, but was removed to Malmesbury long ago and is being carefully preserved. It has never been restored and it is hoped the time may come when it may be heard ringing out in this famous nave, for the abbey was probably the first church in England to have an organ, St Dunstan having given it one. It is probable that the curious projecting box in the triforium may have been made to hold St Dunstan's organ.

There is no old glass, but the tower has four interesting figures in one of its windows—of Maeldub the founder, Aldhelm the scholar, Egelmer the Saxon monk (who is holding the flying machine with which he tried to fly from the tower and broke his legs), and William of Malmesbury, the ancient chronicler who was a scholar here.

Over the porch is a room into which we mount by stone steps through the great wall; it is a little room of treasures, the chief of these being four immense volumes of a Bible written by the monks of Malmesbury in the year 1407. The Bible is richly illuminated and is a very precious work. Here, also, are ancient musical instruments, among them the keyboard of the old organ Alexander Jordan made in 1714 (quite unrestored, but fit for work), some medieval tiles with comical and fantastic figures, an old hourglass, and a penny of

Longleat House.

Above: Giles and Katherine Mompesson.

Above right: Elizabeth and Nicholas St John.

LYDIARD TREGOZE:

three monuments in the church.

Edward St John.

The tympanum on the east wall of the porch at Malmesbury Abbey.

Malmesbury Abbey: the nave.

Malmesbury Abbey: the monument to King Athelstan.

Malmesbury Abbey: the south door.

Edward the Confessor, a very rare coin which we understand is not represented in our national collection.

The great door of the abbey may have been hanging on its hinges all the time. It has about 50 oak panels and is studded with nail-heads, and we may still turn the great key in the lock as it has been turned for about 700 years.

Outside, the long line of nine great clerestory windows is an impressive spectacle. At their west end is the magnificent remnant of the old front, the corner tower among the finest Norman work surviving, and at the east end is a vast arch still standing in ruin, bringing to mind the great arches of Tintern and Fountains. It is a remarkable sight and has stood since the days the Norman builders left it here, supporting the central tower. Altogether there are 20 ruined Norman arches outside the east wall.

Across the graveyard stands the 14th century tower and spire of the old church of St Paul's; it has lost its church but serves today as the bell tower of the abbey. Beyond this ruined tower and the great ruined arch is a curious tombstone which tells the story of a tragedy of long ago; it was in 1703, when Hannah Twynney was slain by a tiger.

At the top of Malmesbury's old street stands its medieval cross; at the bottom is the old hospital of St John. In this street and in the streets about it are many 17th and 18th century houses and some older. Among the inns are three the traveller will wish to see. With its windows looking up to the west front of the abbey is the old Bell Inn, probably once a guest house for the abbey, and still with a 13th century window. Across the road from the churchyard is the White Lion which comes into one of Stanley Weyman's novels, and no less noteworthy is the King's Arms, which has a fine old staircase and a picturesque courtyard reached through an archway from the street; it is a pleasant peep from the courtyard looking on to an old gable and some quaint windows.

On Holloway Hill, on the road from Cirencester, are fragments of the medieval walls which used to surround the town, and there are other fragments near the town bridge. At what is called the Triangle is a stone cross which has been set up in memory of the Malmesbury men who fell in the war. In the town hall is a collection of old maces and seals, the maces 17th and 18th century and of silver, and four of the seals 16th century and in brass. Malmesbury has a modern and an ancient Corporation and the old one still meets now and then under its Saxon charters.

The market cross, reminding us of the crosses of Chichester and Salisbury, though it is not so fine as either, stands about 40 feet high and is supported by flying buttresses with pinnacles rising above its vaulted roof. It has carvings of about 50 extraordinary faces, and in the niches of its turrets are eight figures fading away after being in the wind and rain for centuries. One of these statues is a bishop wearing his mitre, and another appears to be St Lawrence.

The hospital of St John at the bottom of the street was refashioned in the 17th century, but here are still stones the Norman builders must have handled. It has a pointed archway now blocked in and pierced for little windows, and on the floor above this is a smaller arch which may have been a window in Norman days. The arch rises on capitals, but where the window may have been is a stone tablet which tells us that Athelstan gave ten pounds to the free school in this town and ten pounds to the poor of this almshouse to be paid every year; and that Michael Weeks gave ten pounds more to the school and the almshouse every year, and also a pound to the vicar to preach a sermon once a year.

William of Malmesbury was one of the great historians of the Middle Ages. He wrote the histories of the kings and prelates of England and was also the biographer of the Saints, Anselm, Dunstan, and Wulfstan.

William of Malmesbury took Bede for his model but his history is enlivened by his love of stories and anecdotes of the marvellous, and one of his tales is of how one of the monks at Malmesbury in the 11th century, Egelmer, tried to become "a bird man" and having tied wings to his body jumped off the Abbey tower and lived to tell the tale. William of Malmesbury says that he was borne on the air for a furlong and broke both his legs on landing.

One of the greatest scholars William of Malmesbury speaks of is Aldhelm who made a school at Malmesbury in the 7th century and who founded the wonderful little Saxon church at Bradford on Avon. He was also a poet and his poems are said to have delighted King Alfred.

Malmesbury is also associated with that sturdy old gentleman Thomas Hobbes, called by Charles the Second "the beare," who is best known for his treatise on civil government *The Leviathan*—the sovereign power vested in the head of the State by the people.

After Charles the Second's Restoration Hobbes was regarded as dangerous and his doctrines an apologetic for dictatorship and Aubrey says that some of the Bishops "made a motion to have the good old gentleman burned for a heretique." But nothing happened beyond a refusal to reprint his *Leviathan* (Pepys had to pay as much as 24s for his copy) and he was not allowed to publish his *Behemoth*—a book on the causes of the Civil War.

Aubrey knew Hobbes exceedingly well and tells many stories about him. Of how he did most of his meditating while walking, stopping now ánd again to jot down something, having an ink pot concealed in the top of his walking stick; of how "in his old age he used to sing prick-song every night (when all were gonne and sure nobody could heare him)" and of how he played tennis when over 75.

Manningford Abbots. It is in the fine Down country near Pewsey. Its little church has been rebuilt. There is a Norman pillar piscina. The Pre-Reformation chalice is silver and has a beautifully wrought knot ending in lions' heads, with traceried panels above. There are also traces of a Crucifixion on it.

Manningford Bruce. Tidy little cottages below the Downs, a charming old rectory, and a small church with walls of rugged flint. It has two doorways, facing each other, round and high and looking like Saxon, one with a door between eight and nine feet high. The great Norman chancel arch has walls nearly four feet thick, and the light still falls through Norman windows.

The chancel has an apse with no east window, but has three side windows with deep splays. A deep window in the west gable is like a narrow slot through these thick walls. Two round arched aumbries face across the chancel. The timber reredos is made up of 28 medallions and panels, with prophets and angels and emblems, and the Crucifixion in the centre. On the chancel wall a modest tablet with a small but splendid coat-of-arms tells a human story of the Civil War. It is to the memory of Mary Nicholas, who helped her sister Jane Lane to save Charles the Second's life after Worcester. One of the most romantic of all true tales tells how Jane rode pillion behind the hunted king, dressed as a groom, along roads swarming with Parliament troops all eager and determined to find him. Jane led him safely through them, and brought him into friendly hands before she left him. It was in gratitude for this that the king granted the family the rare privilege of bearing on their arms the three lions of England, as well as the scarlet horse seen here on the marble tablet.

A charmingly kept little village it is, with a great house by the church which has neat walls and a lovely thatched roof, a dormer window peeping through the thatch; and beyond the yew hedge is the rectory whose lovely hip-roofs we see from the door, and whose massed gable roofs we see from the east end.

Marden. Barns and stacks and thatched walls—they are everywhere in this Great Plain so rich in stones older than history, halfway between Avebury and Stonehenge. It is said that it was here Alfred's brother Ethelred fought the Danes and died on the field, being carried to rest at Wimborne. So Alfred became King.

The small church was built by Norman and 15th century masons, and a charming place it is. Its embattled tower is 500 years old, with pinnacles, a stair turret, and lovely windows under arches with handsome finials. A rare touch of beauty is in the decorated buttresses, which have panels ending in crocketed pinnacles.

The noble Norman doorway is enriched with a great depth of bold moulding and flowers, its slender pillars having carved capitals. It is superb, flowers carved right round it, with zigzag outside and chevron inside. The door has been swinging to and fro for centuries and has a huge wooden lock. The chancel arch is by the same builders of 800 years ago, wide and round with zigzag and bead mouldings, its four pillars having finely sculptured capitals. The fine roof of the nave is carried on the crowned and mitred heads of ten men and bishops, one peeping over the canopy of the Jacobean pulpit. There are two beautiful old chairs carved with crowns, a fine old font, and an 18th century tablet with cherubs, coronets, and skulls, and a painted coat-of-arms "to rescue from oblivion the memory of one whose virtues were seldom equalled and never excelled."

Market Lavington. The church has been here 600 years, though the tower is a century younger. The high porch has the stout timbers put in its roof by the original builders and broken Norman mouldings built into its walls. The chantry, founded by Robert de la Mere in 1349, has spiral steps leading to the old roodloft. The font is 14th century, and of the same age is the canopied piscina with a flower in its bowl.

On the walls we noticed two stones of interest, one outside to Betty Lambourne, whom they laid to rest here at 107, and one inside with a graceful figure of a weeping woman to a Lord Mayor of London who must have known Betty, for both were laid to rest within a few years of the end of the 18th century.

In the north aisle there is a monument put up by the great antiquary Thomas Tanner, Bishop of St Asaph, whose collections form the Tanner manuscripts in the Bodleian Library, to his parents. His father, Thomas Tanner, being "46 years the diligent, pious resident Minister of this Parish."

Here, in a cottage standing above the stream running past the smithy, we found the last Tom Smith of dewponds fame. For hundreds of years Tom Smiths have handed down to their children and children's children the secret of making a pool on the top of bare and thirsty hills where no stream is, and making it so that it will not run dry. There have been Tom Smiths for 250 years, and every Smith has made dewponds. It is said that there will be no more, yet they leave an enduring memorial near their home, for here is one of their ponds on the hills.

Marlborough. Its great street (shaped from a hillside or an ancient lynchet, and sloping like a cultivated terrace) has been the highway to the West for a thousand years and more, and it remains today one of the finest streets in England. It carries the traffic from London to Bath, and it narrows at each end as if it would have us stay. It is not difficult to stay, for Marlborough is a fascinating place, with a church at each end of the street, with Savernake at its gate, with the great school that everybody knows, and with half a mile of delightful gables, dormer windows, and red roofs. A few survived the great fire in 1653, and behind their charming fronts, looking to one another across the wide street, are interiors with old beams and Tudor staircases.

The world runs through this famous street, yet has never spoiled it, and all about it is a great tranquillity. The mystery of the old world is in the country round, for we are here at a fine centre of Prehistoric Britain. If we would see the great White Horses, or hundreds of burial mounds, Stonehenge and Woodhenge, Silbury Hill and the avenue of great stones that leads to Avebury, the vast earthen wall of Wansdyke, ancient forest, Roman roads, Saxon churches, this street leads to them all. The great mound in the grounds of the College is itself older than history; it was probably a burial place, Maerl's Barrow, which gave the town its name, or it may come from marle burg, meaning chalk town. On it was built the Norman keep, which was a favourite place of kings from the days of the Conqueror to the days when Henry the Eighth came hunting in Savernake. For those who tire of walking up and down this fine old street, there is a wondrous world round about.

The College was built in the middle of last century over this famous mound. Wansdyke, the great wall built across the western side of our countryside just after the Romans left, is the medieval witness of man's everlasting yearning for security. Savernake, the marvellous forest 16 miles round, with avenues that take our breath away, oaks and beeches like giants of the centuries, and quiet glades where the world can be forgot, is an incomparable piece of old England. Silbury Hill, a little way on the road to Bath, is the biggest artificial mound in Europe, leading us on to the gigantic stone ramparts of Avebury, which we may think of as a sort of Westminster Abbey for a race far back in the mists of time. Still there stand within a mile or two of Marlborough remnants of these monuments of British architecture in the days when the Thames flowed through a desert waste where London Bridge is now. But we must look about us in this street.

At the London end of it is St Mary's Church; at the College end is St Peter's. St Mary's was made new in the 17th century after a fire; the fire has left its mark on a Norman pillar which belongs to the vanished north arcade. There is now only one arcade, which cuts the arch of the chancel. The church is chiefly interesting for some of its possessions. The fire most fortunately left untouched the magnificent Norman doorway under its western tower, but let into the wall inside the church are fragments of sculpture by artists as far beyond the Normans as the Normans are from us. They are Roman. One is a fragment of the goddess Fortuna, the other two are grotesque heads let into the sides of a Norman pillar uncovered near the tower. The carving of Fortuna shows her with the left arm supporting a Horn of Plenty and the right hand holding a steering paddle resting on a globe, the idea being to suggest the gifts Fortune has to bestow and the control she exercises over human destinies. It is thrilling to stand in this place and see these fragments of the Roman Empire here in the heart of a world so old that its men were raising temples before the world had heard of Rome. There is another little carving which sets us thinking, for on the 15th century battlements above the south porch is a stone cat which we like to think of as a pretty fancy of the medieval sculptor; the story is that when the church was on fire in the 15th century a cat saved its kittens from the blazing ruins. From another fire in the 17th century come the bullet marks on the outside walls, for they were made by the king's soldiers; one of their bullets was discovered in a beam when the bells were rehung, and it is preserved in the church. A charming small possession is a Madonna and Child in wood about 15 inches high.

In front of St Mary's is the town hall, looking down the long street; it stands on the site of the old market house, and preserves the pillars of that building and also the door of the old lock-up.

It was to the church at the other end of the street, St Peter's, that there came more than 450 years ago a butcher's son from Ipswich to be ordained. His name was Thomas Wolsey, and he had not yet formed within him that ambition to be master of England which was to overthrow him. The church has a magnificent tower 120 feet high, a vaulted porch and chancel, a finely carved reredos, and elegant arches enriched with angels. It is noticeable that one of the pinnacles of the tower is not straight at the top and it is thought that it may be due to a mason's error in repairing it long ago. On the walls of the church are two pathetic memories, a tablet to three children, and a charming sculpture in red and black and gold to three other little ones who died within a month in the home of Charles Stuart's Lord Chief Justice. Sir Nicholas Hyde, their father, lived here but died of gaol fever caught from a prisoner he was trying in London. At the Old Bailey herbs are still laid before the judges as in the days when our courts were so foul that this was a desirable precaution. One of the vicars of this church had a son who, christened at this font, grew up notorious throughout the land, Henry Sacheverell, the Tory High-Churchman who was impeached by the Whigs and after trial in Westminster Hall, suspended from preaching for three years. He became a popular hero, was in favour with Queen Anne, who gave him the Crown Living of St Andrew's, Holborn. Thomas Hearne, the Oxford historian, described him as "a man of much noise but little sincerity."

A little walk by a flagged path from St Mary's brings us to the delightful green with picturesque houses round about; one of the buildings here is the 18th century home of the oldest school in the town, founded as the Hospital of St John for poor people in King John's reign, made into a school in the 16th century, and rebuilt in 1676 and 1790.

A little walk beyond St Peter's brings us to the White Horse cut in the hill about the time of Waterloo by Mr Greazeley's schoolboys, 62 feet long and 47 feet high, a noble steed with tail up and prancing. On the way to it we are brought to a pause by one of the most striking pieces of architecture on the road from London to Bath, the stately columned hall in memory of the Old Boys who fell in the Great War. It is a surprising peep from a country road, and in front of it is a flagged garden fragrant with lavender when we called, and always beautiful. Out of the garden rise long steps leading to the College chapel, and let into the ground at the top of the steps are these words:

Let us make Earth a garden in
which all the deeds of the valiant
shall blossom and bear fruit.

Looking up at the chapel outside we are struck by the curious sight of a hundred odd stone carvings running round it like gargoyles. Inside is an impressive series of wall paintings, a truly striking spectacle in this great place 60 feet high and 178 long. They are by Spencer Stanhope, an artist of great individuality, and form a noble gathering worthy of their setting; they show scenes of the Expulsion of Adam and Eve from the Garden, Ishmael suffering from thirst in the wilderness, the three Marys at the Tomb, the Annunciation, the Visitation, and Gethsemane. There is a stained glass window by William Morris who was a boy at Marlborough College and the windows on the south side of the chapel are in the style of Burne-Jones. The stone reredos shows the Wise Men at Bethlehem and the Crucifixion, with another scene of Our Lord raising His hand in benediction, angels about Him.

The College is built on the site of Marlborough's lost castle, the ruins of which are about the mound. In the old castle King John was married and Henry the Third summoned Parliament. It was given to the Seymours, who then lived at Savernake, by Jane Seymour's son, Edward the Sixth, but it was made into a new house by a pupil of Inigo Jones (John Webb), and in this house were entertained John Evelyn and Samuel Pepys. Charles the Second was entertained in this fine place on his return to the throne, and for 100 years the new castle was a home of the Seymours. It then became the Castle Inn, one of the most popular coaching inns between London and Bath. It received within its walls the famous figures of that great procession of people who went to Bath when that city was at the height of its fame, and many of us have read the story told by Macaulay, and also in one of Stanley Weyman's novels, of Lord Chatham's long stay here shut up in his room. He was on his way home from Bath when his gout got hold of him, and for three weeks he was kept in his room at the Castle Inn. London was expecting him, Burke was thundering against ministers, and Chatham had retired to Bath, but the announcement that he was returning left Parliament expectant. A day was fixed for his arrival, but on reaching the Castle Inn at Marlborough Chatham stopped and refused to move. Everybody who travelled that road, says Macaulay, was amazed by the number of his attendants. Footmen and grooms dressed in the family livery filled the inn and swarmed the streets, the truth being that the invalid had insisted that during his stay all the waiters and stable-boys should wear his livery. His colleagues in London were in despair; confusion grew worse confounded, and though at last Chatham returned to London he might as well have remained at Marlborough, says Macaulay, for he would see nobody, would do nothing, and became "almost as much forgotten as if he had already been lying in Westminster Abbey."

The time came when the railway took people to Bath, and the days of the Castle Inn declined. One winter's day in 1843 this great house ceased to be an inn, and one summer's day in that same year it became the nucleus of the new Marlborough College.

Melksham. In the courtyard is a great yew with about 20 huge limbs held up on 30 props. It is probably as old as the 15th century church, from the door of which St Michael looks across at it, slaying a fierce dragon which is showing its teeth. Above him is a window looking out from the room over the porch. The porch has a vaulted roof, and in it is a colossal stone coffin. Four gargoyles look down from the pinnacled tower, and two grotesque beasts are climbing up and down below the battlements of the walls.

Everywhere are sculptured reliefs. Above an altar is a charming figure of a woman holding a wreath; another, with a weeping man and woman at an urn, is in memory of Richard Jenkins who "closed his sorrows" in 1806. A wife's tablet to her husband by the chancel screen says "oft have we trod thy courts together"; she paved the chancel with marble. Three beautiful green tablets have three items of the history of humanity. One is to John Buckley and a son who followed his friend William Penn to Pennsylvania; another is to a young officer who fell in Mesopotamia; and another is to a Melksham family which perished in one of the saddest tragedies of the last generation, for father, mother, and six children went down in the Titanic.

There are charming brass gates to the chancel, an oak pulpit with six winged angels, a painted frieze of angels round the chapel, and over a hundred painted figures in the windows. The finest windows are in the clerestory, where 18 figures look down in a rich array of costume—Joseph of Arimathea, Aldhelm with his crook, Alfred with his sword, Dunstan with his staff, Richard Poore holding Salisbury cathedral, Chad with Lichfield cathedral, and Augustine with Canterbury.

In this chancel, with a Nativity carved in stone and a roof of gilded bosses, two vicars have served for a century between them, the 18th century Bohun Fox for 53 years, and the 19th century George Hume for 47. We noticed on one of the walls, in memory of an old man of 90 born under Queen Elizabeth, a quaint cherub between a skull and an hourglass, smiling as if he did not care for either time or death.

In this town was born in 1689 the Quaker diarist John Rutty. Wandering far from home, he graduated in medicine at Leyden and before he was 30 settled down in Dublin to practise.

His career was one of modest well-doing. He was a Quaker, and the historian of the Society of Friends, and he lovingly served the poor without fee. He wrote various books on medicine, surgery, and kindred sciences; drank only water as a rule, fasted often, and frequently ate nettles for dinner. Yet he had a healthy man's appetite, and scourges his natural longing for baked meats in the pages of his diary.

The diary covers practically the last quarter-century of his amiable life, and we read his lurid entries as we read John Bunyan's lamentations for his deadly sin of ringing bells. Here are a few characteristic extracts from Rutty's *Spiritual Diary and Soliloquies:*

Indulgence in bed an hour too long.
A hypochondriack obnubilation from indigestion.
A dull, cross, and choleric day.
A little swinish at dinner and repast.
Cursed snappishness to those under me, on a bodily indisposition.
On a provocation, exercised a dumb resentment for two days.

Never was a diariest more candid, never more critical of self, more forgiving of others. When one of his books is savagely criticised in a review all he puts in his diary is that the article is "a wholesome discipline, though severe."

All his life John Rutty devotedly applied himself to the art of healing—John Wesley was among his patients; and it is appropriate, as he would have been the first to agree, that when the Friends burial ground in Dublin had to be disturbed the College of Surgeons should rise over his grave.

Mere. From the top of its ancient Castle Hill one can look down on three counties, for one stands in Wiltshire at the boundaries of Dorset and Somerset.

A 17th century house holds out the Sign of the Ship, a network of scrolls, spirals, and flowering plants with a crown on top and a bunch of grapes at the end. The inn, like the sign, takes its name from the sailing ship badge of John Mere, who founded a chantry in the church in the 14th century. The house as it stands was built by Sir John Coventry, whom a Parliament of Charles the Second nicknamed Boanerges. Pepys mentions the loud-voiced knight, but his name is tacked to an Act of Parliament because of an incident of which he was a victim. One night he was waylaid in the London streets and had his nostrils slit, the outrage so angering the Commons that an Act was passed imposing the death penalty for such mutilation. It was called the Coventry Act.

A neighbouring inn has a more personal recollection of Charles the Second declaring that he dined there after the Battle of Worcester. It is certain that he slept at Zeals, the handsome house with the black hounds at the gate, half a mile away.

A more gracious memory clings to the Chantry, the long low Tudor house near the church, where old William Barnes the poet kept his small school. Its garden slopes down to a stream which escapes in a noisy fall through the garden wall, and trickles across the elm-shadowed meadow. By this stream the poet would sit with his beloved Petrarch. These lawns he kept trim with his scythe. Here is the sedate old coachhouse he turned into the workshop where he worked his lathe. These are the walls from which he took the apricots to carry to his friends. This was the haven where he tended the flowers, this the garden to which he bade so tender a farewell when he had to leave it to seek a better place for his school at Dorchester:

Sweet garden! peaceful spot! no more in thee
Shall I e'er wile away the sunny hour.
Farewell each blooming shrub and lofty tree;
Farewell the mossy path and nodding flower;
I shall not hear again from yonder bower
The song of birds or humming of the bee,
Nor listen to the waterfall, nor see
The clouds float on behind the lofty tower.

No more at breezy eve or dewy morn
My gliding scythe shall shear thy mossy green;
My busy hands shall never more adorn,
My eyes no more may see this peaceful scene.
But still, sweet spot, wherever I may be,
My love-led soul shall wander back to thee.

The church the 13th century built, keeping some traces of the Saxon masons, was rebuilt with greater opulence in 200 years, when they added the tower in emulation of those for which the west country is famous. The tower is impressive and 100 feet high, with carved parapet, pinnacles, and traceried windows. Inside it has a fine panelled arch and a remarkable ceiling, divided into panels great and small, the larger ones with moulded timbers and handsome bosses, divided again into smaller ones, all filled with delicate designs.

The church is one of the best in Wiltshire, spacious and lofty and light. The nave arcades have pointed arches and clustered columns. The clerestory is lit by traceried windows. The 15th century roof is supported by angels along its cornice, some clad in feathers. Nearly all the pews are resplendent with carving. The font follows the example of the 15th century woodcarvers in sculptured stone.

These are ornaments which many a church can show, but this church is rare in having a chancel completely enclosed by screens. It is surrounded on all sides by exquisite 15th century woodwork, and so lovely in its tracery that it is sufficient of itself to make Mere famous. The main screen has two tiers of open traceried panels and lovely fan-vaulting with the roodloft above as in medieval days. In an upright of one of the side screens is a peephole, and near it is a staple with the last link of a chain once holding a book. The seats of the old misericords are adorned with flowers and heads. Among them is an angel and another has a dragon pushing his way through leaves. Four golden angels stand on four posts, lighting with their candles the beautiful new altar which is the peace memorial.

The south chapel was built by Sir John Battishorne in 1350. Old grotesques support the modern roof, and there are fragments of tiles at the altar steps. In one of the fine traceried windows are four medallions of 16th century glass, with colouring subdued but beautiful, showing St Nicholas raising a man from the tomb, St Christopher with the Child, St Martin on a high-stepping white horse halving his cloak with a beggar, and a bishop with a hand raised in blessing. All are set in a background of leaves or flowers. In the middle of the floor, surrounded by a low iron railing, is the fine brass of Sir John himself. He is in armour with chain mail at its joints, gauntlets protected by knobs, and an elaborate belt with a pendant. His sword and dagger are at his side, his feet on a lion. It is a remarkably unblemished brass. Less fine, but still handsome, is the brass of his nephew Sir John Berkeley, also in armour.

There are two porches with rooms over them. The great porch has a vaulted roof whose ribs spring from small heads crowned with flowers and meet in bosses. Under a rich canopy at the entrance is St Michael; over the inner doorway is a battered Madonna. In the room over this porch is a queer possession for a church, a tiny piece of trimming from the bed in which Edward the Second was murdered in Berkeley Castle.

The greatest of all possessions of the church, however, is the alabaster carving of the Adoration of the Wise Men. It was found covered with bright paint in one of the gardens below Castle Hill, and is now restored and so highly valued that when we called it had gone away on exhibition. Other treasures are a carved table, some old seats, fragments of stained glass, and a chest of Shakespeare's day.

Not far from Mere is Woodlands, a manor house of the time of Chaucer, so perfect of its kind, though small, as hardly to be matched. Its great hall is nobly roofed, some of the curved beams meeting in carved cusps. The tall windows, which have carved heads, admit the light to a minstrel gallery with linenfold panelling. Over the porch is a small room which has a big drawing, found on the original plaster wall, of a horse's head with bridle and a well-arched neck. An adventure began at Woodlands which ended in an Act of Parliament (1755) known as Lord Hardwicke's Act "for the preventing of clandestine marriages."

Ridgeway Pitt, son of Thomas Pitt, first Earl of Londonderry and uncle to the great Earl of Chatham, bequeathed Woodlands to his sister Lady Lucy, who was brought up very strictly with her small cousin Miss Cholmondeley, by Miss Cholmondeley's mother, Lady Essex.

One day the children, aged 13 and 14, were hurrying home late when they were passed by their uncle, who said "What will Lady Essex say to your being out so late!" They were frightened at what Lady Essex might say and expected to be punished. When they met two Westminster boys (the brothers Meyrick whom they knew) they stopped to tell their troubles. The boys suggested that they should all marry and escape to France. So romantic a fancy promised at any rate an escape from punishment, and the plan was accepted, though the ingenious young ladies insisted on first returning home to fetch two toys, a pretty bird which came out of its cage when the door was opened, and a dog that barked when squeezed.

Lady Essex could not have been watching from the window, for everything went well with them. A maid whom they commanded, and who foolishly obeyed them, accompanied them. The plan was carried out, and then events began to move. Lady Essex had been alarmed by their absence and had made enquiries, and the happy married pairs were seized when boarding a ship for France. In later years their marriages were properly solemnised, and Lady Lucy Pitt became Lady Pierce Meyrick. The Meyricks lived at Woodlands and we may hope they lived happily ever after; but the Act of Parliament which was the epilogue to their adventure put an end to clandestine marriages, invalidated marriages of infants by licence without the consent of parents or guardians, and required the solemnisation of all marriages in churches.

Mildenhall (pronounced Mynall). There are Roman remains on the banks of the Kennet, under the grass near Folly Farm. In Black Meadow down in the valley is a well they made, now filled in.

One enters the ancient church by a doorway with the stump of the old oak bar still in the wall. The 12th century nave was crowned with a clerestory in the 15th century, when they embattled the 13th century tower, and when the village was still telling the time by the dials on the buttresses. There is much fine sculptured foliage on the capitals and in the roof: on one capital a man holds out a leaf to a woman who extends her hand to receive it; in the roof of the nave leaves spring from richly carved bosses. The chancel roof is covered with flowers and leaves in plaster. The chancel is 15th century, but its arch, with two charming corbels, was made about 1200 and now has a pulpit and a reading desk both of equal height on each side of it, both with canopies. There is an organ in the western gallery and box pews, and it would be difficult to find a more attractive chancel furnished according to the ideas of the early 19th century.

Mildenhall has a curiously built school just over a century old, with four wings round a tower.

Milston. The birthplace of Joseph Addison who was born in the old rectory in 1672. The house has been demolished but its site is marked by a stone in the garden of the new rectory.

He was a politician, serving as Secretary to the Lord Lieutenant of Ireland, and, after the death of Queen Anne, Secretary of State. But he is best remembered as a man of letters; for his work with *The Tatler* (with his friend Richard Steele), *The Spectator* and *The Guardian* and for some of his hymns, many of which are paraphrases of the Psalms. "The Spacious Firmament on high" (Psalm 19)—"The Lord my Pasture shall prepare" (Psalm 23).

The font in the church at which he was baptised has leaves carved on its base and a domed cover crowned with a dove. The church itself is 13th century with 15th century windows.

Milton Lilbourne. It is a rare little place of trees and hills, thatch and gardens, with a fine approach to its treasure house up a steep path, the vicarage one side and cottages on raised pavements all round. The doorway of the church is 700 years old and has massive faces on each side, a woman in a wimple and a man with a beard. There are two square clerestory windows in the nave, and in the middle of the floor is a stone on which we read that under it lie the bones of unknown persons found within the walls. In the 14th century chancel are eight huge stone corbels, among them a king, a queen, and a bishop, and one of the windows has fragments of ancient glass in which is a curly headed lion putting out his tongue. There are 17th century pews and pulpit, and in one of the aisles is a recess with beautiful carving by a medieval mason.

On Milton Hill is an unusual tumulus with two rows of barrows, and there are in the neighbourhood the remains of a village peopled by men and women who lived before the dawn of history.

Minety. It is within easy reach of Braydon Pond, the biggest sheet of water in Wiltshire, and its church is entered by a door about 600 years old, with beautiful tracery at the top.

In the nave are brass candelabra and little holes at the top of the bench-end ornaments were made for holding candles. The pulpit is 17th century with a rich canopy and a carving of the Scottish thistle. The rare little two-branched candelabra is fitted to the edge of the pulpit and has a crown between the branches. It was given by Thomas Browne, who lies in the chancel. On the wall of the chancel is the bust of his grandson, a youth of 17, who, we are told, "died of the cruel smallpox." Another candelabra is for the choir, now in the chancel, with a dove on the top. The third is for the people, hanging in the nave, and has cherubs engraved between its branches.

The best modern window is the Angel at the Tomb, and there is a little old glass with Tudor roses, crowns and flowers, an eagle, and a small human figure faced by a kneeling angel. There are three fine old screens with tracery and flowers and leaves along the top, a richly carved chair by the altar, an old reading-desk, a 15th century font, quaint old pews, a bearded man crowned with flowers among the 12 fine corbels on which the roof rests, and the brass portraits of an Elizabethan family, Nicholas Poulett with his wife and their four children. It was his uncle who looked after Mary Queen of Scots when she was a prisoner of Queen Elizabeth the First.

Resting on a window-sill are three fragments of a Saxon cross with beautiful carving on them, found under the chancel. The porch has two sets of mullioned windows, and a fine barrel roof with oak bosses.

Monkton Deverill. By the River Deverill. In the church and worked into the modern pulpit are four panels of Flemish workmanship representing "The Creation and The Fall of Man." In the first panel God raised Adam to life among the trees and flowers of Eden; the Almighty is also seen on a cloud with Adam in the sky above. In the next picture Adam lies asleep under a tree, and God calls Eve from his side. In the third panel Adam and Eve stand under the Tree of Knowledge and the Serpent of Evil comes writhing out of the branches to tempt them, while in the sky the Creator looks on, apparently sorrowing. The fourth picture is the frightened pair in flight, the flaming sword, and the angry angel.

The church was rebuilt in the 19th century, though the tower has survived from the 15th and the font is 13th.

Monkton Farleigh. It is among the lanes of the quiet country round Bath, and its Tudor manor house has something in it of the

Marlborough College.

Purton: the church with two towers.

The Marlborough Downs and the Vale of Pewsey.

Old Sarum: the castle site.

Old Sarum: inside the castle.

The Grand Avenue in Savernake Forest.

walls of the ancient priory. In one of the fields is a small steep-roofed stone building which housed the water-supply of the monks. Through its locked door we can hear the stream bubbling away, an odd sound which must have been going on since Monkton Farleigh was a famous place and these old ruins part of a stately pile.

The house where Bishop Jewel died, riding here after preaching his last sermon at Lacock, has vanished, but the charming rectory, keeping company with the church, has a lovely oriel window and tall octagonal chimneys.

The church is entered through a Norman doorway with round shafts on which one of the capitals looks like an owl. The old door has hundreds of studs and the curious little tower has two gables and buttresses. In the east window is Aldhelm as a minstrel with a harp, with figures of St Peter and Our Lord. By the altar is a lancet with David minding his father's sheep. There is a Jacobean pulpit with Tudor linenfold matching the 26 linenfold panels at the back of the nave, and elegant iron gates lead into the tower arch.

One curious stone we noticed here to Sara Grant, with the words:

Five pounds she gave unto the poor;
William King gave so much more.

Netheravon. It has lost one remarkable building but has saved another. On the hills above the Avon once stood a Roman house, the foundations of which have been seen. Down below is the Saxon tower of the 13th century church.

The tower stands at the end of a long narrow way, drawing the eye to it as we approach, for it has simple white walls, plain and unadorned except for its great doorway, which rests on four round pillars crowned with crudely carved capitals, the two inner ones having weird beasts with sharp claws and long tails. The tower, of very great interest to the student of antiquity because of the little Saxon doorway high up, has Saxon long-and-short work, and one of the chief authorities of Saxon England believes it was the private chapel of the leading man of the village or the residence of the sacristan who had charge of the sacred relics. The tower was probably once surrounded on all sides and the little door 17 feet above the ground may have given access to a vanished building; the ancient churches of Brixworth and Deerhurst have towers like this. The Netheravon tower has a fine arch opening on the nave, 18 feet high and with three columns on each side.

There are arcades of four bays in the nave resting on Norman columns and the clerestory is 13th century. The roodloft doorway has a gracious woman's head above it. On the wall of the chancel we noticed a tablet to John Kamm who was parish clerk for nearly half a century.

Nettleton. It has one of the oldest monuments in England, and one of the most beautiful towers in Wiltshire.

The monument, the Nettleton Tumulus, is in a field on the Roman Fosse Way, a long green mound with three rugged stones on the top.

The tower is one of the superb group we find in Wiltshire, elegant with windows and pinnacles, and with their upper stages entirely covered with tracery, the centre panels being pierced to let out the sound of the bells. One of the bells in this glorious tower has been ringing half a thousand years, and all this time three wide-mouthed gargoyles have been looking down, and one queer creature has been reaching out. For many generations a splendid chestnut has been growing in the shadow of the tower; it is 14 feet round.

The church has a porch enriched outside with battlements and pediment, winged gargoyles, a quatrefoil frieze all round, and neat buttresses, and dignified inside with a vaulted roof of floral bosses with its stone ribs springing from fine heads. Just outside it are two heads at a window, one appearing anxious to tear his mouth open, and one holding his chin.

In the porch hangs one of the finest doors in Wiltshire, five feet wide and swinging on hinges over four feet long.

The great door brings us immediately in touch with Norman England, for the 14th century arches of the nave rest on round Norman columns, with their sculptured capitals all different and all charming. It has a fine array of Norman and English sculpture, 30 or 40 figures and faces below the roofs and on the arches, mostly human, with a few grotesques. Among them a jester and a bishop, crowned heads, a little face by the chancel arch with a neat head-dress, and a big carving of a woman holding a wrap over her head. Some of them are corbels holding up the roofs. The chancel roof is barrel-shaped with slender oak panelling and a neat cornice. The nave is filled with box pews, and the pulpit is one of that group of about 60 in all England with 15th century stone carving in them.

The tower arch is tall and stately looking along the five bays of the nave into a chancel with fine possessions crowned with a reredos of the Last Supper in stone, a dramatic conception in which the artist has caught the disciples at the moment when they are all

Draycot Cerne:
Sir Edward and Lady Cerne, 1393

Lacock:
Robert and Elizabeth Baynard, 1501

West Lavington:
John Dauntsey, 1559

Ogbourne St George:
Thomas and Joan Goddard, 1517

Bradford-on-Avon:
Anne Longe, 1601

BRASSES OF WILTSHIRE PEOPLE

eagerly listening to Our Lord saying, "One of you will betray me," and Judas is turning away, clutching the bag. There are sturdy altar-rails seeming to be 17th century, a fine carved chair with angels carrying a crown on the top, and a heraldic wall monument which has the only marks of lightning we have come upon in any of our churches.

It is a monument to Samuel Arnold, a 19th century rector here for 40 years, and the marks of the lightning are clearly visible on it. It was struck in a storm in 1842 and was restored by his parishioners. He and another 19th century vicar, Charles Domvile, shared between them almost the whole of the 100 years of the 19th century, Domvile being here 58 years.

There is a Norman font and a stone bell turret on the east gable of the nave housing the sanctus bell.

Newton Tony. A tiny village on the Hampshire border, its 19th century church keeps from the old one a Norman font, set on a stout pillar. On the walls are painted heraldic tablets of the Malet family.

The wall monument of Dame Marian Dora Malet, who died in 1891, has a good portrait-bust of a lady of great serenity. Above the tablet to George Malet hang his sword and scabbard, the sword he carried when he was killed in 1856 while leading his regiment in the attack on Reshire in Persia. Below is a brass inscription on the wall to Hugh Poyntz Malet, writer of several scientific books.

North Bradley. It looks across the fields to the White Horse on Westbury Downs. In its 14th and 15th century church is the tomb of Lady Emma Stafford, mother of an Archbishop of Canterbury, and her chapel has lovely windows, its roof full of fine carving, rich bosses, moulded beams of the 15th century, and 72 oak panels. The tomb is set in a panelled and recessed window and Lady Stafford's portrait is cut in the stone, showing her under a canopy, her feet on a little spotted dog. On the tomb is a small glass case with a pewter paten and a broken pewter chalice. They lay for hundreds of years in the grave of a priest of the 14th century. They laid him to rest in a coffin made from a hollow tree, in which his bones were found with this chalice. He may have christened Lady Emma's son John, born in 1387, made Keeper of the Seal by Henry the Fifth, and Lord Chancellor of England and Archbishop of Canterbury.

Their home stands a little way out of the village, Southwick

Court, a beautiful house still protected by its ancient moat, bushes hanging over it and bridges spanning it. It is now a farm, but inside are many of the old doors with latch-and-bobbin fasteners.

The church has been refashioned since their day; it is 15th century, and gargoyles look down from its embattled tower. The porch has a gilded sundial of 1777. The nave is clerestoried, the timber ceiling is panelled, and there is a fine 15th century font with the bull, the eagle, the lion, and the angel of the Four Evangelists. There is a huge medieval chest and a lovely piscina. In the chapels hang two small brass candelabra. Two of the windows have five figures of familiar characters: William of Wykeham holding Winchester College, Elizabeth of Hungary with an apronful of roses, St Nicholas with the three balls, St Catherine with a sharp-spiked wheel, and Galahad.

In the lady chapel, which has a roof 600 years old, is a wall monument with twisted columns to John Trenchard. Here for 100 years has slept a man who has two fine monuments in the village. He was Charles Daubeny, vicar for 49 years, who built a row of almshouses on the green and the cottages down a lane for six poor folk. They are called Vicar's Poorhouse.

Hanging in the vestry a copy of a prayer offered at the opening of the almshouses in 1818, very much in keeping with the spirit of the time:

O, Father of mercy and God of comfort, who hast in Thy wisdom disposed the different ranks and conditions in life, high and low, rich and poor, look down with an eye of favour on this lowly dwelling dedicated to the more comfortable accommodation for those whom Thy providence has ordained to be fed with the bread of poverty and to have nowhere to lay their heads.

Words which are reminiscent of the third verse (now so often omitted) of Mrs Alexander's famous hymn "All Things Bright and Beautiful":

The rich man in his castle,
The poor man at his gate,
God made them, high or lowly,
And ordered their estate.

Within easy reach of North Bradley is a beautiful neighbour of the moated Court, Brook House, now also a farm. The house is beautifully set in green fields among great elms and stately poplars, with a stream rippling by. The old wing has still original doorways and a magnificent timber roof.

North Wraxall. For 800 years travellers must have been astonished by the beauty of a doorway here, the doorway in the little church in a graveyard full of yews, under a 14th century porch which seems to be falling down with age, and has a pretty timber frieze. The beaded arch of the doorway, with rows of wavy zigzag moulding, rests on shafts with carved capitals, and over the arch is a delightful little figure of the patron saint with a staff and a purse. The chancel arch, springing from the walls with no pillars, leads into the sanctuary with a painting of Christ speaking on the shore of a lake to people sitting about. The altar table is Jacobean, and there is a Jacobean pulpit with a canopy, behind which the old steps to the roodloft are crumbling away. The east window has three small panels of the Nativity, the Ascension, and the Crucifixion. There is a piscina on a windowsill.

An attractive arcade of clustered pillars leads into a raised aisle and a chapel in which lies Paul Methuen, whose family built the chapel. He rests, alone in the middle of the floor, in a white marble tomb of the 18th century, with about 40 painted shields looking down from the roof. In one of the windows of the chapel are four small panels showing Moses striking the rock and holding up the serpent, with scenes of the Resurrection.

Norton Bavant. It lies below the great citadel of Scratchbury Camp.

Towering above the village and looking down on the Wylye Valley from a height of 650 feet, Scratchbury is immensely strong, a fine example of the sort of fort our ancestors were building a hundred years or two before Christ. The ramparts are in places 66 feet high, and follow the outline of the hill all round the summit. The earthen walls are over a mile round, and enclose about 40 acres. There are three entrances. In the middle of the camp are traces of a bank and ditch, perhaps the remains of a smaller camp of the Stone Age men of about 2000 BC. Inside the rampart are seven round barrows of the Bronze Age in which sleep Wiltshire men of thirty or forty centuries ago. Near by is a huge grave of the Stone Age 12 feet high and eight times as long, and in it have been found such relics as fragments of stag-horn, teeth of wild boar, charcoal, and stones, suggesting a funeral mound where bodies were burned.

From the top of the ramparts one can see over rolling hills and wooded valleys into Somerset and Dorset. The church stands in a beautiful park, with a simple 14th century tower and turret, and a chalk arch which has resisted the wear of time through all these centuries. It leads into the Benet chapel, which has brasses of two husbands, John and Thomas Benet, and their wives, one with two groups of children.

Oaksey. It has fine oaks all about it, as the name implies, and at the back of its church a group of earthworks called Norwood Castle.

The small 700-year-old church, with beautiful clerestory windows, has fine patches of medieval colour, which have been restored by Professor Tristram, and it is believed that others are still hidden. On most of the walls are fragments of texts and on the south wall are paintings rich in detail beginning east with "The Christ of the Trades," Our Lord surrounded by tools to suggest the moral that salvation is in labour, the theme of the poem of Piers Plowman which appeared a little while before these paintings were done. Beyond this painting is another painting of the same kind but less complete, having been largely destroyed by a monumental tablet now removed. Farther west is a remarkable St Christopher showing the saint carrying the child across the ford with a hermit holding a lantern; the detail is rich and clear, showing a mermaid, a man fishing, a basket full of fish, and fishes swimming in the stream.

Very vivid is the colour still also in ancient glass, some of it, like the paintings, 14th century. It shows St Anne teaching her daughter, the Virgin Mary, to read. Near is St Catherine crowned, and the same window has also the head of a saint and a pelican perched on the edge of the nest, feeding its little ones, the emblem of the Passion as the Pelican was believed to suckle its young with its own blood. One of the nave windows is full of bright fragments of old glass, in which is an odd picture of a baby in a bathtub, two men kneeling in crimson robes, the crowned head of a saint, and fragments of canopies.

For 500 years strange gargoyles have been looking down on the embattled tower outside, and there is much fine sculpture inside in wood and stone. Eleven stone faces look down from the walls of the lofty nave. There is a fine little head at each end of the arcade and two others on the chancel arch, one a lady in a wimple and one a scowling fellow. Among the old woodcarving is the chancel screen and panels let into the choir stalls of beasts, flowers and birds, a man with toothache, and a man with his tongue out.

Oare. It lies at the foot of the towering Marlborough Downs, among ancient camps and earthworks. Martinsell Hill is a thousand feet high and gives glorious views.

The little red brick church is modern.

Odstock. It has magnificent views from the Roman camp called Clearbury Rings, a handsome manor house with magnificent sycamores at its gates, and a small church founded by the Gerberds who lived here in the 13th century, part of their home built into the house that remains.

Some remarkable knowledge of the civilisation here two centuries before the Romans has come to light. In digging over the 600-acre Iron Age Settlement many storage pits for grain have been found, proving that not only did the farmers of the period grow wheat, oats, barley, peas, and beans, but that they also knew how to prevent the stored grain from sprouting owing to the damp. They toasted the grain in ovens before burying it, the pottery used for the ovens having been dug up. Here, too, have been found the remains of prehistoric timber houses, one 45 feet wide with a verandah outside.

The treasure of the 13th century church is the pulpit, which has panels carved with Tudor roses and marigolds, and one panel with a painted crown and Queen Elizabeth the First's initials and the date 1580; under it are little gilded scrolls with the rhyme:

God bless and save our Royal Queen
The lyke on earth was never seen.

On the book-rest is a carving of a little girl with great wings and curly hair.

In a canopied recess is a tomb believed to be that of the Gerberd who founded the church; on it is engraved a gowned figure of a young man under a canopy. A quaint wooden almsbox is on the wall of the tower.

A bitter tragedy is recorded in a heraldic monument of the 18th century telling of Sir John Webb's tragic loss of four little children, three under and one just over three years old. There was living hereabouts in those days a man who figured in a tragedy more pathetic still, a Scamp who was not a scamp. He lies in the churchyard, his stone covered by rambler roses when we called. On it we read that Josiah Scamp died in 1801, but there is nothing about the story the village tells of this good Scamp. His daughter's husband committed a crime for which he was bound to die, and for love of his daughter Scamp pleaded guilty to it and was executed in his stead.

Ogbourne St Andrew. The tower has weird stone creatures creeping round it, an impressive monster at one corner. Inside it has a vaulted roof with 12 bosses richly carved, two peepholes cut through its pillars and a very old door to the belfry. The two doorways into the nave are Norman, one plain and one with zigzag on its round arch. The nave is a little odd with a single pillar on each side, two Norman arches springing from each, and it is odd also for being shorter than the chancel. One aisle has stone corbels, and the other oak angels; the south aisle has fragments of old glass showing the Instruments of the Passion.

The 13th century chancel has a twin piscina under a canopy, a beautiful old chair and a painted monument with the busts of two kindly looking people of Stuart days, William Goddard and his wife holding a skull between them, their eight children kneeling below with six holding skulls.

The pre-reformation tenor bell weighs 25 cwt.

High up on the hills behind the village is the Horseman's Grave, a cross marking the resting-place of Patrick Francis Hartigan, who was buried here in 1921. On the pedestal is this verse:

Beneath the clean and spacious sky
Here let the sleeping horseman lie,
Nor from his darlings sunder;
And as the thoroughbreds flash by
This dust may quicken suddenly
To hear the gallops thunder.

Ogbourne St George. One of the highest points of the Marlborough hills, with the Wiltshire plain stretched out beneath. It is thought that the rosy brick manor house here stands on the site of a priory founded 800 years ago by Maud of Wallingford. The brasses of a lord and lady of the manor 400 years ago are on the floor of the church, Thomas Goddard in a long furred gown and his wife with an embroidered girdle.

The church is ringed in by great elms, and a pair of giants stand sentinel at the gate, one 18 and the other 21 feet round the trunk. The tower and the porch have grown old side by side, both 15th century, both with gargoyles looking down, the porch with a sundial over the door and a scratch-dial for telling the hours of mass which was here long before the other dial came.

The church has a 13th century doorway and chancel arch with no piers, a 14th century chancel, and the rest (aisles and clerestory, tower and porch, priest's doorway and small traceried screens) all 15th century. The small screens are on each side of the chancel. There is fine carving on the capitals on one side of the nave, a candelabra, an ancient chest, and a lonely face in the corner of the west wall looking a little cynical.

Orcheston. It is known for the long grasses that bear its name, which grow up in two small fields when the fields are flooded. They grow to the top of the water and float on the surface, where the wading cattle feed on them. There is a great thatched barn in the village and we found the wayside bright with strips of flowers.

Two villages now one, it keeps both its old churches. The church of St George, snugly hid among the trees, has a Tudor doorway with neatly carved spandrels, its arch handsomely panelled about 500 years ago. Down two steps into the nave and up one to the chancel. On the wall is a quaint stone face, and in one of the windows is a blue and gold medallion of 17th century glass, a triangle representing the Trinity, scrolls held by cherubs and Latin puns on the scrolls. Set in the wall is a small 18th century gravestone with a winged hourglass and a death's head painted on it, and there is a piscina drain cut in one of the windowsills. The church of St Mary, much rebuilt, has a small gabled tower, a 13th century arcade, a chest 300 years old, a scratch-dial, and a rare little possession in a pre-reformation paten engraved with the Vernicle—the Face of Our Lord.

Patney. It is made an island by the Avon, a tiny stream running here, and it has only its little church to see, looking down from a bank. By it is a gorgeous cedar. In the church is a quaint little organ made in 1786, with painted pipes. The pulpit is older, and a stone seat under a chancel window is older still. Older than all is the font, for it was made by the Normans and has four heads worn away at the base. There is a beautiful piscina with a hooded canopy projecting from the wall. The windows have fine figures of St Oswald and St Edmund in rich jewelled robes, and the Annunciation.

Pewsey. Between the Great Downs and the Great Plain, it is so old that its church stands on sarsen stones which the Saxons probably laid, so old that Alfred owned it. He stands in stone, an attractive figure, crowned and with his sword and shield, at the meeting of the village streets, facing the low bridge over a stream of the Avon, with little gardens and green banks and thatched cottages mirrored in the water. High up on the hill are ancient earthworks, and the view is still as George Borrow found it, with villages, hamlets, farms, towers, steeples, fields, and meadows all about.

The 700-year-old church, set on a hill away from the beautiful village centre, has a 15th century tower with pinnacles and gargoyles outside, and with a stately arch and a fan-vaulted roof inside. There is a scratch-dial on the walls. The church has two old chests and a plain old font, the font remarkable only for its wooden cover, made by Canon Bouverie as a war memorial. The canon was rector here for 30 years and in his day did much carving within these walls. The very elaborate altar and the altar-rails are his, and his are the four patron saints and John the Baptist on the vestry screen. The font cover is his masterpiece. It is an octagon, with eight figures round its base, two tiers of eight angels above, and another tier of figures above them. The figures all stand solidly in the niches, and in the bottom group are types of the men and women in the war.

The church has fine piscinas, a fine west window with a hundred figures in vivid colours, and two others with the shepherds and the kings at Bethlehem; and in one of the aisles and one of the chapels are fine timbers, those in the aisle Jacobean and those in the chapel from the roof of a ruined priory at Ivychurch. The best of all the woodwork here is a splendid chancel screen by Harry Hems.

Pewsey is perhaps unique for having considerable work of a substantial kind done by two of its rectors, Canon Bouverie, whose woodwork we have looked at, and the Earl of Radnor's son who, while he was rector here, sculptured a medallion of Mary and Jesus now on the chapel altar. We may not forgive Canon Bouverie for his paintings on the walls, but his woodwork calls for no apology, and he was interested in so many curious things that he gave his church two strange possessions. One is the lock of the almsbox, which is from the door of a convict's cell on Van Diemen's Island; the other is the fine golden mahogany from which he made the altar-rails. It comes from a three-decker ship, the San Josef, which surrendered to Nelson at the battle of St Vincent in 1797 after which Nelson was made a knight and an admiral.

Pickwick. It is a little bit of Corsham and has no church to call its own. There is a street of cottages which seem to have been sunburnt, with hooded doorways, lovely gables and old stone roofs, overhanging porches, a charming manor house, and a pigeon-cote.

Perhaps Dickens's Pickwick here found his beginning. It was, at any rate, from a firm of Moses Pickwick and Company, which ran coaches through Pickwick from Bath to London, that the novelist took the name.

Potterne. It looks across miles of fields and woods from a steep hill near Devizes. Keep on the lower road and you see one of the loveliest timbered fronts in Wiltshire to look upon and one of the loveliest approaches to any church. Keep on the higher one and you are walking on the level of the tops of some of the houses.

The beautiful timbered house was bought as an inn by Mr George Richmond, FSA, who restored it last century and made it the charming place we see. It is now a private house, with an oriel window looking out on the street at the foot of the hill. It has old furniture in every room, oak rafters mellowed with age, leathern thongs lifting the old-fashioned wooden latches of the doors. The hall door, solid and dignified, has a huge lock with an enormous key. Quaint peepholes in the bedrooms, with stained glass in sliding panels, remain to overlook the central hall below.

The fine church up the hill was built about the time Salisbury cathedral was rising. Its great tower is 14th century and has a pierced parapet, a turret at each corner, and medieval lattice work. The door which brings us in is home again after unknown adventures, for it was rescued from a farm. It is a very big door which is probably as old as the church, yet it has been away for 54 years, an exile in a strange land, and on coming home again it was restored by the village carpenter and the village blacksmith.

But there is something here that was centuries old when the door was set new on its hinges; it is the old font, the glory of Potterne though it is kept as a museum piece, and a medieval font has been allowed to take its place. The new one has little arches round the bowl and still bears the marks of the staples which locked it against witches 700 years ago; but the old one is plain and massive (35 inches across the bowl), and is unique in having round its rim a text from the Saxon baptism service. We cannot be sure whether the font is Norman or Saxon, but the lettering of the Latin text from the Psalms appears to be taken from a version of St Jerome in the 8th century Gospel of St Cuthbert, of which there is a copy in the British Museum. It has the words "Like as the hart that desireth the water brooks, so longeth my heart after Thee, O God," and is written in ancient characters.

Near one of the porches is the Dole Stone, carved with a cross at each end. There are two ancient paintings of Moses and Aaron which may have been part of an altarpiece, a small brass engraved with a skull and crossbones to Hugh Rook who died in 1686, and, in memory of John Spearing, a sculpture of a woman weeping at an urn by the man who made the Nelson Column, E. H. Baily. The elegant oak pulpit is 500 years old, and the organ has been played since 1723; it has beautiful carving round it. The transept roofs are painted and have gold bosses.

There is a fine array of windows in the nave, quaint medallions in the transepts, and two tiny lights high up over the great east and west windows. In these small lights are heads of St Christopher and St Anne; in the medallions are many Bible scenes including serial pictures of the Good Samaritan and the Prodigal Son; and in four great lancets of the nave are splendid scenes in glowing colour of the Annunciation, the home of Joseph the Carpenter, and the Presentation of Our Lord in the Temple.

Poulshot. Its brick-and-timber cottages lie about the green, with elms ringing it round. The church, restored after a fire, has a venerable appearance, for it has rough 13th century arcades, an aisle barely four feet wide, the roodloft stairs still in their place, a 13th century chancel arch with two small heads, and fragments of ancient glass with black and white flowers. There are blocked-up doorways and some Norman carving in the walls. The tower has six very neat faces outside its windows.

Here in this 17th century pulpit preached Izaak Walton's son Isaac. To his vicarage, now vanished, his uncle Bishop Ken came for refuge when William of Orange marched on London. Izaak Walton's son was still rector here when he died, and often the old angler would come here visiting.

Up a lane lined with elms is a rough track leading to an ancient water-mill.

Preshute. A little chalk horse on the hillside above the river here was cut out of the turf by the pupils of Mr Greazeley who had a school for boys in Marlborough; it was cut in the year before Trafalgar and has been kept clean ever since.

Down a little lane a short way from Marlborough College is a 15th century tower with traceried windows, two ancient stone heads, and a narrow sculptured frieze which may be Norman, built into the porch. There are Norman arcades and a huge Norman font cut from a solid block of black marble. It was Camden, in the 16th century, who said that "the people of Marlborough brag of nothing more than of the font in Preshute church," saying that it had come from the castle chapel and had seen the baptism of princes. The font is plain and simple for one with such a high tradition.

There are ten fine small sculptures—corbels of a queen and a bishop, a man with curly hair, a woman with her hair neatly braided, a man with a turned-down collar, and several fine faces of women with hair flowing as in the wind. On a wall sit two cherubs sobbing, with handkerchiefs to their eyes and a skull between them.

On the floor at the top of an aisle are the brasses of John Barley with his wife and their ten children. He is in a full-sleeved gown with fur cuffs, she has a headdress and an embroidered belt. The children are all in severe frocks and the girls have tresses.

Purton. It has a corner of rare charm, shared by a dark pool, a green avenue of clipped box trees, a grey church, gabled vicarage, manor, and a farm. It is one of the few villages with two towers, one crowned with a stone spire and supported by splendid 14th century arches and vaulting in the middle of the church, the other 15th century with a lovely pierced parapet, pinnacles, windows, and vaulted niches, one with an angel. From this fine western tower gargoyles look down.

A hollow yew and the porch have been neighbours for centuries. The porch has a little niche with a modern figure of the crowned Madonna, and on a stone arch supporting its roof are traces of medieval painting. In the room above the porch is a case in which is the latch and handle of the old church door and a 600-year-old key, as well as some ancient coins and an old sword, all found in Purton.

The 13th century chancel has a canopied piscina, simple stone seats for the priests, and altar rails carved by a modern craftsman. By the east window are beautiful modern canopied niches containing a figure of St Nicholas holding a ship in full sail and Aldhelm with a model of his abbey at Malmesbury. Between them is a coloured modern reredos with two angels kneeling above an old painting of the Last Supper, perhaps by a pupil of Rubens.

The nave has an old barrel roof, two lofty 13th century arcades with slender columns and some gracefully carved capitals. The memorial for World War I with its figure of St George, the pulpit with its charming canopy, and the screen in the west tower arch are all modern work. There is a tablet to Nevil Maskelyne, Astronomer Royal, whose home was here. The ancient font, expelled in 1807 and used as a horse trough in a field, is back in its place, with a domed cover of shining copper. Two of the aisle windows have fragments of medieval glass, among them two saints and a trumpeting angel.

But the treasure of the church is the rich-hued old glass and the faded wall painting in the lovely 14th century chapel, panelled with oak, its altar hung with a beautiful frontal embroidered with flowers, birds, and fruit, its reredos adorned with cherubs and an old painting of the Madonna. The fresco is over the door, and though it is fading away we can pick out the daughter of Jairus lying in a red dress, with fading figures waiting for the miracle. The fine glass is a newly made medley of fragments, and it has trees, crowns, roses, canopies, faces, saints and golden wings, and two tiny musical angels.

On one of the piers of the nave is a small stone carving of the Annunciation, half worn away with the centuries but with a graceful figure of the Madonna and the angel still seen.

A little way out of the village is a charming Elizabethan house called Restrop, with gables and dormers and a projecting porch; and hereabouts a Roman camp with two ditches, one of them perfect.

Ramsbury. The church, a magnificent legacy of the 13th century, rests on its Saxon foundations, and a wealth of Saxon stones has been discovered here. The chief of them all stands on a raised platform in the church among coffin stones, old tiles, and fragments of rich carving; it is the shaft of a Saxon cross, covered with lovely linked designs with three medallions of dragons eating their own tails.

Not so old, but interesting, is the carving on the Norman font, faces at the base, about a hundred roses on the bowl, and scenes round the stem in which we noticed Noah in the Ark and a most captivating little face tucked away. The inside is curious for having four fishes carved on the bottom.

The roof of the nave is magnificent, lighted from eight clerestoried windows, and resting on 12 wooden brackets with weird and comical faces and angels looking down, all 15th century. The old pulpit and benches are finely carved. The chancel is without a screen and in it is the tomb of Sir William Jones, Charles Stuart's Attorney General. Here he reclines, with long curly hair, in the fashionable dress of his day, a William Jones of a century later keeping him company with a marble portrait decorated with a skull and crossbones.

The lovely 14th century tomb of William St John has a richly carved canopy, but has been sadly damaged. There is a piscina with a trefoiled arch on little round columns, a tribute to an 18th century vicar for 49 years, and a proud boast on behalf of Elizabeth Batson, whose life was prolonged by cheerfulness and temperance to 92 years, when she departed without a struggle. The tower and clerestory are 15th century.

Littlecote Manor in this parish was the home of Sir John Darell (see Chilton Foliat). The Darell tombs are here but are stripped of their brasses.

The porch is modern but has a fine timbered roof with pierced drop ornaments.

In Ramsbury square still stands a fine old elm, 21 feet round. Everywhere there are delightful gardens, and charming are the quaint thatched inn and the 17th century manor house designed by Sir John Webb. It has splendid gates, with a lion at each side.

A little way off is Axford farm, a delightful homestead with a water mill, fine barns, and a 14th century kitchen wing formerly a chapel. It must have had a noble past, for its windows are lancets, except for one with lovely tracery, and there is a piscina and a priest's doorway.

Rodbourne Cheney. It has stones, one built into the wall of the north aisle, which may be Saxon and is carved with knotwork, and another (in a window in the pinnacled tower) which is certainly the work of a Norman sculptor and is thought to picture the Tree of Life and Knowledge. A cross to a rector outside has been copied from the stone believed to be Saxon. The gargoyles looking down from the tower are emblems of the Four Evangelists, and there are other gargoyles of quaint animals. The church porch is 13th century and the chancel is the same age; there is a small piscina of the 15th century and another double one in the chancel. Most of the rest of the church has been rebuilt, but the 16th century bell is still ringing, there is an old chest, and in fragments of 14th century glass are faces of angels.

Rollestone. A tiny place in the middle of Salisbury Plain, it has the Winterbourne flowing through it. The small church lies hidden

Salisbury Cathedral, from the north-west.

Salisbury Cathedral: the nave.

Salisbury Cathedral: the west front.

Salisbury Cathedral: the choir seen from the south transept.

from the road across the fields, 700 years old, with charming traceried windows and an old plain font with bracketed cover, and fine moulded roof beams. The corbels of the chancel arch are carved heads. One attractive possession is the Ten Commandments, the Creed, and the Lord's Prayer done by some devoted hand in needlework a century or more ago.

Rowde. In the country near Devizes, it has Roundway Down above it with its memories of the Civil War. The nave of the church has charming clustered piers, a clerestory with arcaded beams in the roof resting on eight heads of kings and queens. Also a fine monument to Thomas Spencer (1675), a clothier, and the skull has the clothier's mark cut in it.

Rushall. In that country of the thatcher on the edge of Salisbury Plain, and down a little lane which starts with a great elm 15 feet round, past a tiny island group of thatched roofs and walls, to a church set in a field, with a finely battlemented tower facing us and a medieval west window. The tower has four weird gargoyles.

The nave is 14th century and has many traceried 16th century bench-ends. The charming tower arch is raised on steps with the great Norman font standing under it on a beautiful base; it is said to have been the capital of a pier carved by the Normans. The bowl of the font has 16 small arches round it. Let into the wall is a curious double panel of stone carving.

In a small window in the chancel is some ancient glass. One scene is of the Madonna with the Child in her lap; it is worn by time, but the Crucifixion above it is wonderfully preserved; at the side of the Crucified Christ stand the Madonna in blue, her sorrowful face raised to her Son, and St John turning his head away in grief too great to bear. In the top lights are shields with red stars and a gold lion. In the vestry is a small monument of a woman sitting by a tomb, in memory of an 18th century lord of the manor.

Salisbury. Since the days of Chaucer's pilgrimage to Canterbury pilgrims have been coming here, and Salisbury has not failed them. It cannot fail such pilgrims.

None of our cathedrals stands in a more beautiful Close. It is a tranquil scene unsurpassed in any of our medieval cities, and about it are gathered a group of houses forming a remarkable example of domestic architecture. Built from medieval to Georgian days, these houses are in perfect harmony with the wonderful church that rises in the midst of them. The King's House (in which Richard the Third and James the First both stayed) is 14th century and Tudor, a glorious gabled building facing the west front of the cathedral, and now a teachers' college. Wardrobe House explains by its name what it was in the days when it was linked with the King's House. The gabled house on the north has parts almost as old as the cathedral itself. The bishop's palace is behind a wall and is not seen from the Close, but one may have a glimpse of it through a doorway in the cloisters. The 13th century Deanery, now part of the Training College, is being restored and hidden beauties revealed.

One must go back for the beginning of it to the hill the Ancient Britons used and the Romans made into a fortress, to the fort the Saxons made and left deserted, to the cathedral the Normans set on that same hill where saints and bishops lie, the hilltop of Old Sarum, now waking from the sleep of centuries. Stone Age, Bronze Age, and Iron Age; Roman, Saxon, and Viking; Norman and medieval is this place.

It cannot be missed by anyone who goes from Salisbury to see Stonehenge, whichever road he takes. The Avon Valley road shows it arrestingly as a terraced hilltop, obviously an ancient stronghold dominating the neighbourhood where the river breaks away from the wide plateau of Salisbury Plain. The other road from Salisbury to Stonehenge, across the Plain by Amesbury, rises close to the fortress, so quietly that the nearness of the hilltop may not be guessed, but when it is reached it seems to spring up behind the traveller as the road sinks by it into the Plain. Then it challenges comparison with any earthwork in the British Isles.

Old Sarum has much that Stonehenge has not, for it has a history. It was known as an impressive hill by the Stonehenge men and has played a part in the life of long forgotten centuries. An overgrown ruin for ages, it was investigated in the middle of last century during a dry summer, when the cathedral foundations were so clear that a plan was made of them, and excavations during our own time are unearthing buried secrets and throwing light on the history of this hill for nearly a thousand years.

Nobody doubts that the hill-people who roamed the southern downlands, and are commonly called Ancient Britons, had one of their forts on this hilltop. It is quite clear, too, that this was an important centre of Roman Britain, for here four or five roads converged. Probably it was the station the Romans named Sorbiodunum; certainly after the Romans it was the Searisbyrig of the

Saxons. Alfred fortified it and dug the outer ditch; King Edgar held a Parliament here; the Danes burned it; the Confessor gave it a mint. Then came the Norman Conquest, bringing changes which obliterated the older features of the town. The Conqueror made it a fortress and a bishopric. The summit of the hill was crowned with a castle and a central keep, fortified once more by earthworks with an inner and outer wall. Between the walls the new cathedral was built, and the bishop became the dominant personage in Sarisberie, as it was called in Domesday Book. Roman Sorbiodunum, Saxon Searisbyrig, Norman Sarisberie, and now Old Sarum, it has seen a marvellous procession of the pageantry of life. The town grew in size beyond its walls, and clustered round the base of the hill.

A hundred years more and Old Sarum was in sore straits. The military commanders of the castle were unfriendly; the cathedral was being damaged by the winds; the canons declared that water was scarce; the space was not enough for clerics and soldiers and townsmen. It was one of the clergy who put the case in a nutshell by asking:

What has the House of the Lord to do with castles? It is the Ark of the Covenant in a temple of Baalim. Let us in the name of God descend into the meads.

They were given leave and came down to the meads. The inhabitants of Old Sarum followed them, and the fortress on the hill became so deserted that it had not a single house, and soon the very sites of the castle and the old cathedral were forgotten. Old Sarum sent two members to Parliament till 1832, but there were no inhabitants, and the ten electors met for the election in a field still known as Election Field.

The day of its desolation is over. The Society of Antiquaries has excavated the summit of the hill and discovered the foundations of the buildings which lost their uses and began their fall into destruction 700 years ago. The ground plan of the Norman cathedral on the hillside has been marked out, and from the summit of the hill one can see where and imagine how the 12th century clergy and soldiers and townsmen lived. It is now in charge of the Department of the Environment.

Out of Old Sarum came the Salisbury to which all travellers come in time. Here are the very stones of Sarum, in the long wall and gateways of the new Cathedral Close. Every day the wind blows in Salisbury on Norman carvings in her streets, on stones consecrated to faith and prayer 800 years ago. On Easter Monday in 1219 they put up a wooden church, and in 1220 they laid the foundation stones of the new cathedral. The bishop laid one for the pope, one for Stephen Langton, and another for himself; and William Longespee laid one for himself and one for his wife the Countess Ela, who founded the abbey of Lacock.

Before the cathedral was half ready they buried Richard Poore at Tarrant Crawford 15 miles away, and in 38 years from the laying of the foundation-stones the cathedral was complete without the spire. Here are the stones the bishop touched when he consecrated it, 19 of them still left of 24, with patterns of flowers and stars cut in circles on them. Before the century was out they added the spire, raising it from the tower as a veritable triumph of design, so that it seems to grow out of the great mass as a flower grows out of its foliage.

From west to east the total length is 473 feet, from north to south 230, and it covers an area of 55,000 square feet. It rises tier above tier with porch, pediment, and pinnacles, its traceried tower springing from the centre and the spire soaring over all, 404 feet high.

In the capstone of this marvellous spire is a tiny lead box a child could hold on its hand, with a fragment of woven fabric in it put there in 1375, when people believed it to be a relic of the Virgin and that it would guard the spire from lightning and all harm. In the spire (of which the walls are two feet thick at the bottom and nine inches at the top), is the scaffolding on which the workmen stood to build it, still left inside to give it strength; but in spite of this it has listed a little, and a hundred years later they added one or two flying buttresses and noble stone screens which have saved it from listing more. It was Elias of Dereham, the Norfolk man who built this place, and Richard Farley, the Wiltshire man who crowned it with the lovely spire.

There has been much anxiety about the safety of the spire in our time. It has cracked and moved in a gale, and there has been too much reason to recall the fact that when Sir Christopher Wren surveyed the spire he found that it was leaning 23 inches out of straight. For the guidance of architects who should follow him he set a piece of metal in the floor below to show the extent of the leaning, and it was not until a few years ago, that the movement increased. Wren declared that the cathedral should not have been erected on the spongy bog on which it stands, and that the slender seven-foot-wide high piers could never have been intended to support the tons of masonry in the tower and spire. It has been the aim of the restorers to stabilise the spire and tower and redistribute the weight of 6000 tons which falls on the base. There has always been a weak spot at the top of the tower just above the ridge of the roof, where the weight is 4500 tons. The tower has four sides, and when the octagonal spire was set on it the tower was altered so as to give the spire an octagonal base. Brick corbels have been built at the base of the spire into the four corners at the top of the tower, and these will take the weight off the centre of the walls and transfer it to the corners. At each corner at the top of the tower is a spiral staircase, and all these have been filled in and made solid. Eight windows of the tower are filled in with brick, and the work is strengthened by a band of steel invisible from the outside. The effect of all this strengthening is to remove the dangerous outward thrust which has endangered the spire so long.

The west front is famous, but it is not so good as the rest of the cathedral. It has still its characteristic features of the 14th century, with the familiar ballflower ornament, but the tiers of bays and niches have lost nearly all their 120 ancient statues, and all but a few of those now there are 19th century. They are arranged in lines across the front as at Wells, on the plan known as that of the Te Deum, with Christ above, archangels, prophets, martyrs, and the church below, and local saints and notables at the bottom.

The interior height is 115 feet from floor to roof. It has been said that no building anywhere is more logical, more lucid in expression, more restful to the mind and eye. It was built with 12 doors into it, 365 windows giving light, and 8760 columns holding it up—that is to say, a door for every month in the year, a window for every day, and a column for every hour. It was Thomas Fuller who met a rustic centuries ago wondering at it all, saying he had never believed that there could be a church with as many columns as there are hours in the year, but now he could never believe there are as many hours in the year as there are columns here.

The clustered columns of the nave, surrounded with slender shafts, support ten great arches, which support the triforium, which supports the clerestory. The arches are pointed and graceful, with masses of carved foliage where they join. Stone benches run round the base of the pillars all the way along and on them rest impressive tombs, taken from all parts of the cathedral and from chantries that have vanished. Those on the right of the nave begin with a conventional figure of Hibernia by Rysbrack, the fashionable sculptor of the 18th century, but they end with the magnificently mailed figure of William Longespee, in armour as he stood at the sealing of Magna Carta; he may have handled the very copy of it kept upstairs; his name is mentioned in it. He lies here with six prancing lions on his shield, a stirring figure in stone resting on a base surrounded by an oak arcade. These arches carved in wood have been here about 700 years, and the diaper work has still its silver sheen on some of them. It is the finest tomb of its kind in England.

This king's son (for he was the son of Henry the Second) became Earl of Salisbury on marrying the Countess Ela in 1198, and he lies here with their son the second earl. The father sailed out and destroyed a French armada prepared for invading England, and he was one of John's supporters at Runnymede. The son witnessed the confirmation of Magna Carta as his father had witnessed its signing.

William Longespee was the first man buried here, but behind him in the south aisle lie the monuments of bishops from Old Sarum, older than he. The great coffin lid near the door is the cathedral's oldest monument, and next to it are coffin lids with two Old Sarum bishops deeply engraved by the Normans. Lying in a fine suit of armour of the time of Agincourt, richly decorated with a girdle which has lost its jewels, is Robert Lord Hungerford, his dog still with him wearing its rich collar; the dog has lost its tail, but it is lying close by.

The shrine of St Osmund a little behind William Longespee has three oval openings on each side and no figure on it; the six openings are where cripples used to rest their limbs to be cured the quicker by being a little nearer the relics of the saint. On the wall facing this shrine is the black figure of Eleanor Sadler, who was buried in 1622 under the pew she sat in daily for almost half a century. She is kneeling at prayer, and on a shield above her clasped hands is one of the rare bits of heraldry seen only in two or three places now; it shows a tiger looking at his face in a mirror and the idea is that, the tiger imagining the reflection to be its cub, the hunters were enabled by the delay to carry off the cub to safety.

The north side of the nave has a giant lying facing William Longespee—a giant indeed, for his remains have been seen and his thigh measured 21 inches. He was Sir John Cheney, who saw the famous fight on Bosworth Field which ends in Shakespeare with the line, The day is done; the dog is dead. It was the end of the Plantagenets and the beginning of the Tudors, and Sir John Cheney had borne the victorious standard of Richmond. Here he lies richly apparelled, with a little angel still left at his head looking mournful. Lower down the aisle is William Longespee's son in chain armour, with legs crossed and hands on his sword. Behind him is an extraordinary little figure described (wrongly, we believe) as a boy bishop of the 13th century; he has iron rails above him. Such bishops were elected by choir boys and wore vestments and performed service as real bishops once a year; the custom is still practised here in modified form on St Nicholas day.

Higher up the aisle lies an old warrior in mail and chain armour, his head on a helmet, a fine lion at his feet, and a belt with the handle of his sword hanging to it. His tomb has lovely arcading, his armour is wrapped about him, and we can only just see the face of Sir John de Montacute, whom they laid here in 1390.

Following the wall round to the north transept we come upon some famous names. There is a brass set up by British architects to John Britton, who was historian of this cathedral. There is a figure by Sir Francis Chantrey of the first Earl of Malmesbury, who is shown sitting, and close by is a figure of Benevolence by Flaxman, who shows her lifting a veil from a relief of the Good Samaritan. On a bust of Richard Jefferies we read that he enriched the literature of his country and won for himself a place among those who have made men happier and wiser.

A graceful figure of John Bacon suggests Moral Philosophy mourning over a medallion of James Harris, and there are two Flaxman wall sculptures in a transept chapel in memory of two brothers; Justice and Literature mourning one and Science and Benevolence the other. At the end wall of the transept lies a 15th century Bishop Blythe, and near the bishop's canopied tomb sits Sir Richard Colt Hoare in white marble. He was a Wiltshire historian, and this statue by a native of Salisbury shows him writing with a quill. Near it is the rare old clock without a dial which dates from 1386 and is thought to be the oldest in England.

Set round the choir are graves and monuments of varying value and interest, including a fine effigy of Bishop Wordsworth, the poet's nephew. It is by Sir George Frampton, and shows the bishop sleeping calmly with his hands clasped and his crozier tucked under his arm, a white figure on a black base at the side of the lady chapel. Near it is the tomb of a maid-of-honour to Queen Elizabeth the First: she is with her husband Sir Thomas Gorges, under a canopy resting on twisted pillars. In the north choir aisle are two of the skeleton figures which mark the curious fancy of the 16th century, and in a chapel close by is the brass of Bishop Edmund Guest, with a walking stick, who assisted Archbishop Parker in the drafting of the XXXIX Articles of Religion in the Prayer Book. He was Almoner to Elizabeth the First and "he must both be a wise and a good man", says Fuller, "whom she would trust with her purse."

Next to Bishop Guest's brass is a most unusual one to the 14th century Bishop Wyville looking out of Sherborne Castle. Wyville was involved in a lawsuit concerning the possession of the Forest of Bere in Dorset and appealed to trial by battle. But as it was not proper for Bishops to take up arms he appeared by champion and the champion is shown on the brass standing at the door of the castle ready for the ordeal of battle.

At the end of the south choir aisle lie a son of Protector Somerset and a sister of Lady Jane Grey, both at prayer, with one of their sons at their head and another at their feet. A modern sculpture designed by Sir Arthur Blomfield shows Bishop Moberly in four scenes, teaching, preaching, blessing children, and opening the first Diocesan Conference which he started. The bishop's wife is remembered in the south choir transept in a splendid wall relief of the Angel of Dawn with a trumpet, and by this white monument is a beautifully cut stone in memory of a friend of hers, the wife of Archdeacon Carpenter, who lived all her married life in the Close and was buried here on her fiftieth wedding day.

A little way removed from these rare simplicities is a classical monument, with gold leaves twined round stone pillars, to Sir Richard Mompesson, who reclines a little higher than his wife, suggesting his higher rank. Round the choir are three beautiful chantries, the best of them, exquisitely lovely, that of Bishop Audley, with original blue paint in the fan-tracery of the 15th century roof. Facing it is the chantry of Walter Lord Hungerford, with its rich heraldry, and a little way off lies Bishop Giles of Bridport in a 13th century tomb with a chantry built in the style of the cloisters and the chapter house. It has scenes from his life in the spandrels and lilies running round the canopy.

The choir has stalls which incorporate a little medieval work, notably the carved misericord seats, but most of the work is Victorian and later. The removal of the incongruous metal screen and the reredos has greatly improved the general effect of the choir. The bishop's throne is a lofty timber structure with two lions at the armrests, saints crowning the pillars, and medallion portraits round. The organ is one of the masterpieces of Henry Willis, and its case was designed by G. E. Street. The vaulted stone roof is painted with roundels showing 24 prophets and saints, with Christ and the Evangelists, and panels representing the twelve months—January warming at a fire, July reaping, November cutting wood; they are modern reproductions of the 13th century paintings which faded away.

The choir is the last resting-place of the Countess of Pembroke, Philip Sidney's sister. When they brought her from her great house at Wilton and laid her here it was William Browne of Tavistock who wrote the memorable lines:

Underneath this sable hearse
Lies the subject of all verse:
Sidney's sister, Pembroke's mother.
Death, ere thou hast slain another
Fair and learned and good as she,
Time shall throw a dart at thee.

She lies under a tiny square brass before the altar.

Salisbury, famous for her matchless exterior and her superb natural setting, misses some of the glory that we find in other cathedrals, and it has little beautiful glass. But it has much glass that is interesting and some of it with a romantic story, and a few windows of our own time which are fit company for anything here. One of the best of them is the Powell window in the north choir transept showing the Heavenly Jerusalem. It is magnificent in red and gold, with over a hundred figures, many of them wrapped in wonder at this solemn scene, while little children, not knowing, are pulling flowers on the banks of a stream. In the south choir aisle are two windows designed by Henry Holiday, both fine, one with the four Marys and four other holy women in white and pale gold. Close by these is a Burne-Jones window with four angels high up in red, blue, green, and gold. It is considered one of his masterpieces; the chalk cartoons for it were sold for 50 guineas.

In the north aisle is a window to the fifth Earl Radnor, painted by his countess; it has saints and bishops against a background of vivid red wings. High above the high altar in the choir is an unusual painted window remarkably rich in colour showing Moses lifting up the serpent in the wilderness; it is 18th century and is given an unusual effect by being apparently unbroken into sections.

In Saint Michael's Chapel, which has become the war memorial, and has a richly gilded reredos and a bronze relief of Bishop Ridgeway, are four modern windows ablaze with colour. In them are our four national saints, and in the next chapel to them a fine portrait of Alfred looks down among other national figures.

Most of Salisbury's old glass was destroyed in the 18th century, but a window in the nave has a collection of fragments recovered by Dr Stanley Baker, who lived in a 13th century house in the Close. The best remaining glass is in the great west window, where are fragments from a 13th century Tree of Jesse and a throned bishop set between ovals of Christ and the Madonna. As we stand looking at this great west window we may turn to the south aisle of the nave and see what is perhaps a more important window still, for it has in it some of the best 13th century glass, forming a Jesse Tree. Its colours are rich, though we can no longer see the vine springing from Jesse and covering the window, with the kings of Judah in its branches and Christ at the top.

The east windows of both choir aisles are old, the great south transept window is all old, and there is ancient glass in patches round the choir, most of it black and white made up in mosaic form.

We have yet to come to what most people believe to be the most remarkable interior in Salisbury, the Chapter House, reached from the cloisters.

The arch of the chapter house doorway has 14 small niches with sculptures showing the battle of the Virtues against the Vices, a noble entrance into a noble hall. On the floor are tiles copied from the old medieval pavement; on the roof the paintings have been done again after the originals. The central pillar from which this vaulted roof springs is 52 feet high, and the hall is 52 feet wide. The pillar has carving probably copied from books of fables in the Middle Ages. The roof bosses are elaborately carved with figures of armourers, musicians, apothecaries, and grotesques.

But it is the walls all round, the 49 niches of the canopied arcading, which attract every eye that looks on here. In the spandrels of this arcade, looking so fresh that it is difficult to believe it has been here about 600 years, is one of the most remarkable sculpture galleries in England, 60 scenes with about 200 figures, as well as about 60 carved heads on the slender columns of the arches. There are melancholy heads and merry ones, tender ones and pensive ones, heads whimsical and scowling, and three heads in one with three noses, three mouths, three beards, and four eyes. It is an odd collection.

But the captivating spectacle of the chapter house is in the 60 tiny sculptured groups which tell the Bible story from Creation to the Commandments. It is all marvellously wrought by the medieval artist, and now and then we smile at his wit, now and then we wonder at his exquisite skill, while all the time we are drawn to his work as one of the masterly legacies of the 13th century. There is the Creation of Adam and Eve and the animal kingdom, the Tree of Good and Evil and the expulsion from Eden; the story of Cain and Abel, the building of the Ark, the setting up of the Tower of Babel and the destruction of Sodom (in which one of its citizens is buried alive). There is the meeting of Jacob and Rachel, and the long and wonderfully pictured story of Joseph and his brethren, ending with Jacob's journey to Egypt and leading on to the days of Moses with the passage of the Red Sea, the destruction of the Egyptians, and the Tables of Stone.

In the cathedral library is one of the original copies of Magna Carta. It may or may not have been made for William Longsword, but he is mentioned in it, and here he lies with it under the same roof, the man who saw it sealed and the copy of it neatly written on a single sheet of about 1000 words. It is one of only four copies known, one other being at Lincoln and two in London. It lies with many priceless documents.

One of the books was bound for Henry the Eighth by his own binder, and it was the king's own copy of that book against Luther for which the Pope gave him the title of Defender of the Faith which is still on our coins. Another was a 9th century copy of the Psalms. Another was printed by Wynkyn de Worde from Caxton's own type. Another has Isaak Walton's handwriting in it with a couplet something like this:

To this blest man let this just praise be given:
Heaven was in him before he was in heaven.

Another volume has on its fly leaves a long list of all the dances of the day, written when they were no doubt short of paper. One of the charters here gives the cathedral a right to use the stones of Old Sarum for the building of the wall running round the Close in 1331. Altogether there are here over 8000 books, about twenty 15th century ones and about a hundred of the 16th century.

It is the fate of much of the beauty of cathedral cities to be neglected, for in the shadow of the great the small is easily lost. In Salisbury is much it would be a pity to lose, and especially it has three churches about as old as the cathedral; they are St Martin's,

St Thomas's, and St Edmund's. St Edmund's has lost its six chapels but is still big enough to hold six; it has a St Christopher tapestry and a charming modern stone pulpit with open arches. The other two churches are treasure-houses which all should see.

The treasure of St Martin's belongs to our own time, four new windows set in four ancient walls. They are original and charming, with delicate colouring and a gallery of most attractive scenes peopled with figures of great beauty, the work of Mr Christopher Webb. In the ride into Egypt Mary, in a blue robe, is sitting on the donkey with the Child, and Joseph is turning round looking proudly at them. In a scene in the Temple the faces of the Elders are captivating; all these faces, indeed, are exquisitely drawn, and the serenity of the groups is unusual. In the Nativity scene Mary is kneeling by the side of the Child lying on a bed of straw, a little lamb looking up at Him; the shepherds are looking on, the donkey and the ox are peeping through, and Joseph is holding a lantern so that they can see. In another scene the Madonna is shown as a country maiden receiving the good news. One of the curious things at St Martin's is a corbel of a nun's head with spectacles, a very rare thing in sculpture; the corbel is supposed to be 15th century.

The church of St Thomas is a spacious and stately place worthy of any town. It has magnificent 15th century arcades and one of the most notable Doom paintings in England, covering the great wall space above the impressive chancel arch. The picture is quite recognisable after 500 years, having been uncovered and preserved at the end of last century. Its mass of figures are clear (notably the Dishonest Alewife and the miser, she being the only one clothed), and are all being consigned to the lower regions by the Lord of All, with a row of angels below. The picture is one of the important legacies of medieval art, and below are two ancient portraits of St Osmund and a pilgrim. There are more wall paintings in the beautiful chapel on the right of the chancel showing the Annunciation, the Salutation, and the Adoration. The chapel has a lovely roof decorated with heraldic emblems, merchants marks, and prayers for the founders. Above the altar are two alabaster tombs raised high on the wall, with two kneeling figures on each. The magnificent nave, with its clerestory windows and its beautifully carved roof, is 15th century; the clerestory runs over the chancel. There is a brass of John Webbe with his wife and six children, all born before the Spanish Armada; and kept in the vestry is a piece of embroidered altar cloth and a fragment of a funeral pall about 500 years old.

A chest which may be older still is bound with about 50 yards of iron bands. The clock in the tower has been telling the time for more than 300 years, and has two fine helmeted figures in mail striking the bell. In the porch is a queer piece of woodcarving done by Humphrey Beckham, one of the old carvers of the city whose work is in many of its houses.

Some of the old houses of Salisbury are going the way of many of our beautiful places, and the fine Hall of John Halle, for ages one of Salisbury's show places, has become the entrance to a cinema, though it is splendidly kept and its 15th century work can still be seen. The house of John A'Port (in Queen Street), was built in 1425 by a merchant who was six times mayor. It has a glorious front with curved and upright timbers in its two gabled wings, the top storey overhanging. There are over 500 diamond panes of glass in its windows, and indoors are magnificent stone fireplaces, one representing the Sacrifice of Isaac, and a carved oak mantelpiece. The Hall of the Shoemakers Guild, built in 1638, owes its existence to the good heart of a schoolmaster, Philip Crewe, who lived next door and left his house and garden to the Shoemakers hoping they would extend it to make themselves a hall. The cottage next door he left to his servant. The Shoemakers built the hall, and have hung a copy of Philip Crewe's will on the wall. The Joiners Hall is one of the neatest timbered fronts in the city, with six square windows divided into squares, two on the street level under the overhang's great beam, two smaller ones in the two gables, and two great windows centred in the house; these are divided into 15 compartments each, and each projects on three carved oak brackets by Humphrey Beckham. The Old Bank in Queen Street has a fine restored front with two gables, and in its chief window are seven triple panels in which the old trade guilds of the city are represented: the Goldsmith, the Joiner, the Weaver, the Cutler, the Clothworker, the Tailor, and the Cordwainer, all shown at their work. The building is now the office of an insurance company. The Tailors Hall has also stained glass windows. The George Inn is one of the delightful spectacles of the High Street, its immense beams and its projecting windows looking today as they have looked for ages; inside it is a sight for all to see, and parts of it must be as old as the cathedral. The finely timbered Pheasant Inn, joining the Hall of the Shoemakers, is one of the oldest timbered houses in the city.

Salisbury has a Guildhall and a Council House, the Guildhall standing in the marketplace, the Council House on Bourne Hill off the London Road. The Council House joins St Edmund's Church, and was formerly the College of St Edmund, a 13th century foundation for the maintenance of a priest and six canons which came into the possession of the crown in Tudor days, and was made into a private house at the time of the Restoration. In the grounds is the only remaining fragment of the City Rampart, a great ditch made for defence about 700 years ago; there is a memorial urn set up in 1771 to mark the discovery of 30 bodies slain in battle here. It is thought it may have been a battle between Britons and West Saxons, and weapons were found with the bodies. The Corporation took over the house as civic headquarters to mark the 700th anniversary of the granting of the charter in 1227, and the ten acres round it are delightful to walk in, with stretches of lawn, shaded paths, and relics here and there.

The Guildhall in the marketplace was built in the last years of the 18th century and is characteristic of the time, a long low building with a heavy portico resting on six stone columns. It was designed by Sir Robert Taylor, the stonemason's son, whose father's death left him penniless but who was so successful as an architect that he was able to leave a fortune to Oxford to encourage the teaching of languages. In the banqueting hall hangs Hoppner's portrait of the second Earl of Radnor who gave the Guildhall to the city; with it are many other portraits of notabilities. In front of the Guildhall stands the city's war memorial, a stone screen in the shape of a crescent with the names in panels, surmounted by a lion in bronze. By it stands one of the two bronze statues in the marketplace, Lord Herbert of Lea, the devoted friend and champion of Florence Nightingale, by Baron Marochetti. The other bronze statue in the marketplace is of a man beloved by the nation in his time, born in a house in Queen Street close by where he stands, Henry Fawcett the blind Postmaster-General.

It was in this marketplace that the second Duke of Buckingham was beheaded one Sunday in 1483. It was the end of a career in which he had been the chief supporter of Richard the Third on his march through murder to the throne. He had been the most magnificent of all the figures about the king at his coronation, but in a few months Richard declared him a traitor, Buckingham was a fugitive, and was found hiding in a hut in Shrewsbury, to which somebody noticed that an unusual quantity of food was being taken.

One may walk for hours about Salisbury and never be tired, so varied its appeal to the eye and the mind. The entrance to the

Cathedral Close is by three gates: the High Street Gate with the first statue of Edward the Seventh on the cathedral side and the 17th century college for widows on our left; St Ann's Gate with the ancient chapel over it and the house near by in which Fielding wrote much of *Tom Jones*; and Harnham Gate, which links the Close with Harnham, which has perhaps the oldest building in the city, the lovely little Hospital of St Nicholas standing by the 13th century bridge. The old bridge and the new stand side by side, the new taking the traffic, the old one scheduled as a national monument. It was built in 1245 and still stands on its island. The north side of it is 88 feet long with two arches, the south side is 134 feet long with six. The bridge was widened in 1774.

The Bishops Palace, now a school, has a great hall of the 15th century with Jacobean woodcarving, and portraits of all the bishops since the Reformation. The Poultry Cross is reminiscent of the cross at Chichester, of which it is a copy, the top being modern. The lower part was built in the 14th century, probably as an act of penance, and it has six arches with pinnacled buttresses and a canopied niche over each arch, the roof supported by a central pillar with angels round it, and above the roof an openwork parapet circling round over the arches, with modern flying buttresses meeting at the pillar, which is crowned with a tabernacle and a cross.

It was from the meadows over a long white wooden bridge to old Harnham Mill that Constable painted his famous picture. The mill has been here 700 years and must have been known to the cathedral builders.

Salisbury has one of the finest museums in the kingdom, finely housed not far from St Ann's Gate to the cathedral. It has been built up for the city by the devotion of a father and son, and is still maintained by the son, Mr Frank Stevens, whose knowledge of Salisbury is probably unrivalled. Few museums are more attractively arranged. Standing at the door there is one of the finest views of the cathedral spire.

One of the most attractive groups in the museum is the series of water colour sketches in the Kemm collection of Wiltshire churches; they are admirably arranged, with a map showing the position of the churches and houses shown on the screen. It is a plan that all county museums might well adopt for creating interest in the countryside. For examples of everyday things used in Salisbury for six centuries there is no better place to come to. There are cases filled with things recovered from the open drains which ran through the streets in olden days—keys, knives, seals, daggers, bells, forks, spoons, buckles, and what not. Here is the watchman's horn dated 1675, and a leather jug marked with the cypher of Charles Stuart, and dated 1646. There are clay pipes and wig curlers, both of which were made in Salisbury long ago, and hanging on the walls are man-traps, spring guns, chimney cranes, and kettle tilters. There is the pillory from the marketplace, the bell from the old Guildhall, an old fireplace, a pump, and a pikeman's suit of armour worn in the Civil War.

There is a model of Old Sarum, with cases all round the model filled with things found on the spot; rings, pottery, coins, chessmen, and relics of the Roman occupation. There is a similar Stonehenge room with models and maps and photographs. This prehistoric heart of England is nowhere set up with greater care and clearness. There are models showing sections of the burial mounds, charts of tools and implements in chronological order, an Iron Age village, and things found in ancient camps, such as the skeleton of a dog which is perhaps the oldest known in England.

For those whose interest is in civilised things and not in stones there are rich pieces of colour and delight in this great place. There are few quainter figures in Wiltshire than the medieval St Christopher here, apparently a sort of cousin to Gog and Magog at the London Guildhall. He is a Processional Giant, the only remaining example of the "Going of the Giants at Midsummer" in this country, and he dates from 1496, having been rescued from the Guild of Merchant Taylors in 1872 when the guild was on the point of death. The founder of this museum gave 30 shillings for this distinguished representative of medieval Wiltshire, and still the Giant appears in the streets of Salisbury on days of great rejoicing, Jubilees, Coronations, and the like, riding immediately behind the Mayor at the head of the procession.

Here with St Christopher in this museum is pageantry arranged like West End shop windows, but far more entertaining and a thousand times more educational. We look into Wiltshire cottages and Wiltshire drawing-rooms of long ago; we see a bridal party in all its glory, soldiers and sailors in their ancient uniforms showing the changes for a hundred years. There is a beautiful round room which was once a dining-room in a Salisbury house, with a rich domed ceiling, French windows, and mahogany door three inches thick. The room is built into the museum, an appropriate setting for its fine collection of pottery and porcelain—porcelain figures of

Salisbury Cathedral: the cloisters.

Salisbury Cathedral: the monument to William Longespee.

Salisbury Cathedral Chapter House: the roof.

Salisbury Cathedral Chapter House: "Noah's Ark," one of the carvings on the w

Salisbury: a corner of the Close.

Salisbury: the Matron's College, in the Close.

St Thomas's Church, Salisbury, with the Doom painting over the chancel arch.

the Five Senses made at Bow, and typical Derby and Chelsea work among which we noticed a figure of John Wilkes. There are miscellaneous exhibits in thousands, and groups of objects representing the old trades and guilds, especially a long series of shoes and shoe buckles, and another of trade tokens and Maundy money. There is a dressing-case which belonged to Prince Rupert, a doll which belonged to a French princess, and a pair of gloves embroidered in silver and spangles.

Savernake. It is on the Bath road. One of the natural glories of England, the only ancient forest left in the possession of any subject of the king, it covers 4000 acres, is 16 miles round, and has a Grand Avenue four miles long (with eight roads meeting in it) where we are free to walk or ride through as fine a collection of elms and beeches as any man may want to see.

It belongs to the Marquis of Ailesbury, who lives at the 18th century Tottenham House which looks down an avenue of elms and beeches to the Ailesbury Column, an obelisk crowning a noble height; it was erected to mark George the Third's recovery from insanity. The house takes the place of the old home of the Seymours and the Esturmys; the Seymours lived here when Marlborough Castle was given to them and Savernake fell into disuse. Lord Ailesbury has still in his keeping the old hunting horn blown in those early days when kings came hunting here; it is at least 600 years old. Near Tottenham House is a small church set up in 1861 by the marchioness of that time; it has a window with two angels in the porch, and a stately figure of St Catherine chased in the wall. There is another little church built in the middle of last century on the edge of the forest, at Cadley.

Seend. It has a long street with green verges, and by a little humpbacked bridge at the bottom of a lane is a low timbered house with a gabled wing. It was the manor house of Humphrey de Bohun, who fortified it in the 14th century, and it belonged to Lord Berners, who translated Froissart and was at the Field of the Cloth of Gold. Encouraged to come to England by Henry the Seventh, a company of Flemish clothiers settled in Seend and stayed long enough to leave their mark in the shape of a beautiful aisle added to the church they found here.

The church stands on the brow of a hill and we see it from afar, nobly set in the trees, for it looks across a glorious wooded valley to the distant Downs. It has a fine pinnacled tower, beautiful clerestory windows and the aisle the Flemish John Stokys built in the 15th century with fine gargoyles running along it outside, among them lions, dragons, an ape with a baby on its back, a fierce creature with a baby in its claws, a wild animal eating another, and two men blowing bagpipes. In the shallow moulding round the west window, inside and out, is the clothier's mark of John Stokys, a pair of shears, and the inside moulding has a tiny sculpture of the Madonna. There is a room over the porch reached by a flight of outside steps. On the wall are the brass portraits of John Stokys and his wife Alys, he in a fur-trimmed gown, she with a headdress and a belt with an ornament hanging from it.

The nave has graceful pillars and an ancient roof with carved bosses and tracery above the beams; the beams rest on stately stone corbels sculptured with bishops and angels, women wearing wimples, and grotesques. By the chancel arch are remnants of a wall painting and the remains of what seems to have been a Madonna, with traces of colour still left. Over the south door is a charming window of the bringing of the Child to the Temple. There is a splendid candelabra.

Among the wall monuments is one of the 18th century to George Husey with a delightful little woman gracefully leaning over an urn, and there is a mourning damsel for William Locke, who died in the last months of the 18th century.

Semington. It is in a charming corner of the fine high country round Melksham, with a simple little church built seven centuries ago, now standing among black and white cottages. At the church door, in the archway, is a stone with a Norman–French inscription which has not faded away in 800 years. In the churchyard are numerous handsome 18th century table tombs.

Semley. It is a little surprising here to come upon a noble horse in bronze, a small statue in the churchyard of a young soldier on horseback. It is a mother's tribute to her son, Lieutenant Armstrong, who gave his life for his country in 1915. The horse is raised on a fine block of marble and stands at rest with his master on his back wearing a sun helmet and carrying a sword; it is the work of Henry Pegram RA, one of the two Pegram artist brothers, Henry being famous for much fine sculpture and especially for his Cecil Rhodes's statue at Capetown. He did also the statue at Shanghai of Sir Robert Hart, the Englishman who built up the Chinese

Customs, the statue of Sir Thomas Browne at Norwich, and the monument to Nurse Cavell standing by the cathedral there.

Semley was given a thousand years ago to the Abbess of Wilton. The church is modern but has the plain bowl of a Norman font and a battered stone figure of a priest lying on the floor under a canopy, his robes hanging in graceful folds.

Shalbourne. Near the Berkshire border in a valley surrounded by trees and hills, filled with delightful hamlets of thatched roofs.

Much of its Norman church has been rebuilt, but the embattled tower with its pyramid cap and its gargoyles is old; the Norman doorway sheltered by the timbered porch has still its handsome chevron arch, slender pillars, and carved capitals, and in the north wall is a very early Norman doorway. The font, probably 600 years old, has a 17th century wood cover still showing traces of colour. The pulpit has old linenfold and the lectern has flowers and wheat, with four tiny birds, two in flight and two picking up food.

Fragments of Tudor glass still grace one window, and among the pieces are golden Tudor roses.

There are fine painted roofs, with cornices of roses and suns between ropework; and in the chancel are 66 charming painted panels of roses and gold stars. Above the dignified oak chancel screen rise great spandrels of open panel work with gold tracery enclosing the handsome roof beyond the nave. In the chancel are stone monuments to Sir Francis Choke, who died in 1562, and Elizabeth Mayott, who died in 1722. The tomb of Sir Francis has a fine pillared canopy crowned by his arms upheld by winged figures. He lies here a handsome old man with flowing beard, his head on his helmet and his feet on a lion, wearing rich armour and resting one hand on his breast and the other on a book. Elizabeth Mayott stands under an arch wrapped in a classic garment, her coat-of-arms above her and a winged skull and cherub below.

Shaw. The church is modern, 20th century. All the buttresses of its tower go up to its top and each one has a life-size statue on it: David, Daniel, Isaiah, and Zephaniah. Over the west window is the Good Shepherd, and by the doorway the Annunciation. The nave has great oak pillars up to the open oak roof, and the clerestory windows have oak mullions. A very high oak reredos is richly carved with Christ and two angels under a canopy, with the archangel Michael over all and the Twelve Apostles below.

There is a fine brass candelabra brought here from an older Wiltshire church. The chancel has an elaborately canopied sedilia, and four good windows in the nave have fine figures of Alfred and the Saxon bishop Aldhelm, with St Osmund and St Osburgha. The great west window is a war memorial, and has the four patron saints at the bottom and the four archangels above.

Sherrington. Its narrow roads wind about its watercress beds, and it has a small mound near the Wylye River covered by bushes and surrounded by a dry moat. Here was a castle in the days of the Plantagenets, the home of the Giffards of Boyton, one of whom was a crusader with William Longsword. The church has an old scratch-dial, a plain chancel arch 500 years old, a 15th century font, some curious 17th century wall-paintings, old pews, and a panelled pulpit. Two reading desks are made of panels from the old pulpit, and the fine old altar-rails are carved with a chain design, enclosing a pair of old chairs.

Sherston. Associated with the legend of John Rattlebone whose stone effigy, 3 feet high, is round the corner of the south doorway of the church, and the 13th century chest in the church is called "Rattlebone's Chest" for the initials R.B. on it, and it is said that it once contained the armour worn by him when, according to tradition, he won a great victory with Edmund Ironside over the Danes in this place in 1016. As the saying goes:

Fight well, Rattlebone
Thou shalt have Sherston.

The old Tudor rectory has a wall with heraldic stones, on which are such things as three owls, a buck and a bear climbing a tree together, and a tree growing out of a barrel. In the rector's garden is the base of the old village cross.

Near the church are traces of earthworks and the church itself has a Norman central tower, handsome with its elegant pierced parapet and pinnacles and its splendid corbel table. The old porch, with a room over it, has also a lovely parapet, a sundial, a canopied stoup, and a stone roof with ribs springing from angels to meet in faces and roses. The nave arcades are Norman with zigzag carving, and the impressive arches of the central tower are by our first English builders. They have a fine set of ancient sculptures, in which we recognise Simon de Montfort, the founder of our Parliament, handsome and crowned with flowers; Henry the Third and his Queen; Ela of Salisbury wearing a wimple; Richard Earl of Cornwall bearded and in a cap; and some moderns. The nave arcade has zigzag moulding round the arches, and a curious head looking out to the door from one of them, shaped like an old-fashioned kite with its pointed beard. The font is that at which the Norman builders may have baptised their little ones. There are ancient wall paintings of the Madonna and St Thomas, now hidden by the organ. The pulpit is Jacobean, simply carved.

A gay old lady dressed in black kneels on the transept wall under a canopy, her monument bright with gilded flowers, ribbons, and ears of corn; she is Joyce Hitchings, who died about the time of Queen Anne. There is a robed figure of a priest at prayer, his feet resting on small beasts, one with its paw on the hem of his garment. He lies under a window with detached and projecting black columns, its arches neatly carved with tiny heads; it is one of the charming effects of this church that some of its windows are set back with dainty heads and corbels. One window has a dazzling Resurrection scene.

The new oak reredos is striking with fine tracery in red and gold, and carvings of the Crucifixion in which a group of fine figures stand about four winged angels holding candles at the corners. By the altar is a painted monument of the 17th century.

The old roodloft doorway and stairs still remain, and there is a short passage leading from the north transept into the chancel.

Shrewton. At the corner of the bridge spanning the river which runs through the village is the Blind House, a round stone building with a domed stone roof and an iron-sheeted wooden door. It has stood for over 300 years in the heart of the village, having been built as a prison house. Shaped like a beehive, it stands 16 feet high, its diameter inside being 7 feet. The entrance is so narrow and low that a big man could hardly push his way through. Inside is an old wooden bench against the wall. In this extraordinary little place people found guilty of theft and other offences were imprisoned before they were led away to the place called the Gibbet, about half a mile from the village, for execution.

The church was largely rebuilt in 1855 but retains much of interest. The nave arcades and the responds of the chancel arch are late 12th century and the tower 15th century. There is a 15th century carved stone panel with the Crucifixion and in a window of the south aisle exquisite painted glass by Sir Ninian Comper which alone would make the church worth a visit.

Slaughterford. More beautiful than its name, it climbs a steep hillside above the little Box brook by the Gloucestershire border; it has an old farm group, a rebuilt church, and an old elm. There is a cottage on a raised pavement, with mullioned windows and dormers; a fine farm group with 20,000 stone tiles in its roofs and timbers a foot square in its barn; and the church high up in a field looking down on the village.

The church was Norman but was entirely rebuilt in the 19th century. It has a pinnacled and embattled tower, and a Jacobean altar table. Round the venerable elm in the churchyard is a stone seat for the old folk to rest on after climbing the hill; the elm is 14 feet round its trunk.

South Marston. The home of Alfred Williams, the Wiltshire poet, who continued into the 20th century so much of the spirit of those Rural Poets—John Clare, George Crabbe, Robert Bloomfield, and the Wiltshire Stephen Duck and William Barnes—who belonged to an earlier period.

The Rural Poets were always very much at one with that part of the country they knew best. John Clare was never happy away from Helpstone and Alfred Williams loved South Marston.

When he was eleven he went to work on a farm but soon transferred to the railway works at Swindon where he became a hammer man, and after working hard all day he and his wife would read and study together and learnt Latin, Greek, and Sanscrit; he writing his poems and she copying them out.

Then came the First World War. He was called up and sent to India, to a place called Ranikhet. On his return he bought an old cottage at South Marston and he and his wife rebuilt it with their own hands. They called it Ranikhet and there is a tablet on it.

The churchyard in which he and his wife are buried is within sight of their home. The church itself has pinnacles on its battlemented tower, a little Norman arch, and a 12th century font.

South Wraxall. It has a house and a church five centuries old.

One view of the house is at the end of a long green avenue, but its best approach is by its 15th century gatehouse, with an oriel window which has looked out on all the comings and goings here since Tudor days. Sir Walter Raleigh came this way walking with his friend Sir Walter Long, whose name is linked with his in the story which makes this house famous. It has a Raleigh Room in which it is believed Sir Walter Raleigh and Sir Walter Long sat smoking their pipes, the first two smokers in England. The pipes were of silver, and they were smoking the strange new weed Sir Walter Raleigh had brought home from one of his expeditions, the weed called tobacco. It was the first time it had been smoked in any English house.

The house is rich in sculptured figures and carved cornices, and the gatehouse, a small doorway, and the hall are as Raleigh would see them. A 14th century guesthouse is now part of a farm.

The 15th century church has an older tower with a saddle roof, so rare in Wiltshire, with a pinnacle at each end and a ball in the middle. Inside is a tomb with an effigy of an unknown lady. In front of this tomb in the Long Chapel is a winged angel standing serene between two lions which seem to be pawing her in a friendly way. Two canopied niches in the chapel walls have faces below them, one with its mouth open, the other a bishop with more dignity. The niches have vaulted roofs with Tudor roses in the vaulting. There is a peephole from the chapel into the chancel. The font is old and beautiful, the piscina has a charming canopy, the chancel arch has low black and gold iron gates into it, and there is an old stone to William Jones (1660), the epitaph ending with the words:

In life he taught to die, and he did give
In death a great example how to live.
If Wisdom, Learning, Knowledge cannot dwell
Secure from change, vain bubble Earth, farewell.

Standlynch. It is in the pastoral country near Downton, a few scattered farms and a house called Trafalgar House, set high in a green park, built of brick and stone and given to Nelson's brother in 1814 as an act of national gratitude for Trafalgar. Round about it grow beautiful beeches, and in the park is a small chapel founded in 1147 and rebuilt in 13th century style.

The house has, of course, a collection of intimate possessions of Lord Nelson, among them the couch and armchair which were on the Victory at Trafalgar, a cane the admiral carried at Naples, one of his telescopes, his log and navigation books, the seal he used in settling the terms of peace after Copenhagen, a naval coat and waistcoat that he wore, and two vases which belonged to him.

Stanton Fitzwarren. Set among elms and pretty gardens, stone walls and cottages, and down the drive to Stanton House, through a 50-acre park, is a church in which the oldest parts of the nave walls are Saxon.

The walls have two early Norman doorways now built up and a deep little Norman window. The Normans also made the splendid chancel arch, high and wide and finely carved, though the chancel itself is later, with one 13th century lancet, three 15th century windows, and a modern clerestory. It has one piscina on a Norman pillar and another with a canopy.

The font has a picture of Virtue conquering Vice; under the arches round the sides of the bowl eight Virtues are trampling down the bound and writhing figures of eight Vices. Some of the Virtues have lost their faces but all but one have still their swords with which they impale the Vices; the swordless Virtue carries a torch instead. The Church Triumphant is symbolised by the figure of a woman with a chalice and a cross standing on a winged beast, and by her stands a flying warrior.

On a wall is an ancient stone carving of a man's head under a canopy. Under the west window is a 16th century German woodcarving said to have come from Cologne cathedral and showing the Adoration of the Wise Men with the Child dipping his hand into a casket. The wealth of modern carving is the work of a rector, Caldwall Masters, who was a friend of Alfred Williams, the Wiltshire poet.

This church also has some fine carving by Owen Thomas, a friend of Caldwall Masters. The figures of Christ, St Leonard, and two angels in the niches of the modern porch, the oak lectern with its pelican in piety, and the fine cross, are all his work. The cross, a model of the ancient one at Cricklade, has angels on its canopied head and niches with figures of St George, St Alban, St Michael, and the Crucifixion; it was set up in memory of "the brave lads of Stanton Fitzwarren."

Stanton St Bernard. It lies by Marlborough, with a pinnacled tower which has been guarded by its splendid gargoyles for 500 years, centuries older than the church itself, which is a centenarian only. One gargoyle is a wild-looking man crowned and armoured. The round font has been here eight centuries.

Stanton St Quintin. A well worn figure of St Christopher is above the door of the 12th century church. The chancel was rebuilt last century but was made beautifully, with an arcaded parapet and elegant pinnacles, one of the pinnacles springing from a niche above the east window, in which is a sculpture of the Crucifixion. About a dozen animals and faces run round the outer walls, one a woman covering her face with her hands, and a curious trio tucked away in a corner, where a big surly fellow keeps company with a hooded monk and a woman with a wimple. An odd possession of the church is a curious little room built on to the nave, lit by one small circular window and another with tiny twin lights.

We come into the nave through a Norman doorway with a carved arch and crowned heads on the capitals, and are greeted by a brave array of nine delicately carved faces on one of the piers. Two handsome arches have chevron mouldings, prim foliage on the capitals, and a little head on each spring of the arches. The central tower has a Norman arch on the west and an English arch on the east. The font is Norman, charming with two tiers of leaflike pattern and a ring of carving round the bowl. The charming piscina is carved with a head of flowing hair, supported by a knight in chain mail in company with a short-haired youth.

Stapleford. A delightful little place, with green banks and thatched cottages clustering about the way to church. The church was built of flint and stone 800 years ago, but most of what we see is 14th century. The doorway is Norman, its arch decorated with fine mouldings, and one of the nave arcades has the rich moulding of the Norman masons, resting on stout Norman piers with carved capitals. From the 14th century come the pinnacled and embattled tower, the charming clerestory, and the chancel, and there are two pointed arches with small heads on their capitals in the nave. The sedilia in the chancel have handsome canopies, well carved with human heads. One of the windows has a small piece of old glass with floral design.

The plain round font is Norman, and in the sanctuary is a little old chest. n the nave are two carved stools, and in the porch a great stone coffin, with an ornamental cross. An old stone crucifix is let into the wall outside, above the east window.

Across the river is an earthwork approached through an opening called the Slay Gate.

Steeple Ashton. It is four miles from busy Trowbridge, and has a long street with old timbered houses, red brick herringbone, and all the lovely places about the little green. The cross on the green is set on stones believed to have been here when the Norman families were settling down after the Conquest; the cross was established in 1071 and repaired in 1714, and it stands here, by the little lock-up, with four sundials on the top of the shaft and above them a ball, a cross, and a crown. The lock-up has a domed roof and no windows, only a little opening in its nail-studded door. Looking on to it is the fine old manor house, which has an 18th century granary on high stone mushrooms. The vicarage has a 14th century hall, and we come to it through the porch of those far off days.

The church is magnificent, 500 years old, with its fine tower and lovely turrets, its embattled roofs and traceried windows, and its spectacular array of pinnacles and sculptures everywhere. The slender buttresses mount to the top of the tower, the pinnacles running round the parapets, 60 or 70 of them, and twice as many heads and sculptured figures. Round the walls are terrifying creatures that draw the eye to them again and again, one with a man in its mouth, weird beasts peeping up and down and north, south, east, and west at all who come. The tower is enriched with tier after tier of doorways with carved spandrels, windows, canopied niches, blind windows, and stone tracery. Of the two fine porches one has a magnificent vaulted roof and a stone carved with the Coronation of the Virgin.

It brings us into the church by a great door blistered with centuries of sunshine, crowded with studs, with four panels running from top to bottom, swinging on two hinges five feet long, locked with a lock in a case 28 inches long and a foot wide. We come into a nave of mighty bays resting on great clustered piers with 100 slender columns clustering round them, some of the columns rising to break into fans for the roof, passing on their way the great clerestory windows with 88 lights.

The sunshine pouring through these fine windows lights up a marvellous roof with 350 carved oak bosses. There are 42 stone fans, a noble array of craftsmanship, for they spring from floral corbels in the chancel, from heads and shoulders in the nave, and from canopied niches in the aisles. The walls of the aisles are enriched by these niches, resting on great brackets carved with heads and shoulders, each niche with slender sides beginning in grotesques and rising to the canopy, which grows into a fan for the vaulted roof.

The great chancel arch rises from huge piers of clustered shafts, and has a blind window above it in two tiers. The chancel is modern but has been fashioned with a splendour to match the nave and aisles.

There is a fine font and a reredos elaborately carved with eight wooden figures and three paintings, three handsome candelabra, and windows aglow with light breaking through jewel-like fragments of medieval glass. Thirteen windows have old glass in them, over a thousand pieces in all, the effect being mainly of golden light with crowns and mitres, suns and roses, a king in a blue robe, and a queen in purple, both on golden thrones, a winged lion, a winged bull, and an eagle. In the great west window are eight saints in two rows.

One small possession of much interest has this great church, a palimpsest brass hanging so that we can see both sides; it is on the north wall. On one side is a tribute to Deborah Marks, who died in 1730 at 99 after living under Cromwell and seven kings and queens of England. On the back is a picture showing a stout figure of Queen Anne standing with upraised sword by a scale in which is a Bible, her crowned consort and two bishops behind her. A roughly drawn church labelled "the Church of England" is in the background, and a queer little cowled figure is running away from the group saying "Burn the heretic book," the remarks of other unseen persons floating above him. Below is a verse showing that the brass, of which this is only half, was a vigorous Protestant attack on Roman Catholicism in the days of Queen Anne. The brass was engraved by Samuel Farley, who produced Wiltshire's first newspaper, printing it himself.

Steeple Langford. The River Wylye threads its way through the meadows, wandering in many streams crossed by small bridges, and edged with reeds and willows. The story of the village has a chapter for most of our great building centuries. The 12th century gave the church its font, standing on five pillars sculptured by a Norman artist, who gave it heads of a man and a bear, a shield and a badge. The 13th century gave it a fine chancel arch with many rows of plain moulding and beautiful capitals. The tower is from the 14th century, and the belfry from the 15th century. In the 16th century was born here Thomas Merriott, a famous scholar and writer of grammar books who was driven from his living.

It was probably in the 17th century that the carved pulpit was made; we may wonder if Joseph Collier preached from it. We see him in the church, a painted wooden figure wearing a black gown with a red book in his hand. He would be rector here when Shakespeare died, and his son Henry would follow him. The story of

Henry Collier and his family is the most pathetic page in the history of Steeple Langford. He was turned out by the Puritans, who declared him to be ignorant, scandalous, and inefficient, and he wandered homeless with his wife and their 11 children. They slept in a barn and the children gathered sticks in Grovely Wood. Two of these boys grew up to join the Penruddock Rebellion; and they suffered an appalling fate, for they were taken captive, sent to Jamaica, and sold as slaves.

After the Restoration their father returned to this small place and must have preached from this pulpit. He must often have looked on a gravestone in the nave engraved with the portrait of a hunter wearing a long gown and pointed shoes, a horn hanging at his side. It is thought that he may be Waleran, descended from the Conqueror's huntsman Waleran, who was Ranger of the New Forest.

In one of the aisles are four old benches on which men may have sat listening to Henry Collier preaching. The beams and bosses of this aisle belong to the original roof; the bosses are carved with animals and leaves. Let into the front of the prayer desk are old panels carved with an angel and a monster. In the sanctuary is an old carved armchair. There is a table tomb sculptured with the Mompesson arms, a recess filled with stone heraldry, and a splendid heraldic frieze carved in stone. It is blazoned with the pierced hands and feet and the heart of Christ. Another treasure, brought to light in our time, is a fragmentary Saxon cross with cable ornament.

Stockton. A lovely group of almshouses, each with a pinnacled window looking on to a flower-bordered court, with paved pathways and a fine heraldic gateway. It was all laid out by John Topp, who built the handsome manor in the 17th century.

The church is partly Norman and partly medieval. John Topp's effigy has a long pointed beard and wears a deep ruff and square-toed shoes; his wife has a simple frock with a curious headdress. Behind them kneel six children. Guarded in a glass case is a beautiful blue, gold, and brown patterned velvet dorsal curtain John Topp gave the church 300 years ago for the back of the altar. It was probably made about 1500. The chancel it adorns is 13th century, remarkable for being almost cut off from the nave by a solid wall pierced by a small archway and two peepholes. The wall is now covered by a lovely oak screen with small figures in canopied niches, 20th century work.

There are two Norman arcades whose low round piers have square sculptured capitals; a plain Elizabethan altar; two old carved chairs; a 15th century clerestory; a 700-year-old bowl. Above the 17th century wooden cover of the font hangs an 18th century candelabra. A delightful little wood angel brought from Wimborne Minster kneels with spread wings on a bench-end. A Jacobean aisle roof has moulded beams, and another roof of cedar has good beams and little decorations in the panels. The roof has a story, for it was made from the cargo of a ship wrecked off the Isle of Wight village where Bishop Wilberforce was curate. He helped to save the crew and they gave him the cedar wood.

An unknown 13th century lady simply clad lies on her side, in a recess, a headless dog at her feet. On the wall is a golden-haired cherub with green wings to John Terry, a rector who, according to his wish, was buried among the poor in the churchyard opposite the rectory.

There is a marble wall monument, decorated with cutlasses, pistols, nautical instruments, cherubs weeping and wringing their hands, and a winged skull crowned with bay in memory of John Greenhill. He went to sea very young, his epitaph tells us, and travelled the world over. He burnt some French ships and was well rewarded by the Dutch Admiralty in 1680. He became Governor of the Gold Coast, where he was sent by the Royal African Society, and came home to be one of the Commissioners of the Navy, laying the foundation stone of the dockyard in Plymouth.

Here also lies his ancestor Jerome Potticary, who died while Shakespeare was writing his plays. He, like good John Topp, was a clothier, and like Topp he built a manor house. His clothier's mark is sculptured on his tomb, which has brasses of himself, his two wives, and their children, all kneeling.

The tower, most of it 700 years old, has four gargoyles; in the graveyard are two gravestones that were here when the tower was new, one with a tiny cross at each end. Among the gravestones is one much worn at the entrance to the porch, and its inscription is almost invisible from the passing of many feet. It covers the body of Anne Raxworthy, a lady's maid who was pensioned off in the cottage close by, which has a handsome porch. From this cottage every Sunday she would walk to church in a black silk gown, a fact which troubled her when she came to die, for she felt that she had been too proud, and asked to be buried where everyone would walk over her.

Stonehenge. About ten miles northward of Salisbury, it is the most finished work of a mysterious race of men who scattered circles and avenues of stone, stone places of burial, and stone monuments over many parts of the world. Most of these memorials are primitive, but Stonehenge is elaborate and massive, with signs of design and a fixed purpose.

The place chosen for this monument had a deep impressiveness when the Plain was an open, wild, lonely, and barren waste; now it is crossed by modern roads and is largely cultivated. As Stonehenge was approached on foot fifty years ago across the open thinly grassed plain, with no one visible for miles around except a shepherd or two, the wide stretch of the Plain broken here and there by groups of prehistoric burial mounds, the uprising of this massive open-air circle, weathering in decay, partly overthrown by the tempests of many centuries yet retaining signs of order and grim strength, brought to the thoughtful mind a feeling of intrusion into an unknown past. The traveller was an alien back in a world he could not realise.

This prehistoric world of Old Stonehenge, which expressed itself crudely in stone, is still unrealised. Modern man has done his best with it. He has dug round it. He has found the tools with which it was constructed. He has reconstructed its plan. The National Trust has safeguarded its seclusion by purchasing the land surrounding it.

It has been said of Stonehenge that it is an Ancient British work, a Druidical work, a Saxon work, even a Danish work, and a scholar has in our time suggested that it was erected by immigrants from Egypt. But modern study of it is generally much more modest. It puts the date of Stonehenge's erection back to at least 3500 years ago, and makes no profession of exact knowledge of the purpose which it served.

What do we reasonably know of this monument of antiquity perhaps (with Avebury) the most elaborate effort of the race which tried to express its beliefs and feelings by piling up stones? We know that, with amazing labour, they brought huge stones, from 8 to 22 feet high, 6 feet broad and 3 feet thick (the tallest probably weighing 50 tons), and set them up in two immense circles and two gigantic horseshoes. In the outer circle with a diameter of 99 feet on the inner side—almost equal to the inner dome of St Paul's—there are thirty such stones in pairs, with a ten-foot slightly curved stone placed at the top of each pair and hollowed out to receive a shaped knob from each of the upright stones. Inside this outer circle was another circle of small unlinked stones, forty in number; and inside the inner circle was a horseshoe-shape formed by five separate pairs with horizontal stones on them, and then another horseshoe of about 19 unlinked stones 8 feet high inside the larger one. Then, inside this horseshoe on the south-west wide of the circle was a large flat central stone. Round this massive open temple they made a circular earthwork and a ditch with a circumference of about a thousand feet, and beyond the whole circle they placed a sighting stone on the north-east side, over which the sun would rise as viewed from the flat altar stone on the morning of the summer solstice, and four other stones symmetrically placed so as to serve a similar purpose at sunset and sunrise on other days, so that all this arrangement had astronomical observation as its foundation. The sighting-stone does not now exactly fit the sun's rising at the summer solstice, but astronomers tell us that it did 3500 years ago, and so they establish the date.

Careful study and excavation have revealed that the linked stones of the outer circle, the sighting stone, and the five pairs forming a horseshoe are of local origin, but that the circle and horseshoe of single upright stones and the flat altar stone come from Pembrokeshire, photographs from the air having shown the very track by which they were brought up from the river at West Amesbury. The flint axes, rounded hammer stones, and heavy mauls used in shaping the stones and smoothing their surfaces so perfectly have been found embedded with both the Welsh and local stones, together with the picks of stag's horn used for excavating the holes in the chalk in which they were embedded. A tiny stain on one stone also shows that one of the builders dropped a small bronze ornament upon it. All this proves that the monument was built as a whole at the end of the Stone Age, when the Bronze Age was beginning to overlap it, about the year 1800 BC, and thus the result of independent study by the archaeologist coincides with that of the astronomer calculating the date from the known change in the earth's tilt.

There appears to be little doubt, therefore, that the practical service rendered to the agricultural community of the Stone Age by this monument was the fixing of the calendar. Here the wise men would calculate for the primitive tribesmen when they should sow and plough and reap. Yet Stonehenge must have stood for more than that. We must conclude that it was also a place of worship. What rites were performed in this place so strangely constructed?

No one knows. That is the heart of the mystery. It was here at Stonehenge that apparently the men who expressed themselves in stone reached the height of their endeavour, whatever its purpose was.

Stourton. It is in the country not far from Mere. Few churches have a more delightful setting than this, lying in a quiet hollow with a tree-covered hill climbing sharply behind it, a noble group of beeches opposite its gate, the wonderful cross in Stourhead gardens facing it, with a glimpse beyond of clear water, deep woods, and a small stone temple on a green bank.

It is a fit resting-place for a man who loved Wiltshire as Sir Richard Hoare did; he loved its old and precious things so much that he spent much of the 18th and 19th centuries searching them out; learning all that he could of them and describing them in a great work on the county. He lies in a small mausoleum.

The chiefly late medieval century church has pierced parapets on the roofs, an embattled tower with gargoyles and traceried windows, a window in the chancel with beautiful panelled splays, pointed arcades on round piers, charming corbel angels carrying the roof timbers, and a small piscina under the tower. In one of the windows are some fragments of ancient glass, with golden-haired saints under purple, gold, and green canopies. There are many monuments. An unknown Tudor lady lies facing the door, and by the walls are 18th century memorials of Henry Hoare, topped by his handsome bust, of brother Henry who is mourned by two small angels, and of Hester Hoare, wife of the famous Richard, who left him a widower when she was only 23. Their little boys weep over a black and white urn, seated on a granite sarcophagus. The monument was made by Italian craftsmen fashioned out of granite brought from Egypt.

The finest monument the church has is that of Edward, Lord Stourton, who died in 1535. The sides of his tomb have exquisite niches, with remains of what seem to have been dogs sitting up between them on small ledges. Lord Stourton wears fine armour, is bearded, and has long hair; his wife Agnes lies at his side, and at their heads kneel three small figures, a bearded man with a chain about his neck, a headless lady, and a youth in a furred gown. The Stourtons held this place from Saxon times until 200 years ago, and many of them are buried under the tower.

Near the church is a low stone building with an embattled tower

Salisbury Plain,
near Devizes.

Stourhead House.

(National Trust)

The gardens at Stourhe

Silbury Hill.

Midsummer sunrise at Stonehenge.

Stonehenge: one of the trilithons.

graced by a tall oriel. A war memorial in the form of a village hall; Sir Aston Webb built it out of part of an old inn.

Just inside the gate leading to the beautiful grounds of Stourhead is the medieval cross which for centuries looked down on the passing throng at the meeting of the four chief streets of Bristol. It is 50 feet high, with pinnacles and statues of King John, Henry the Third, Edward the Third, and Edward the Fourth under fine canopies; and above these 17th century figures of Elizabeth, Henry the Sixth, James the First, and Charles the First. Higher still are cherubs with shields, a delightful spire crowning them all. The cross was first set up in Bristol's streets in 1373 and heightened and repaired nearly 300 years later. In 1733 it was thought to be in the way and was removed to College Green, where it stayed for 30 years, only to be taken down again and kept in the cathedral cloisters. Finally it was given to Henry Hoare, who had it restored and moved here.

The great house of Stourhead and its wonderful grounds are unparalleled in Wiltshire as a spectacle. It is good to come when the rhododendrons are in bloom, but, rhododendrons or not, its pleasure grounds, two miles round, give us an hour never to be forgotten. In a little valley of the park are six wells from which the River Stour rises, and everywhere about these grounds are temples, caves, and grottoes, with a profusion of sculpture among which are statues from Rome and Herculaneum. There is a Temple of Flora with an ancient vase, a Pantheon on the banks of a lake where Somerset and Wiltshire meet, a grotto with a sculptured nymph, and a cave with a statue of Neptune, while in front of the house itself, and on the portico, are statues by Rysbrack and mythological scenes. In the Pantheon, which is 36 feet across, is a statue of Livia by an ancient master; it was she to whom Augustus said, when dying, "Livia, remember our happy married life." In the house itself is a superb collection of art treasures, a mantelpiece by Grinling Gibbons, and 26 chairs made by Chippendale himself for Marie Antoinette.

On a height reaching 1000 feet above the sea is Alfred's Tower, which the motorist sees for miles. It is built of a million bricks with a top of stone, is triangular with round towers at the corners, has 222 steps, a statue of Alfred, and an inscription saying that on this height Alfred set up his standard against the Danes in 879.

The house was burnt down in the present century, but Sir Henry

Hoare rebuilt it with the help of Sir Aston Webb and Mr Doran Webb, and presented it to the National Trust.

Stratford-sub-Castle. The village lies in the hollows, looking up at Old Sarum towering above it; the castle is one of those ancient camps that lie everywhere in Wiltshire. The small church is 700 years old, with a Norman font and a canopied pulpit handsome after its 300 years. It has an hourglass in an iron bracket made by the local blacksmith in the 17th century, as was the roof which rests on corbels of gilded angels, grotesques, demons, and people carrying coats-of-arms. The chancel screen, delicately traceried and decorated at the top with angels and flowers, comes from the 15th and 16th centuries. The chancel roof, though made by the 17th century craftsmen who roofed the nave, has corbels 200 years older, small and gilded, with a mermaid and a strange crowned head among them. This head has two tiny heads in place of ears, a crude way of representing the Trinity.

Much of the beauty of the church is due to Thomas Pitt, the Blandford rector's son who became a rich East India merchant and is known as Diamond Pitt because he bought for £20,000 a diamond since valued at half a million sterling, and now one of the national jewels of France. He gave the panelling for the chancel and built the embattled tower in 1711. He probably gave the 18th century clock, which has only one hand, and has in the corners of the dial the gilded signs of the Zodiac.

The home of the Pitts, now the vicarage, reached by a lime avenue, is a fine 17th century house with projecting wings and a porch between. At the back is a handsome room added by Diamond Pitt, but the house is chiefly famous because the first William Pitt, the Earl of Chatham, was born in it. He was the first son of Diamond Pitt's first son.

Stratford Tony. It is named after Ralph Toni, who founded the Toni family and bore the Conqueror's standard at the Battle of Hastings. It was historic ground even before then, for Stratford is where the Roman street from Old Sarum to Badbury Rings forded the Ebele.

The church stands above the pretty cottages on a steep green mound, about whose foot winds a stream full of swaying water plants, shaded by willows and crossed by tiny bridges. Brick, flint, and stone weathered to perfect harmony make up much of its charm.

Its low tower has gargoyles and a little spire. Its plain font is Norman, and the lovely traceried windows of the chancel are perhaps 600 years old. All the pews, the panelling running round the church, the chancel screen, and the choir stalls, are topped by delicate railings. The original stone altar is still used, and there is a scratch-dial by the priest's door. It has been given a modern pointer to cast a shadow on the dots.

Stratton St Margaret. Its oldest possession is a Norman doorway in the north wall of the church. Its tower has been here 500 years, and the beams put in the porch by these 15th century builders are still in their place.

The windows of the clerestory light up the fine moulding of the ancient beams in the nave roof. On each side of the chancel arch is a peephole, one with a trefoil arch adorned with leaves. There is a recessed tomb under a lovely canopy adorned with pinnacles, flowers, and a quaint head.

On the windowsills when we called were bronze coats-of-arms saved from the 17th century bells. Three heraldic monuments are in memory of 17th century folk; one of them is painted on wood in a frame enlivened, so to speak, with skulls, hourglasses, and crossbones. In an aisle is an elaborate altar tomb to Susanne Van Acken who died in Bengal in 1783, her embalmed body being kept there until she was laid to rest here four years later.

Sutton Benger. Here is a piece of work done by a woman about 500 years ago, a strip of embroidery once brightly coloured but now mellowed by exposure to quiet greens, yellows, browns, and blues. It is part of a 15th century vestment which at some later time has been cut up and pieced together to serve another purpose. It has rows of little figures under elaborate canopies, 22 in all, with faces all wonderfully clear and full of life. Among them is a golden-haired prophet in a rich ermine robe carrying a scroll, Moses with his white beard holding the Tables of Stone, St Andrew with his cross, the grey-bearded St James dressed as a palmer carrying his staff, a deacon with a heart in one hand and two swords in the other, and two graceful St Catherines.

The font by which this hangs is Norman, with a simply carved bowl, and is the oldest possession of the church. The walls are 14th century, the pinnacled tower 15th; the short bell-turret rises above the parapet of the tower with an ancient bell in it, and there are three stone heads over the traceried west window. The 15th century porch has a vaulted roof and six windows in pairs, and along the south wall runs a handsome corbel table. Near the east window a gargoyle leans out, projecting about three feet.

On one of the arches leading into the nave, is a sculpture of a man's head with foliage coming from his mouth and birds perching among the leaves. It is a huge stone bracket, and there are two other brackets near by with birds among foliage.

There are old beams in the aisle, a piscina with two bands of ballflower, a little old glass, and windows of much interest. One is above the pulpit where the wall has been pierced to make room for a small angel in red, green, and gold; another has four pictures of the Good Samaritan; another has three women at the Tomb, and the Ascension, in charming colours; and the east window of the aisle is remarkable for its structure, having set in the bottom of it a beautiful stone canopy with a vaulted roof, the splays of the window itself being rich in the ballflower of the 14th century.

Sutton Mandeville. Under the widespread branches of a yew planted in 1780 lies an ancient gravestone, carved with the Madonna and Child and a praying figure below. The small church has been here since Norman days; the Norman tower remains, with belfry windows added by the English builders, and with a 13th century chancel arch resting on clustered columns with simply moulded capitals. The angels in a small chancel window were painted by a vicar. Two tablets tell of vicars who spent nearly all their life in the village. John Wyndham was here as curate and vicar for 60 years of the 19th century, Henry Fricker died in 1792 after being here 56 years. The beautiful carved pulpit is dated 1631.

Sutton Veny. The church is 19th century, but its bells are from the ancient church, which has become a ruin. There is a carved eagle on the lectern, and an old almsbox. Up the path a white marble cross to Jane Major who died in 1896 aged 105.

The ruined walls and arches of the deserted church are a pathetic witness to the treasure the village has lost. The chancel has been restored and has lancet windows, a plain Norman font, and the tiny bust of a praying woman by a tablet to Margaret Bayley, who died in 1693.

Down the lane to the old church is a white house with a great sloping roof. It was once the parsonage, and parts of it are said to be 600 years old. It has beautiful traceried windows. Among the ancient graves and earthworks on the hills is one called Robin Hood's Bower.

Swindon. A century ago it was a village on the top of a hill, with about 500 families and one big house in which lived the lord of the manor, Mr Goddard, whose family had been here since 1560; the ruins of the ancient church are in the grounds of their house.

Then there came a man whose statue should be in Swindon's streets, Daniel Gooch. He was one of the apprentices in George Stephenson's workshop, and when he was only 21 the great Brunel recommended him as Superintendent of the Great Western Railway, and he held this post while Swindon rose from a hamlet to a busy town.

One summer's day Daniel Gooch set out with his chief engineer to prospect in the fields where Swindon now stands. They picnicked by the line, and one of them picked up a stone and threw it. They put in a peg where the stone fell, and on that spot began the Swindon railway works. It has been noted that these two men had seen only 58 years of life between them, but they were far-seeing enough to lay the foundations of a town by the throwing of a stone. Today the little village they knew has grown into a town of 80,000 people. The railway works cover 323 acres, 73 acres roofed over. They repair a thousand engines every year, and one workshop alone has a floor-space of half a million square feet. When their people go on holiday they fill 30 trains with 1000 people in each train.

The day must surely come when Swindon will set up a statue to Sir Daniel Gooch; at present it preserves a monument of his energy more interesting than a statue, a copy of his first engine, the North Star, which is kept in the Works and may be seen by anyone. It has in it the original driving-wheels and buffers and a maker's plate with the date 1837. It was made when Gooch was only 21, and is described today as a marvel of symmetry and compactness. Gooch was a great experimenter and inventor as well as an organiser, and his inventive genius was famous in the early days of railways, when so many difficult problems were being worked out. He did much to solve them. But in 1864 he was attracted by the new idea of the telegraph, and left railways to become Superintendent of Communication with America. He dispatched the first cable across the Atlantic in 1866, but in 1865 the GWR had suddenly found itself nearing bankruptcy, and Gooch went back as chairman and put it on a sound footing.

Since those days Swindon has become the biggest town in Wiltshire, and we may all see over its great railway works, which remain the chief of its many industries. It is one of the healthiest industrial towns in the kingdom, and its station, though almost at the lowest level of the town, is the highest point on the railway from London to Bristol, and stands level with the top of the dome of St Paul's. It is also the driest town in the county. It is well placed, and has easy access to such towns as Salisbury and Gloucester, Chippenham and Bath, Oxford and Reading, Newbury and Devizes.

It has little that is old except in its fine museum, but it has much that is interesting. St Mark's Church, the mother church of the town, was built by the GWR in 1846, and Christ Church, which is Swindon's parish church, was built a few years later by Sir Gilbert Scott, who also designed St Mark's.

The cenotaph in the centre of the town has on one face a winged sword symbolising Protection; and on a panel in the town hall are the names of 900 Swindon men who did not come back from the war. One man who did come back was Alfred Williams, of South Marston, the poet who has a tablet on the town hall giving his name and dates (1877–1930), and the words:

Lyrical poet, classical scholar, master of English prose, who self-taught, self-inspired, while toiling at the forge, illumined all around him with
The light that never was on sea or land,
The consecration and the poet's dream.

The town is keeping for itself delightful open spaces, and has, a mile away, what is known as Coate Water, down the Marlborough road. It is a reservoir of 72 acres, and is a fine lake, with a smaller sheet of water hidden among the trees close by which is kept as a bird sanctuary. Here is the home of Richard Jefferies, the house he was born in, now belonging to the town. There is a tablet on it, and another tablet has been fixed on the house in Victoria Road where he lived as a journalist writing for the Wiltshire papers.

The museum has five rooms full of interesting things: musical instruments of the world, relics from Pompeii, old china and exhibits showing its evolution from clay, one of the best collections of British shells in existence; a gallery of Wiltshire pictures; a metals and minerals room much used by children in which an exhibit shows the formation of coal; and a facsimile of Shakespeare's Folio. Here also is one of the biggest crocodiles in England, 15 feet long, one of the ugliest things with one of the most beautiful looking down on it, for on the wall is a peacock's tail. With the crocodile of 15 feet is a python of 20 feet. The museum has also the best work of art in Swindon, a white marble statue of Charlotte Corday, sitting meditatively looking over the back of a chair. It is the work of an Italian sculptor, and he has given her a beautifully chiselled lace cap.

Teffont Evias. It has fine trees on the hills about it, a running brook adding to its quiet charm. There is a beautiful Tudor manor house with a battlemented porch, where lived a man whose fame John Milton knew and who became Lord Chief Justice, Sir James Ley. He lives in literature and in history too, for Milton mentions his death in one of his sonnets, and it was he upon whom the painful duty fell of pronouncing the judgment of his peers on Francis Bacon. He is buried at Westbury.

The church, rebuilt a century ago, is neighbour to the manor house, and has a spire beside a tall yew with a great spread of branches. In nearly every window of the nave are small Flemish pictures of Bible scenes, probably the work of 17th century artists. It has a simple old stone font and a small carved chest. In a chapel side by side lie three proud sons of Teffont Manor, the father and brothers of Sir James Ley, bearded and fine looking men. Henry, the father, is in black armour of the 16th century, and carries a small shield, his feet on a lion. The sons, William and Matthew, are in the armour of Shakespeare's day, and wear ruffs, their feet also on lions.

Teffont Magna. Here the stream rises from a chalk pit and passes through the village on its way to join the Nadder; the simple little church has a 13th century porch and what is declared to be one of the oldest English bells.

The bell stands in the nave. Also fragments of a Saxon cross with interlaced carving. There is also a lovely old traceried screen carved with flowers, and a plain round font perhaps as old as the screen.

Tidcombe. Wansdyke runs past and there are ancient graves on its hills, and through stately trees a charming Queen Anne house near a church which has been here about 700 years. It has a low pinnacled tower and clerestory windows, and is an attractive little place with a group of 21 windows of all sorts and unexpected shapes. It has a raised chancel longer than the nave, and in the south wall is a curiously raised doorway three feet from the ground, half built up with steps, the top half opening. The font is Norman. The elegant 17th century pulpit has beautiful carved panels and a handsome sounding-board. In the tower is a modern traceried oak screen with linenfold panels, and in a small recess in the wall are some ancient patterned tiles.

Tidworth. The church is mainly late 15th century; its battered tower is lit by charming windows 500 years old; its tall arch looks down on a nave with 18th century panelled seats, painted with the names of those who sat in them long ago. There is a big Norman font, a chancel piscina with a chalk canopy and a fluted basin, and a canopied piscina in the nave by which is a lovely niche decorated with tiny stone carvings of a monk and a king. In the nave also are two tiny sundials which have been set in the splay of a window.

Gone is the ancient priory, but the small door which opened on the path leading to it remains near the pulpit. Gone also is the ancient home of the Mompessons, and a new house stands in its stead set in fine gardens.

Tilshead. A rough trackway climbs the Downs near this pretty village, and leads past White Barrow, a prehistoric grave 255 feet long. From its summit the Plain is seen unfolding, dotted with graves and streaked with the ancient trench running for miles across the Plain; it is called Old Ditch. Silver Barrow bears a flag-staff, and Long Barrow, away behind White Barrow, rises majestic at the top of a hill between dark masses of trees.

In the church nave massive square piers support arcades of the plainest Norman arches, and the great walls of the tower appear strong enough for all time. They lead from the aisled nave into the narrow chancel, the tower walls continuing all the way. The only two arches of the tower are east and west and have been pointed; the north and south walls have deep Norman windows fitted with narrow lights. The nave is dark in spite of the quatrefoil windows in the clerestory, but the light falls finely in the east as we look from the west.

The lancet windows of the chancel are all deeply splayed; two are very small and one is closed by an odd wooden shutter, apparently a relic of very early days. A curious feature of these two tiny windows, and of the doorway near one of them, is the big arched beam in the top. The three beams are full of old nails broken off. The big font

Salisbury (St Thomas):
John Webbe, 1570

Salisbury Cathedral:
Bishop Wyville, 1375

Salisbury Cathedral:
Bishop Guest, 1578

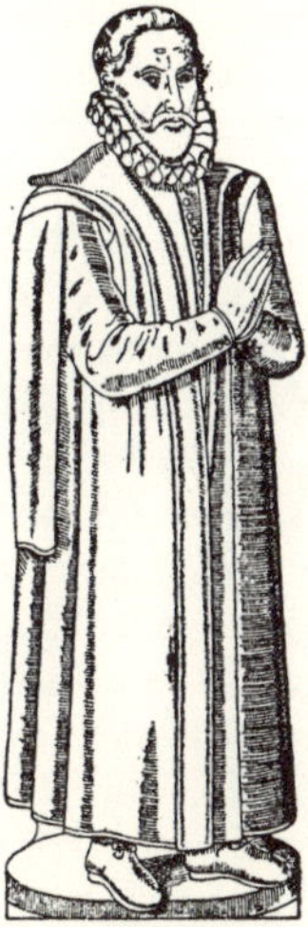

Westbury:
Thomas Bennet, 1605

Tisbury:
Lawrence Hyde and Family, 1590

Seend:
John Stokys, 1498

BRASS PORTRAITS OF WILTSHIRE PEOPLE

is boldly chiselled, and round the top is a band of herringbone carving. The 17th century altar is handsomely carved, and there is a canopied piscina. One vicar died in the 18th century at the altar, for his epitaph tells us that

Amid his pious labour (grief to tell)
He sank, and in the altar service fell.

On the highway hereabouts is a stone set up as a warning to those who think to escape the punishment of thieves. It tells of the attack on a Mr Dean by four highwaymen, who were beaten off and hunted so hotly across the Downs that one of them fell dead on a spot marked by another stone. The other three were captured and transported for fifteen years.

Tisbury. It is one of Wiltshire's oldest towns and has one of England's biggest barns, a grey giant of a place with two thatched porches and massive timbers looking young after 500 years. On a farm is the 15th century kitchen of a manor house with a beautiful stone chimney, given with the church and the village to the nuns of Shaftesbury about a thousand years ago. There are two delightful gate-houses still standing, with impressive buttresses.

Up through winding and climbing lanes is the wooded hill on which two castles stand—the ruined late 14th century Wardour Castle which figured bravely in the Civil War, and the 18th century Wardour Castle which Lord Arundell of Wardour filled with his treasures and is now a girls' school. It is a magnificent house, and stands in these wooded hills as one of the proud domestic monuments of its period. The chapel, one of the few we have seen with its altar at the west end, has a splendour to match the house, vaulted roofs richly decorated and walls with valuable canvases, but the rarest thing here is the red velvet chasuble embroidered with pomegranates fleur-de-lys, and Tudor roses, said to have been among the treasures of Westminster Abbey. The Glastonbury Cup, another beautiful possession of this place, has the Twelve Apostles round it and three lions at the base, its lid being engraved with the Crucifixion. The domed west end of the chapel is a small architectural masterpiece by Sir John Soane. This glorious building serves as the church of the surrounding Catholic population.

The ruins of the old castle, famous for their defence by Lady Blanche Arundell in the Civil War, stand as they were left by that Lord Arundell who blew up his own house because he could not eject General Ludlow (occupying it for the Parliamentarians) in any other way. Lady Blanche Arundell held out heroically against the Parliamentarians only capitulating when granted honourable terms of surrender which were not kept. She is buried at Tisbury. It is set in a scene of great beauty, with cypresses and cedars about it. This shell of a noble building has still over its entrance a head of Christ in a niche, and the words, Under Thy protection may our race and house stand. The ruins are now in the care of the Ministry of Works.

The church is a fine cruciform building with central tower, the top stage of which was rebuilt in 1762 after the fall of the spire. The nave, transepts, and crossing are late 12th century; the chancel, aisles, and north porch 14th century; the arcades and nave roof are 15th century; the aisle roofs are 16th century, though the south bears the date 1616.

The nave, with fine clerestory windows, has a fascinating roof of blue and white panelled into squares, with painted mouldings on which are about 150 carved bosses. Everywhere small heads peer down, and six great angels spread their wings and hang out above us from the walls. They have been here 500 years. Both aisles have ceilings carved by 16th century craftsmen, rich and handsome with about 300 bosses.

Here behind the altar rails is a brass engraved with the portrait of Lawrence Hyde, who died when Shakespeare was writing his plays. He is kneeling with his wife and their ten children, and the brass is remarkable because it shows an arcade, a group of windows, an eagle's head, and a shield on which is a queer hairy beast gazing at its reflection in a mirror. We see the reflection. One of the ten children in this fine brass was Henry Lawrence, who grew up to be the father of Lord Clarendon, from whom two English queens descended. In an aisle are the brass portraits of a 16th century lord of the manor and his wife who are thought to be members of the Davies family to whom belonged John Davies, the poet born hereabouts in the days of Shakespeare. The altar rails are fine, the 17th century pews are carved delightfully at the ends, the chancel is panelled in ancient linenfold. The Jacobean panels in the pulpit and the ends of all the seats were probably carved by the men who made the painted and gilded cover for the 13th century font, which is shaped like a pyramid of blue, white, and gold, and is raised by a wheel and chain.

On the wall of the chancel hangs an old helmet belonging to the first Lord Arundell. The original stone mensa remains, with its five consecration crosses, but over it now is a modern altar with a reredos of Christ and Mary Magdalene after the Resurrection.

Rudyard Kipling is buried in the churchyard near the grave of his parents. His father, Lockwood Kipling, provided some of the illustrations for his son's books.

Tisbury was the birthplace (in 1589) of the forgotten poet Sir John Davies who was best known for his poem *Nosce Teipsum* (Know Thyself), a philosophical argument in favour of the immortality of the soul.

Tockenham. It has a beautiful brick and stone manor house which Richard Danvers built when the Stuarts came to England; it has the font at which the Normans christened their little ones; and it has a Roman god.

They are monuments of three great periods in our island's story, and the Roman god in his niche on the wall gives Tockenham the oldest possession that any church in ancient Wiltshire has. We have come upon many Roman altars and other Roman stones but only once before (at Compton Dando in Somerset) have we come upon a Roman god. There Jupiter holds up the church at a corner where he may be missed; here Aesculapius stands on the wall looking at all who come. He stands under a canopy as if he were walking, a battered figure in beautiful drapery, just by the south doorway. To the Greeks he was the god of medicine, and in Homer he is not a divinity but simply the "blameless physician"; but the Romans represented him as a stately figure with a staff and a serpent, and so he is seen at Tockenham. The centuries of sun and wind and rain have worn the beauty off his figure, but the symbol of the serpent twisted round his staff is plain to see. He was supposed to have power not only to cure sickness but to bring back the dead to life, and Jupiter, fearing that man might find the power to escape death altogether, killed Aesculapius with a thunderbolt. Remarkable it is that these two gods from ancient Rome should be found on our village walls not far away from one another, Aesculapius with his mystic powers at Tockenham, and Jupiter, who slew him with a thunderbolt, at Compton Dando.

The tiny church, restored last century, has a small shingled spire and a scratch-dial, a plain Norman doorway, and its Norman font, battered but sturdy for its 800 years, has tiny arches and is set on an aged-looking base. The west wall is unusual for having oak timbers in it, and it is curious also to find the roodloft doorway framed with timbers and the steps inside it timbered at the edge. On the wall of the chancel is the bust of a beautiful girl who died in 1726; she is Mary Goddard Smith who died a few weeks after her marriage.

Tollard Royal. One of the delightful places among the hills and woods where Wiltshire meets Dorset, it is royal because King John had a hunting lodge here, but it is famous because of a man who restored King John's house and made his name known far and wide for the great things he did. He was General Pitt-Rivers, whose work all travellers hereabouts come upon across the Dorset border at Farnham, where his marvellous collections are. There is no greater surprise in our countryside than the wealth of history there displayed before our eyes. But it is here that the General is buried, his ashes in a little black casket carved with the instruments of the excavator, and in the middle of his monument on the wall are some of the things he found.

Close by are the magnificent grounds known as Larmer Gardens, high above the village. The grass walks are bordered by trees, and all lead to something charming—a pool in a hollow with two bronze cranes, or a spirited bronze Chinese horse eagerly expectant of adventure, a little stone temple, or an open-air theatre. It is open to all, a fine memorial of a noble life. The Pitt-Rivers home was at Rushmore Lodge, the chief lodge of Cranborne Chase when it was divided into six walks.

A tablet in the 13th century church to Lord and Lady Rivers tells us that they were both born in the same year (1810) and both died in the same week in 1866. Near them hangs a wooden cross which was made by Swiss peasants to mark the place in the Bernese Alps where their daughter was killed by lightning on her honeymoon; one of the windows of the church is to her memory. There is a charming tablet to a rector of 1710, old altar rails, a simple font, and (oldest of all the possessions of this small church) a stone knight in banded mail. He is Sir William Payne, who died in 1388, and he is drawing his sword, his crossed feet on a lion.

General Pitt-Rivers won his military rank in the Crimean War, but is remembered as a scientist rather than as a soldier. The curious story is told that while examining a new rifle he was struck by the fact that weapons of war advanced in precision and value by small and continual changes, and not by any sudden burst of invention or creative effort. The idea of evolution was then in the air and this thinking man suspected that it should apply to everything made by human hands. He began to look into it and to collect tools and weapons made in all ages. He dug up arrowheads and spears and flints, relics of the Stone Age, the Bronze Age, and the Iron Age; he collected pottery, idols, mirrors, spoons, combs, tools, coins, and games—nothing was outside his range, and he came to the conclusion after studying these things that human progress has been like a game of dominoes, like fitting on to like, with sequence as the first rule of the game. He began to study the history of peoples and led the way in determining the character and age and movements of races by the things they left behind. He made immense collections of objects, which he offered to Oxford, where they are now in the Pitt-Rivers Museum. He excavated his own estates and showed that hereabouts in the primeval forest was the cradle of a race of Britons of small stature, men and women both standing about five feet high. They were probably the first cultivators of our English soil. The last generous act of this generous man (who gave much of his life to social work for the good of the people), was to build a museum at Farnham over the Dorset border, and this and the museum at Oxford are the monuments of his indefatigable and industrious life.

Trowbridge. It is a handsome and ancient place, one of the fine group of old towns in which Wiltshire is so rich. The town's chief glory, its spacious church, has been partly rebuilt and is hemmed in by houses and shops in the heart of the town. Trowbridge has become the administrative capital of the county, and is adding new industries to the cloth-making for which it has been famous through the centuries. But it keeps the atmosphere of the past about it, and in its square, about the old George Inn, medieval stone faces look down from under the eaves.

The great church has seen seven centuries, but has been disturbed in half of them. Begun in the 13th century, its famous spire was added in the 14th, and all but the spire and tower were taken down in the 15th and built again. The work of the medieval builders lasted 400 years, but in the middle of last century the structure began to fall to pieces, stones fell out of the spire, and in the end the church was made new on the old lines—chancel, nave, arcades, clerestory, and the upper half of the spire. The spire rises 160 feet, a striking spectacle with three bands of panelling round it; it is often said to be the best spire on any parish church in Wiltshire, and is not unworthy of the county which has the famous Salisbury spire. It rises from an embattled tower richly gargoyled with all manner of strange birds, beasts, and demons.

The church has three porches, the north and south porch having rooms over them. In the south porch are some medieval gravestones found in the ruins of the vanished castle; they are 12th century, and one of them has on it the words "Here is buried our daughter Acelina." The western porch in the tower has in it a curious stone ball three feet round with an iron spike in it which was familiar to Trowbridge for centuries, for it crowned the market cross which disappeared in the 18th century. The ball was lost sight of for nearly 100 years and was then discovered in a garden, and given a home where it now stands.

The great church is light and handsome. The old timbers of the medieval roof still look down on the nave, for it was restored and recreated on the new walls. The roof is divided into five bays to match the nave, the beams having carved spandrels and angels with outstretched wings. The roof of the north chapel (its beauty lost to sight now that the organ is here) has 30 stone compartments filled with tracery and carved bosses. There is fine carving on a stone mantelpiece in the vestry which was once a priest's chamber; the mantelpiece has old carving with heraldic crests, including a white hart, a lion, and a queer creature with a sheep's head. The floor of the baptistry has engraved tiles of the Baptism of Christ, and the font has 15th century carvings of shields with the Emblems of the Passion on them: the cross, the coat without a seam, the spear and nails, and so on. Near it hangs a dainty set of 25 painted shields.

The windows have a splendid array of portraits, the finest being the great transomed window in the south chapel. It has 23 lights in four tiers with fine figures of St George, Richard Lionheart, St Martin, and Joan of Arc, and a group of three in white and gold showing Our Lord sitting between the archangels Gabriel and Michael. The chapel which has this memorial of Trowbridge men who fell in the war was once a chapel of the seventh Duke of Somerset who was at the fall of Mons in 1709. On the chancel wall is a pathetic memorial to a major who gave his life in the war; it is his sword hanging in its sheath. What is called the Historical Window in the baptistry has portraits of famous people in the history of the town; it shows Ela Countess of Salisbury, who laid a foundation-stone of the cathedral in which her husband William Longsword was the first to be buried; Queen Philippa, who begged the life of the

Burghers of Calais from her lord; her son John of Gaunt, and Humphrey de Bohun, Constable of England, one of the Magna Carta barons. The west tower window is interesting because it was set here on thanksgiving day in 1847, when the nation, having been threatened with famine, was overjoyed to find itself with a good harvest.

There is elaborate carving on two chairs in the sanctuary, both from the continent, and the stone reredos is carved with Leonardo's Last Supper. The church has lost an old chantry, but kept among its documents is still a deed by which a merchant founded the chantry 400 years ago.

In the chancel is the monument, by E. H. Baily, for the poet George Crabbe who was rector here for the last 19 years of his life, 1814–32. The epitaph says that though "he broke through the obscurity of his birth he never ceased to feel for the less fortunate." He was born of a poor family, had been a farmer's boy, an apothecary's apprentice, and an unsuccessful physician, but when his poetry attracted the attention of Edmund Burke, who took him under his patronage, helped him towards Ordination and a career in the church, he never forgot from whence he had risen; and in an age when so many of the Rural Poets spoke of country life as an idyll George Crabbe was the first to write about *The Village* as it really was. The Rural Poets peopled the countryside with "gentle swains" and "quilted shepherdesses" but they did not survive the scorn Crabbe poured upon them in his poems *The Village*, *The Parish Register*, and *The Borough*. He had not met them in his early life in the country which he knew to be one of hard unremitting toil.

He had been a rector in Leicestershire and it was at Trowbridge during his last years that he put together the most voluminous of all his works, *The Tales*, *The Tales from the Hall*, and a further volume of *Posthumous Tales* was found in manuscript after his death. He really belongs to Suffolk and it is to that East Anglian countryside, and to his home town of Aldeburgh (The Borough) which treated him badly but for which he had a lasting affection, that in his poems he always returns. The Rural Poets were tied to their localities and George Crabbe is the laureate of that East Anglian countryside which he depicted with the same realism and invigorating freshness as those painters of the Norwich School who were his exact contemporaries.

It was while he was a rector in Leicestershire that Crabbe got to know the Rev Edmund Cartwright, the inventor of the power loom, and long before Crabbe became rector of Trowbridge Cartwright's invention was beginning to revolutionise the weaving industry. A

Wilton House.

The "Double Cube Room" at Wilton House.

Wilton House and the Bridge.

Wootton Bassett: the Town Hall.

manufacturer at Lyttleton, near Trowbridge, installed machinery in his mill and a crowd of workmen came to smash the machines. Among them was Thomas Helliker, a cloth finisher. Information was given that he was the ringleader and he was arrested and tried at Salisbury where he asserted his innocence but refused to give away his accomplices. He was found guilty and was executed on his nineteenth birthday.

The clothworkers of Wiltshire and Somerset were much impressed by Helliker's loyalty and fortitude. They considered him a martyr to their cause, and erected the tomb in Trowbridge churchyard with the following inscription:

Sacred to the memory of Thomas Helliker, the thread of whose life was cut in the bloom of youth. He exchanged mortality for immortality, March 22, 1803 in the 19th year of his age.

The fatal catastrophe which led to this unfortunate event is too awful to describe; suffice it to say that he met death with greatest fortitude and resignation of mind. Considering his youth he may be said to have but few equals. He died a true penitent, being very anxious in his last moments that others might take a timely warning and avoid evil company.

This tomb was erected at his earnest request by the clothmaking factories of the counties of Wilts and Somerset, as a token of their love to him and veneration for his memory.

Tytherton. It lies at the end of winding lanes rich in trees and between two rivers. Across a field from its handsome old farmhouse with a coat-of-arms over the door, its little church is guarded by a row of elms. Its gable ends have sculptured ornaments, its bell hangs in an open cot, its plastered ceiling has charming oak bosses carved with flowers, its pulpit has a simply panelled canopy, and its font, big and deep, has fine arcading by a Norman craftsman.

At East Tytherton there is a school and a church built by John Cennick for the Moravian Brethren.

Originally called the Bohemian Brethren who traced their history back to the Hussite Schism in Bohemia in the 15th century, the Moravians became a pietiest movement in the 18th century under the influence of Count Nicholaus Ludwig von Zinzendorf. Von Zinzendorf was resident in England from 1749–55 and Peter Bohler established a Moravian Society in Fetter Lane in 1738 where he exercised a great influence on John Wesley. The Moravians retained a form of the episcopate and the Moravian Episcopal Church was recognised by Act of Parliament in 1749.

Wesley severed his connection with the Moravians in 1740 but John Cennick, who had been one of his lay preachers, seceded from Methodism, joined the Moravians, and established the Moravian place of worship here.

Upavon. A quiet village on the Avon with bare Downs above it and trees to shelter it, it hems in its church with thatched walls, cottages, and barns. On the Downs is Casterley Camp, the biggest prehistoric fortress in Wiltshire.

The handsome tower is 700 years old, with a 15th century parapet; the lofty arch of the tower has seats round the base of its piers. It looks on to arcades as old as itself and on to a richly moulded chancel arch which introduces us to Norman England, for the chancel was built in those last days when the Norman was beginning to give way to the Gothic.

The chancel has a very quaint charm, its walls as the Normans left them, with one round doorway built up, the light falling through a Norman window. The arch itself has the Norman chevron carving and the dainty capitals the Normans gave it, but it has been reshaped and pointed by the English builders in the new style. On each side of the great arch is a small round arch which has been partly built up so as to form a tiny pointed arch on the chancel side—all a little curious. One of the windows has been made into seats.

There is a Norman font, with floral crosses and raging lions in its panels; in another panel is a graceful and charming Annunciation, with the lily in a pot between the angel and the Madonna.

Upton Lovel. The Lovels, who lived at the manor house in the charming Wylye valley, come into a famous Scottish ballad, the hero of which went abroad to strange lands seeking high adventure while his Lady Nancy died of grief for him at home. The grief of it killed him too, and the ballad goes on to say that after they had laid him in her grave a rose and a briar sprang up from the tomb, wreathed together, and that,

They grew and they grew, to the church steeple too,
And then they could grow no higher,
So there they entwined in a true lover's knot,
For all lovers true to admire.

Another Lovel took part in the Lambert Simnel Rebellion after the end of the Wars of the Roses, escaped to this manor house, and hid in a cellar where he is said to have starved to death, his skeleton being found seated at a table at which he was writing with a book beside him. This tale is also told of Minster Lovel in Oxfordshire.

It is believed that one of the Lovels lies in the 13th century chancel of the little church. A fine stone figure of a knight lies there in armour, with his visor closed, his gloved hands at prayer, his sword hanging from a handsome belt, and his feet on a dog. In front of the altar is the brass of a good-looking 14th century priest, probably Richard de Popham.

The choir stalls have old carved panels at the ends, and a sanctuary chair has a prancing unicorn carved on the back. In the tower is an old panelled chest. The nave roof has moulded timbers, and bosses carved with foliage, and is about 300 years old. The low tower with its crocketed pinnacles was built about the same time. The simple font made about 800 years ago has been lost and found; it was used in the vicar's garden as a vase.

Upton Scudamore. It is 800 years since the Scudamores came to the manor house, but their village is charming still, 400 feet high on its hilltop in the splendid country of the Downs near Warminster.

Two battered effigies of Scudamore knights have lain in the small church about 700 years. They lie on the floor of a chapel, their faces worn away, one having lost an arm, the other with his hands still on his sword. Above them hangs a small flag of red and gold. We come to them through a magnificent doorway made by the Normans, its arch resting on slender columns with Norman capitals but with a pointed arch set within it 700 years ago. The Norman arch has three depths of carving, a band of zigzag between two bands of chevron. We come into the chancel also through a Norman arch with carved crowns on its capitals, and the children are christened at a Norman font. One of the windows has stone seats for the priests in its recess, and facing it by the altar is a neatly cut stone telling us that William Seaman "enjoyed the rectory 52 years" in the 17th century. A brass inscription of 1632 is set in a charmingly carved stone panel.

Urchfont. Called, it is said, after a stream that never runs dry. A lovely place with fine Downs, it has a pond on its green with a glorious cedar throwing its shadow over a wall, and a wonderful little church built about 600 years ago. Its embattled tower, gargoyled and pinnacled, with a stair turret and graceful windows, was added in the 15th century, when the pinnacled porch was built.

The porch has a beautifully panelled stone roof, an inner doorway with exquisite pierced moulding, and an image niche. The roof of the chancel has fleur-de-lys on its gable, quatrefoil in its parapet, and buttresses with gabled heads.

The 500-year-old arcades of the nave are high and carried by round piers; the clerestory and its charming windows have kept them company all the time. The vaulted chancel roof has richly carved bosses bearing dragons, a mermaid, Abraham with the ram caught in the thicket by his horns, St Michael and the dragon, and a pelican.

There are lovely traceried windows, two charming canopied piscinas, and part of an old pillar piscina lying in a peephole; a little wooden door with tracery and a sunflower carved on it; a font on pillars about 700 years old; a handsome Jacobean roof in one aisle with moulded beams and carved pendants; a case of old floor tiles; and fragments of 14th century glass. But there is more old glass looking down from a window where it has been 600 years, enchanting red and gold angels of many wings, each holding two crowns. The tomb of Robert Tothill, Clerk of the Privy Seal to George the Second, has excellent portrait busts of himself and his wife, by Thomas Scheemakers.

In a field a mile or two away, guarded by a rail and watched over by three great elms, are three Plague graves, and the sight of them brings back to the memory of Urchfont a tragic tale of its rectory. One of its rectors was seized with plague when his son and four grandchildren were living here and all six caught the plague and died. The brave little maidservant who alone was spared buried them all in the rectory, where their bones were discovered long after.

Wanborough. We turn to it from the Swindon road at a little thatched cottage which says E.A.K. 1672; the lane brings us to what was once the Key of Wessex, where met three Roman roads. Here in Saxon times was an important point of vantage, and here two battles were fought.

Its church has something peculiar to itself as far as we can remember—a pinnacled tower at the west end built in the 15th century, and a stone spire of the 14th with two rows of windows set in it.

The north porch has pinnacled buttresses and a lovely doorway with a moulding of flowers, and near this door is a board which is not afraid to say that all females are requested to take off their pattens on entering this door.

There is a Norman tub font, a medieval painting fading on the walls (in which we could still distinguish Christ riding on an ass into Jerusalem), and brasses of Thomas and Edith Polton. They may have built the tower. He has a small moustache and a forked beard, and she is in a plain gown.

There are fine figures of St Andrew and St Catherine in the chancel windows, and on the roll of honour are 14 names.

At Nythe, a little way off, is the site of a Roman station on Ermine Street, a town which was about a mile long. Here runs the little River Cole, beloved by Richard Jefferies.

Warminster. It lies close to Somerset, 400 feet above the sea in the widest part of the Wylye Valley. It is rich with four churches, a 19th century town hall, and an 18th century grammar school, with a dignified front and seven small dormers in its long roof. An obelisk at the crossroads comes from the same century as the school; it is in memory of a visit of George the Third to the town.

There are Wren houses in the old part of the town, one known as the Chantrey and one in Vicarage Street. The town hall was built in 1830 in Jacobean style; facing it is a striking clock carved to represent Agriculture and Produce, a souvenir of the Great Exhibition in 1851. The arcade of an hotel in the street is the only relic of the great Corn Market here.

The oldest possession of Warminster is the 14th century nave of St Lawrence, a church with the spire in which hangs a bell cast in a field close by in the days when bells were made on the spot and people would throw bits of silver in. Three flying foxes look down from a queerly twisted parapet above the nave, evil gargoyles look out from the tower, a king and queen greet us at the door, and there are other sculptured heads inside and out. The font has been here since the church was almost new and it is its chief possession. The windows have quaint little scenes.

The new churches are Christ Church, standing in a noble position with fine roof timbers, lofty arcades, and a noble cedar 12 feet round; and St John's at the end of the long street, a light and spacious place with a handsome interior, mosaics on its walls, and beautiful windows. The mosaics are great and small and are made of great and small pieces. Those in the nave show Gabriel bringing the good news to the Madonna and the kings bringing their gold caskets to the Manger, Christ in the Temple, and the Good Shepherd. Those in the chancel, covering the walls by the sanctuary, show Moses with the serpent in the Wilderness, groups of stately figures of archangels, Christ in Majesty, and a heavenly choir. There is a brass on the chancel wall with the portrait of George Temple; it is one of the few modern brasses in Wiltshire, being 19th century, and it shows him kneeling by the brass screen set across the chancel in his memory. The two best windows in St John's are a fine lancet of the Madonna in a blue robe, with a small Annunciation panel below, and the glowing west window with six scenes in dazzling reds and blues.

At the other end of the long street stands St Denys, the parish church, with a noble yew 15 feet round throwing its branches over the porch, from which angels reach out to it. The tower is 15th century and the lady chapel has kept it company all the time, but most of the rest has been refashioned. The organ was built for Salisbury cathedral in 1792.

There is a fine iron grille in the chancel and two splendid old chairs in the sanctuary, each with four faces finely carved. The reredos has carved and painted figures under gilded arches. In a glass case hangs a book used by King Edward when he came to a service here as Prince of Wales in 1856.

The church has much fine oak and stone carving inside and out, with strange winged animals, angels reaching out from the walls, floral pendants hanging down from the heavily timbered roof, angels at prayer holding up the beams, and below these a stone choir of angels with a fiddle, a harp, and two trumpets. The chapel roof has old timbers with carved spandrels and winged angels.

There are two old gravestones, one to a faithful servant, Jeremiah Cruse, who served for 67 years at the great house of Longleat under five marquises of Bath; the other to Alice Alcock, for 60 years the faithful wife of the headmaster of the grammar school. A stone on the wall tells us that a member of the Townsend family left £3 a year for ever for the singing once a year of an anthem by Roger Townsend, and somewhere here there lies Nathaniel Butler, who comes into books of odd scraps of knowledge because the total ages of himself, his wife, their three daughters, and his wife's mother reached five hundred years. The daughters died halfway between the Battle of Trafalgar and the Battle of Waterloo, and they remembered their grandmother who was born in the first year of the Civil War (1642).

Westbury. It is famous for its view of the white horse on Bratton Hill, familiar to every traveller for miles round. It is thought that there has been a horse on this hillside for over a thousand years, since Alfred beat the Danes, but the old horse was destroyed and a new one cut in the turf in 1778. The old one was of the carthorse breed, and has been replaced by a more prancing steed, 175 feet from head to tail and over 100 feet from foot to shoulder.

The beautiful churchyard is distinguished at both its gates, for at one an old chantry looks down, and at the other is a group of four chestnuts. The path runs between them, and in the shade of these trees every villager of Westbury must have walked for many generations. One of the trunks is 18 feet round. Huge winged gargoyles look down from under the battlements, and everywhere are queer stone faces. On the wall by the south porch, which has a carved stone roof and a huge sundial, is an extraordinary corbel of three faces with four eyes.

The cruciform church is mainly 15th century The old porch has stone seating. Spacious and light, the nave has lovely peeps through its arcades, and is rich with old and new craftmanship in wood and stone. There are many stone faces and bosses on the cornice—of men, women, and beasts, with a fine figure of a minstrel among them; and the arches in the two chapels are charmingly moulded inside. The timber roofs of the chapels are panelled in squares with oak bosses. The stone reredos was carved by Gloucestershire masons in our time, and has figures of St Peter with the keys, St George with the dragon, St Catherine with the wheel, and a bishop with four musicians. There is a brass of Thomas Bennet and his wife, who died soon after Queen Elizabeth the First, and have little lions and dogs with them; and a bust of William Phipps, an 18th century Governor of Bombay. A tablet to Surgeon Shorland has hanging above it a chain which was saved from the wreck of the Invincible at Jutland, when the surgeon, a very gallant gentleman, went down with nearly all the members of the ship's company. The chancel screen is a magnificent piece of modern craftsmanship. The eagle lectern is on a pinnacled base with four figures, and the pulpit is adorned with figures of Paul and the Evangelists.

The west window has a little original glass in the tracery panels in purple, green, and gold, and there are good pictures in some of the modern windows. The baptistry window has stately figures in ruby and gold of Thomas Becket, St Augustine, and St Alban, with a small scene from each life; two big aisle windows face each other with six big figures, and in the north transept window is a curiously attractive picture of Abraham Laverton of Farleigh Castle, kneeling at a desk reading with 40 figures about him in small panels. There is an old chest, an old Bible, and an old font.

In an ornate tomb carved with cherubs and symbolical figures lies the most famous man buried in this place, James Ley, first Earl of Marlborough. He lies with his wife, he with a beard and bows at his knees, she holding up her gown which has a chain and a girdle. Ten fierce lions keep guard round their tomb, as befits a judge of such fame that he pronounced sentence on Sir Francis Bacon. He sat in Parliament for Westbury, was one of King James's first knights (knighted on a royal visit to Wilton in 1603), and he made himself hated throughout the kingdom by his bitterness as a judge. He is said to have offered £10,000 for the Attorney-Generalship but he failed to get it, and was made Lord Chief Justice. When Bacon fell from power Ley took his place as Speaker of the House of Lords, and it was he who declared the sentence on the fallen Chancellor—a fine of £40,000, imprisonment during the king's pleasure, disablement from holding any public office, and prohibition from coming within 12 miles of the Court. Ley became a decrepit old man, but Milton regarded him as an honourable judge, and in a sonnet addressed to his daughter Margaret described him as

> *That good earl, once President*
> *Of England's Council and her Treasury,*
> *Who lived in both unstained with gold or fee* . . .

West Dean. It is a charming hilly village with a stream running through it. It has lost its great house, but it keeps a chantry chapel 600 years old, built by Robert de Borbach in 1333.

Hidden by trees on the top of a hill, it is a pathetic monument of the past, with its founder sleeping in a canopied recess. It is kept as a funeral chapel for those of this ancient place who follow him. In it is a group of impressive monuments to the Pierreponts and the Evelyns, the biggest of them a handsome piece of work in memory of Robert Pierrepont, Earl of Kingston, who married a daughter of the Evelyns and lived through the Civil War. This great tomb has doors of wood which, on opening, show the lifesize statue of the earl, a stout man with curly wig and classic drapery. He is kneeling on one knee, and a tiny angel flutters behind him. His strange epitaph is engraved on the gilded copper lining of the doors, one door dealing with his soul, the other with his body. We are left to gather from this curious form of words that the earl suffered the cutting off of his legs with heroic valour, but that before this his body had passed healthy and sound through Italy and France and Spain, unmutilated, undiseased, without the marks of Sin or Chance. It is good to know that he returned with a lady of whom nothing was too good to be said.

On a lovely alabaster and marble monument kneels a man with the famous name of John Evelyn, living in the famous diarist's day; he and his wife both in black, she with a long black veil over her hair, and their 11 children kneeling below. The arches are carved with bunches of flowers bound with ribbons. Looking out from a small recess with marble curtains drawn back and secured to two little columns is Elizabeth Tirell, who married John Evelyn's son. She has short curly hair and wears a pretty bodice, a necklace, and ear-rings. We see the handsome face of another 17th century Evelyn, old Sir John, behind the iron doors of a monument on the wall, and there is a brass portrait of George Evelyn, a dear impish-faced boy with long hair, square tippets, a frock down to his toes, and a collar and cuffs as in Van Dyck's pictures. He was six, and died in 1641. On the floor lies an old tapering stone coffin shaped for the head.

A little way off stands the tithe barn of an old abbey, a fine red brick building which received the tribute of the cornfields 400 years ago. Down the hill is the modern church, where the people listen to the reading of the Bible from a lectern made of a column about 700 years old, with a sculptured capital and a tiny consecration cross, one of the oddest lecterns we have seen. Let into two recesses in the sanctuary are old tiles with fleur-de-lys.

West Grimstead. It is on the Hampshire border and has a charming little church with a brick tower. In the church is a plain stone font at least 800 years old, and possibly Saxon. The arches of the nave were set up by masons of the 13th and 14th centuries, and the roofs have still massive beams which these men put in their place, some of them having a carved boss in the centre. The Jacobean pulpit has brackets carved like eagles to support the ledge, and heads of strange birds peep out of the foliage on the sides.

There is a very big stone coffin and in the vestry a 17th century carved altar table.

West Harnham. It has something unusual in its church, a long and narrow window running along the wall. It is a relic of the 14th century when the church was not apparently big enough for the people, and what was called a lean-to shelter was set up for those who could not get in. The wall, now sheltered by a modern porch, is covered with letters and symbols these people scratched on it (for there were litter louts in those days). On the wall beside the porch is a well-preserved scratch-dial.

The old church has windows the Normans made in the nave and chancel, and the pillars of a small Norman doorway. The deep font bowl is the work of the English builders who followed them and built the chancel arch with its simple capitals and clustered columns. One group of columns stands on the fragments of an old stone altar, and in a niche behind it are traces of a fresco seeming to show Mary Magdalene anointing Our Lord with her pot of ointment. The chancel roof has very good bosses and heads of the 15th century, painted and gilded; the heads are considered to be portraits. A graceful Jacobean screen separates the nave from a chapel with a Jacobean altar and a modern oak reredos to match the screen. On each side of the altar is medieval woodcarving by German craftsmen, showing the Presentation in the Temple and the Entombment of Jesus, both vigorous pieces of work.

Across the way from the church, where the Nadder spreads into a wide pool sheltered by willows, is an ancient mill. It has early windows and Tudor doorways, and a mighty network of timber. It is not known who built the millhouse, but it may have been a rest house for the cathedral, or perhaps a hospital. It is a lovely walk from the mill to Salisbury, through the water-meadows.

West Kington. A tiny village near the River Box. The church stands on a hill and has a fine 15th century tower, the belfry windows being filled with tracery, the centre panels acting as "sound holes" for the bells. The pulpit is late medieval.

The village is associated with the Reformer Hugh Latimer who was rector here for five years in the fifteen twenties. In 1535 he became Bishop of Worcester. On the accession of Mary Tudor in 1553 he was committed to the Tower after his refusal to recant his Protestantism and he was burnt, with Nicholas Ridley, Bishop of London, at Oxford on 16th October 1555.

West Lavington. It lies among the hills on the northern edge of the Plain, and its fine clerestoried church has the work of all our great building centuries. In it is an impressive array of sculpture, and perched on one of its parapets is a dancing bear.

The nave has two noble arcades, the font is 14th century; its makers cut two curious little heads on its base. One of the windows has bright-coloured fragments of enamelled glass from the 17th century, but the little pieces with a chalice are 500 years old. There is an odd window high up at the roof of the east wall, with a tiny figure set in blue glass. From the 17th century also come seven or eight heraldic brasses, two of them palimpsests, brasses used on both sides for different people. England has probably a few scores of these.

The Beckett Chapel has a beautiful Elizabethan altar, a canopied pillar piscina, an ancient chest, and an old door in an archway carved with flowers. The Becketts lived in the house at the top of the village, and it was here that one of their guests met with a tragic end. He was Captain Henry Penruddock, a Royalist who was resting in his chair when soldiers came upon him and murdered him in his sleep.

Three people who lived in two dynasties sleep here, their tombs filling the chapel wall, a remarkable spectacle. Two are in shining marble, with sculptures of fashionable people of their day, and one is in old stone, beautiful and serene. In 1430 the Dauntseys were living at the manor house; they built the charming south chapel, to which in another 200 years they brought Elizabeth Dauntsey, who lies on her side, a stout and kindly looking lady in snowy marble, a book in her hand. She has a fine lace-edged veil and is handsomely dressed in the fashion of Cromwell's day.

Near her is the ornate tomb of Henry Danvers, who lies with a book in his hand, quaintly dressed in a Stuart wig falling over his shoulders and lace cravat, with a cloak and sandals. He is a good-looking youth who died when England was a republic.

The dainty little lady in stone is an unknown Elizabethan, a charming figure with her head on cushions and an ornament hanging from her belt. By her recess on the wall is the brass portrait of a knight in Tudor armour, John Dauntsey.

Westwood. It is a captivating place by the Somerset border with Iford manor as well as its own to give it dignity, and one of Wiltshire's rarest little churches to keep both company. Westwood's manor house, standing by the church, has gables, dormers, and rich plaster ceilings; Iford's is famous for its Italian gardens.

The church has brought its beauty unspoilt from the 15th century, the nave has a Georgian roof with fine plastered bosses. The roof of the chapel keeps its splendid old timbers, panelled and with rich bosses.

Indoors and out it is charming. Its beautiful tower (the only way in) has traceried windows, gargoyles looking down from an embattled parapet with pinnacles at each corner, and a stair turret crowned with a superb little dome. There are dragons looking down outside the east window, and the window is filled with most precious glass.

The tower doorway brings us first into the charming little nave by the fine font, above which is a winged dragon looking down on a font cover, and an exact copy in wood of the lovely stone dome of the turret above the tower. It is the finest bit of woodwork in a church with much fine work, the dome being divided into eight panels by ribs carved with what look like buds, all meeting in a graceful finial. The panels themselves are carved with hundreds of overlapping scallops. It is the work of a 15th century craftsman, a little older than the lovely pulpit of Jacobean days and the sturdy altar-rails.

It may have been that as the carpenter was fashioning the cover of the font the glass makers were making the east window, for both come from the 15th century. There is probably no more interesting glass in Wiltshire. Our Lord hangs on the cross in the centre of the window, the shaft rising from a vase and blossoming triumphantly with lilies and stars. At each side are angels with shields on which are symbols of the Passion, and one of the shields is unusual for having on it the head of a man with his tongue out; he is the man who mocked at Calvary. In the tracery is Michael weighing a soul with two disciples between him and another saint, and altogether there are about 20 figures in the window. In other windows of this small 700-year-old chancel are more angels with shields, all in old glass, and with them is a later medallion of the Crucifixion by a Flemish artist; in it the Madonna and St John are mourning at the foot of the cross over which the clouds are hovering above the towers of the city.

The clustered columns of the nave are graceful with very slight capitals. The walls on the east are enriched with lovely canopied niches. The double piscina in the chancel has fine carving round it, and there is a double peephole in the chapel wall. The splays of the tower arch are beautifully panelled.

On the chapel wall is a charming monument with 29 little

heraldic creatures, and near it is a stone to Charles Francklin with a line for every letter of his name. It tells us of his virtues and winds up:

Crowned with his native innocence he fell;
Kings crowned with laurels seldom die so well.
Let age and youth from hence this maxim know:
If Heaven commands the best are forced to go;
Nothing that's good is permanent below.

Whaddon. A little church on a low green hill with the Avon running by. For eight centuries people have been coming through this Norman doorway, summoned by the bell in this odd little stone turret, passing between these pillars with their carved capitals and the stones carved with beaded zigzag. For centuries they have been pushing open this very door with eight great iron strips across it; it is sad to see that the Norman doorway in the north wall has lost not only its door but its very self, for it has been shut up in a coal house.

In the chapel opening off the Norman nave by the stairway to the old roodloft are the memorials of Walter Long, who died just after Trafalgar at 95 and his sister Katherine just before Waterloo at 97. Three other sisters not far away, one having died at 66, one at 70, and the other at 89. This brother and his four sisters shared between them 417 years of life. The monument to Katherine is the work of Westmacott.

Whiteparish. In the 13th century church of this border village is a tablet in memory of Sir Giles Eyre. He lived at Brickworth, a Jacobean house now modernised, and while there was "plundered by soldiers and imprisoned for refusing to pay money illegally demanded of him under the privy seal." There are two tablets to 17th century members of the St Barbes family, gruesomely decorated with worms writhing out of the mouths of skulls.

Wilcot. The lovely roofs of its manor house are a fine sight over the churchyard wall. There are old stone faces at the window of the tower and there is an ancient scratch-dial. The 13th century arch into the chancel has six carved capitals on its clustered columns, and a peephole cut through for the altar. A 16th century tomb of John Berwick has a daintily carved canopied recess with elegant flowers and heraldry. Let into the wall of the sanctuary is a tiny painted oak medallion with the assurance that a good conscience is more than great riches written small in the middle of a wreath of flowers.

Two memories of the village are preserved in tablets on the walls, one recording the faithful service of a servant at the manor house for nearly 41 years, and the other telling us of the young son of Admiral Sir John Gore, who was coming home on his father's flagship in 1835 when he leapt overboard in a great storm to save a sailor's life and was himself drowned.

Wilsford. It is a village of the Avon within easy reach of Salisbury and has a lovely Elizabethan manor house by the wayside built of chequered flint and stone, and a little church rebuilt last century which keeps the tower the Normans gave it. The manor house was the home of a great discoverer of antiquities, Edward Duke. A Wiltshire man, he gave his leisure to exploring the burial mounds of his own estate and afterwards on the Wiltshire Downs, concerning which he formed a remarkable conception held by no one else before or since, for he suggested that the early inhabitants of Wiltshire had devised these prehistoric monuments as a vast planetarium on the face of the downs, the earth being represented by Silbury Hill and the sun and the planets by stone temples and earthworks round it.

The church, into which we come by a doorway resting on pillars with sculptured capitals, is the last resting-place of one of the founders of the Wireless Age, Sir Oliver Lodge, who ended his remarkable life of discovery and invention at Wilsford in his 90th year. It was on the basis of his coherer that Marconi was able to build up his own wireless system, and make broadcasting a practical business.

Wilsford. It lies off the road to Devizes, under the high Downs on which lie so many Ancient Britons, a neat little place where not only the cottage roofs are thatched but the tops of the garden walls. A fine row of elms looks across the lane to the old church built by the Normans and the first English builders. It has a handsome tower with gargoyles and sculptured friezes, and an arch all askew inside. There are ten fine stone corbels in the nave and chancel with men in crowns and mitres, ancient timbers in the chancel roof, a canopied piscina, an old plain font, and a priest's doorway. The chancel window has a picture of Eunice with her little son Timothy, and another has a woman with a bunch of flowers, standing in a flowing robe in a landscape with sunset on the hills.

Wilton. Once the capital of Wiltshire and of Wessex, it has lost that high distinction, and today, an hour's walk from Salisbury, although it still has the carpet industry that has made its name famous, it is a quiet place with three things for the traveller to see. There is one of the very greatest treasure-houses in England, Wilton House, the home of the Pembrokes for many generations; there is the chancel of the old church, off the marketplace, which has been brightened and given a new lease of life after being long neglected and forlorn; and there is a modern church not like any other we have seen, a Byzantine structure a little over-splendid, a gorgeous example of the architecture of the Victorian Era, built regardless of cost.

For nearly seven centuries Wilton was the seat of one of the four most important nunneries in England—the other three were Barking, Shaftesbury, and Winchester—whose abbesses were peeresses of the realm though being women they had no seat in the House of Lords. It stood on the site of Wilton House but the only visible remains are to be found in some outbuildings nearby.

The old church has been restored and hallowed as a place of rest in memory of Robert Bingham, the American ambassador, and his ancestor Robert de Bingham, second Bishop of New Sarum, who was consecrated here 700 years ago.

The remarkable new church is raised above the street on steps 100 feet wide, with a tower 100 feet high linked with it by a cloister. Its west front (which is not really west, for the church is one of the very few not laid out east-to-west) has three deeply recessed round arches, the central one with four orders of moulding and pillars resting on lions. Inside everything is remarkably rich. There is much mosaic, rich carving on capitals, fine marble monuments, mosaic chancel steps, a sanctuary floor of agate and marble, an enamel chalice covered with scenes and figures by a 12th century craftsman, two massive monoliths brought from Italy, and two twisted marble pillars which were part of a shrine in Rome in the 13th century and in the 18th century in the collection of Horace Walpole.

The monuments, an interesting group, have often the high quality of genius. There is a lovely white figure of Lord Herbert on a black marble tomb sculptured with scenes from his life, and near him is a lovely sleeping figure of his mother. There are sculptures by Rossi and Westmacott, one of the Countess of Pembroke with a mourning woman over an urn, the other a big wall sculpture to George Augustus Herbert, showing a beggar with his dog, a woman with her child, and a man leaning on his staff, a symbol of charity and good works. Over the cloister door is a Jacobean monument of William Sharp kneeling with his wife, their three children below in tiny recesses. There is a marble bust of the ninth Earl of Pembroke and a brass of John Goffer three years older than the Spanish Armada.

Among much ancient glass the most extraordinary piece is a panel brought from Wilton House with the arms of Philip and Mary, a piece of heraldry rarely met with in a church window. In the same window is a portrait of the Earl of Pembroke and his countess with their two sons and a daughter kneeling. The east window has some pieces of glass among the oldest in England, 12th or 13th century; the picture of Stephen is supposed to be 1200. In this window is St Nicholas, the Flight into Egypt, the wedding feast at Cana, the driving-out from the Temple, and Gethsemane. Other glass is from St Chapelle in Paris. The east windows of both chancel aisles have also rich old glass, much of it 13th century, and many of the figures are quaint and charming. There is an old Venetian chest, a wheel window showing the Flight of Time, and a reading desk with old Flemish carving.

Over the gateway of Wilton House sits Marcus Aurelius on his horse, a copy of the famous bronze statue on the Capitol in Rome.

The full tide of English history has flowed past this stately house and through these lovely gardens, leaving behind it noble works of art and glorious memorials. Here stood the nunnery in Alfred's time, here the Confessor's wife was educated, and when their habitation like themselves had passed away a new life was conferred on Wilton by the Earls of Pembroke, the first of whom received the site as a gift from Henry the Eighth, part of his ill-gotten gains from the destruction of the monasteries. Others of the line enriched it with every gift of architecture and art, and not least with the art of gardening, and the noble home they created has been the casket of noble memories. Statesmen and soldiers, men of chivalrous hearts, poets, painters, thinkers, left their footprints in these gardens, or found a home within these walls.

Sir Philip Sidney sat in the avenue bearing his name to write the first part of Arcadia, which he dedicated to his sister, the Countess of Pembroke, of whom Spenser, another visitor here, wrote:

The gentlest shepherdesse that lives this day
And most resembling both in shape and spright
Her brother deare.

Here, according to tradition, Shakespeare himself with his troupe played *As You Like It* for the first time, before James the First in the great hall, and here certainly was born William Herbert, son of the immortalised countess, to whom (with his brother) the Shakespeare Folio was dedicated. He was a great patron of arts and letters, and many think he is the mysterious W. H. of Shakespeare.

If Inigo Jones studied in Italy at his expense that supreme architect well repaid the debt, for the Wilton House that we see was refashioned from his designs. It is said that Holbein also had a hand in

Pembroke's princely dome, where mimic Art
Decks with a dazzling hand the magic powers.

The Holbein Garden House, once part of the mansion, is named as a tribute to his association. But it is the boldness, sureness, and grace of the hand of Inigo Jones that gives Wilton House its beauty, though the garden front was enlarged by another hand, and the southern front was rebuilt by John Webb (his nephew by marriage) after his designs.

The gardens were laid out by Isaac de Caux, a nephew of the rebuilder of the southern front, and they have a beauty no less renowned than that of the house. To them Nature gave a setting which Art could hardly fail to adorn. The river Wylye bounds the park, the Nadder flows through the pleasure gardens and is spanned by a fine Palladian covered bridge. There are 70 acres of lawn with stone-edged flower beds, stretching from the river to set out the stateliness of the southern front. There are Italian gardens with fountains, statues, terraces, and the rich foliage of the trees sets off the riot of colour in the flower beds. There is a noble group of ancient cedars of Lebanon, probably the earliest of these cedars planted in England, older even than the monarchs of Goodwood and Warwick. There are copper beeches, a noble ilex that Philip Sidney may have seen, a walk of lofty yews, and fine vistas everywhere. One of them commands at its end the spire of Salisbury cathedral, a view which Constable (we may be sure) would see.

Plain to every eye is the treasure of the house. It has noble rooms. Behind the Inigo Jones front are seven, of which the double-cube room, so called because of its dimensions (60 feet by 30 feet), stands out pre-eminently as the work of the great architect. It was specially designed to receive the famous Van Dycks still adorning its walls, and is one of the most beautiful rooms in any house in the country. Its walls of white and gold have a domed ceiling with panels of the legend of Perseus. Other notable apartments are the corner room with a portrait of Prince Rupert over the mantelpiece, the single-cube room, and the colonnade room, with its long line of fluted columns.

The Van Dycks are one of the glories of Wilton. Besides the masterpiece of Philip Earl of Pembroke and his family in the double-cube room, there are others of the royal Stuarts, who at all times were honoured patrons of the house, of which Charles said he loved it above all other places. He came there every summer, and he was not the only monarch who knew it well. Queen Elizabeth the First was a visitor, and here still is kept the lock of hair she gave to Philip Sidney, and the manuscript of a poem he addressed to her. That is only one of Wilton's priceless heirlooms. The Earls of Pembroke were always collectors, beginning with the first of them, and they made their home one of the richest in the land.

William Herbert, third Earl of Pembroke, born at Wilton House, enjoys immortal fame as the friend and patron of Shakespeare. Son of Philip Sidney's immortal sister, he was born here on a day in 1580, when Sidney was a guest.

Samuel Daniel, the poet, was his first tutor, Massinger the dramatist grew up on his estate; he was the hero of Ben Jonson, Inigo Jones, William Browne, and George Herbert. Jonson confessed to Drummond that in his poverty he had often eaten his library (that is, sold his books). Their renewal was made possible by Pembroke, who sent him money for books (equal to over £200) every New Year's day.

A youth of precocious intellect, Pembroke reached Oxford at 12, and left it two years later. As a young man at the Court of Elizabeth the First he was involved in a discreditable intrigue with a maid of honour, and was banished to the country, where he married the heiress of the seventh Earl of Shrewsbury.

His career under Elizabeth and James was now that of the typical scholar-statesman; accomplished with lance and pen, skilled in diplomacy, a good actor in masques, a resolute spokesman for popular rights, a lavish host of royalty, and above all the stay and succour of men of genius. There seems little doubt that his mother invited the king to Wilton to witness a performance of *As You Like It*; and still less doubt that Pembroke, as Lord Chamberlain and therefore supreme arbiter in the affairs of theatres, plays, and players, must have been in fairly close contact with Shakespeare.

All his contemporary fame as courtier and scholar might be forgotten, but Heminges and Condell, when they published the First Folio of Shakespeare, conferred on him a patent of immortality by dedicating the Folio to Pembroke and his brother, the Earl of Montgomery.

The two immortal nobodies who preserved Shakespeare for posterity knew not how inestimable was their gift, but sought credit for it from the names of the men to whom they inscribed it in these words:

When we value the places your highnesses sustain we cannot but know their dignity greater than to descend to the reading of these trifles; and, while we name them trifles, we have deprived ourselves of the defence of our Dedication. But since your lordships have been pleased to think these trifles something heretofore, and have prosecuted both them and their author living with so much favour, we hope that . . . you will use the like indulgence towards them that you have done unto their parent. So much were your lordships' likings of the several parts when they were acted, as before they were published, the Volume asked to be yours. We have but collected them, and done an office to the dead, to procure his orphans guardians.

The wedding of a kinswoman of Pembroke is believed to have occasioned the writing of *Midsummer Night's Dream*; but Pembroke himself was indirectly the occasion of the play with which Shakespeare took leave of the drama. Pembroke, who was deeply interested in colonisation, which he promoted with money and expeditions, was responsible, with Shakespeare's other patron Southampton, for the voyage of Somers, ending in shipwreck on the Bermudas, from which Shakespeare took his idea for *The Tempest*.

All his life a supporter of Raleigh, Pembroke had a major part in the voyage to Mexico that was to bring his luckless hero to death. He had a prominent share in the investigation of the charges against Francis Bacon, who thanked him for his moderation and affection.

Pembroke gave his name to Pembroke College, Oxford. He died in London in 1630, and is buried in Salisbury Cathedral.

Winkfield. A small village on the Somerset border, its 500-year-old church has magnificent views of the distant hills. It has an embattled tower with pinnacles.

In the porch is preserved the only stone which is known to remain of a lost parish. Centuries ago there was a parish of Rowley, but all records of it have disappeared and its church is gone except for this piece of stone from one of its windows, for the sake of which Winkfield is called Winkfield-cum-Rowley.

In the wagon-roofed nave, panelled and plastered, is a heraldic monument with twisted columns, a cherub, Tudor roses, and a horse on a shield; it is in memory of John Bayley who died in 1665, and in a tiny chapel is a charming small stone to his brother Christopher. In this chapel stands the little font with its bowl curiously cut in folds. The chancel, with nine Tudor roses in its roof, has tablets on its walls to two men who must have known each other in the 18th century, an eminent clothier who "lived virtuously and died piously" and a magistrate "inferior to few and superior to many." The altar table was made from wood brought from the Andaman Islands.

At the cross roads is Winkfield House, a charming gabled home awaiting a tenant when we called, and not far off is a house called Midway which was the home of a man whose name has a grim significance, for he was the artillery officer who invented a shell named after him, Shrapnel. The gates of the park have a group of the projectiles on the top of each post and the names of some of the battles where Shrapnel was used on the faces of the post.

Winsley. In this high country near the famous Saxon town of Bradford is a hollow in the hills called Dane's Bottom, said to have witnessed a terrible encounter between Alfred and his Danish enemies.

The church was rebuilt in 1841, but has still the old tower beside it, joined by an arch. The tower has a packsaddle roof, a stair-turret with a pointed cap, and four gargoyles looking down with their great mouths open, three of them with ears like rabbits. The medieval font has shields in its carved panels.

Winterbourne Bassett. On the hills by the village can be seen the White Horse of Broad Hinton, 90 feet long and 90 feet high.

The treasure of the 14th century church lies on the floor under a canopied recess in the chapel wall; it is a stone coffin lid over six feet long with two exquisite figures of an affectionate couple of about 700 years ago. They are slim figures with faces of great serenity, he with curly hair and she with a veil, each with the left hand on the heart, their right hands clasped.

In the fields of Manor Farm, the pleasant old house by the church, is a stone circle. At Manor Farm lived Captain Budd who served under Nelson and lived 64 years after him; he is buried under a big tomb between his home and the church. A bearded man and a crowned lady look down from the chancel arch, and there is more fine sculpture in the foliage of the 13th century font; its cover is 17th century. In the chapel is a canopied piscina with a flower in its bowl.

Winterbourne Gunner. It was probably Gunnora de la Mere who gave her name to this dear corner of the Downs, her husband owning the manor in the 13th century. The small 13th century church is in a green field. Its short tower has a humble spire. There are 14th century beams in the roof, a 700-year-old chancel arch, and a plain old font.

Winterbourne Monkton. It is one of the villages of long thatched roofs. Its little church has an oak shingled belfry resting on stout timber piers; it looks down on a farmyard through which one approaches it. It has an old carved pulpit and a lovely 800-year-old font, covered with all sorts of patterns, among them a queer creature, part human and part plant.

Winterbourne Stoke. Its 13th century church has two Norman doorways, one rich in moulding, the other more simply decorated and blocked up. On the wall of the nave is the iron bracket which used to hold the hourglass. There is a Jacobean pulpit carved with foliage. The tower is embattled, and has gargoyles and charming windows. On the floor by the font are some old tiles with foliage.

About three miles away on the Plain is Yarnbury Castle, a huge earthwork with triple ditches, one 50 feet deep. It is thought to have been one of a line of strong fortresses built to protect the southern Plain. It was thrown up in the Iron Age 2000 years ago, and is the second biggest prehistoric fortress in Wiltshire, the biggest of all being Casterley Camp near Upavon. It covers nearly 30 acres. In the original entrance was excavated a ditch 12 feet deep, and V-shaped, so that the attackers could not fight one behind the other. Above the ditch was found the skeleton of a man in leather boots with iron hobnails.

Winterslow. Its fame has gone out from its inn, far and wide across the world. We pass it on the wonderful ride across Salisbury Plain, and those who love fine writing pause with delight at the neat little inn, with a pond and a group of trees, where William Hazlitt did much of his thinking and wrote many of his essays.

Hazlitt's wife having property here, they spent some months of each year in this fascinating corner of Wiltshire, staying towards the end of his life at the Winterslow Hut. He loved the woods all round him, famous for the home of the Clarendons which was once sheltered in these stately trees. He loved to walk to Stonehenge, which stirred his imagination. He loved the sound of the bugle which meant that the mail was arriving at the Hut. The inn stands in the valley between two hills, and on either hill the horn of the approaching coach was blown. On the walls of the Hut hang pictures of a terrifying adventure which marked the arrival of the mail coach one day. It had just drawn up one night when a great beast leapt upon the horses from the shadows. In the confusion the coachman could not see, but suddenly to his horror he found it was a lion. At that moment a mastiff flung itself into the fray so that the lion turned and pursued it, then fortunately retreating under the granary, where the terrified people barricaded the king of beasts. By this time the keepers of a travelling menagerie had come to the rescue. To the horror of the onlookers, they lit candles and crawled under the granary to where the lion crouched, and, recognising them, the beast quietened down and returned with them to captivity. The granary is the small tarred wood building still standing on stone mushrooms in the yard.

In the quieter hours at this inn William Hazlitt would sit writing; for months every year towards the end of his life he would come here.

A pleasant thatched cottage in the village, a mile up the hill behind the Hut, is said to be the home of the Hazlitts, and if so its roof has sheltered Charles and Mary Lamb, who used to come and visit them. We found the roses growing over it as they would love to see it. They must have seen the little church as we see it, with windows from the 14th and 15th centuries, a big Norman font like a tub, 13th century arches, and some fragments of old carving. The fine 17th century pulpit has reliefs of prophets and saints.

Woodford. There are Upper, Middle, and Lower Woodfords, all in the lovely Avon Valley with Downs on either hand. The old church was mostly rebuilt in 1845, but the tower and south aisle were spared. The south doorway is Norman. There is a fine old chest but the best possessions are the three windows of painted glass by Sir Ninian Comper. Under the gallery in the tower is an old carved screen with two brackets strikingly carved with angels. There is a 16th century brass showing Gerrard Erington in a long gown and ruff. Heale House, where he lived, is a lovely place with a fine elm avenue and an enchanting water garden; it once belonged to the Hydes. Charles the Second sought refuge here after the Battle of Worcester, and was hidden in the priest's hole. It was from here that he rode out to see Stonehenge.

A few carved stones are all that remain of the old palace of the bishops. They are at Court House, a charming building standing on the site of the palace.

Wootton Bassett. Its best known possession is the quaint town hall rising on 15 stone posts in the middle of the street, with a fine 17th century oak staircase inside, and under it the old stocks, a ducking stool, and a fire engine with wooden wheels looking something like the picture of George Stephenson's Rocket but a hundred years older. It must have been a thrilling sight to see it rushing to a fire.

The 13th century church, with a priest's room over the porch, has much of its fine old roof left, painted with a thousand stars. It was enlarged by Street in 1870. The Elizabethan pulpit has red and green panels to match, but the old wall painting of the murder of Becket, seen for 30 years last century, is now covered up. The reredos is an astonishing piece of sculpture showing the Wise Men and the shepherds arriving with their camels to adore the Child, who sits on His mother's knee and has long hair. The Wise Men are bringing their caskets and offerings of birds, and the ass is eating from the manger.

The font is striking for its mass of roses, carved in little squares, covering every inch of the bowl. They have been recut to look like new, but are probably the work of Tudor craftsmen. There is an 18th century candelabra. The west window shows the martyrdom of St Cecilia, St Lucy giving charity, Catherine with the doctors in the temple, and the Madonna teaching her Little One. The old rood stairs are still running up through one of the piers.

The White Horse of Wootton Bassett has been looking down from the hillside since Farmer Simmonds cut it in the turf, the most northerly of Wiltshire's white horses.

Wootton Rivers. Jack Sprat's curious clock was telling the time in the quaint little wooden tower when we called, not an atom worse for having been made by the faithful local craftsman from odds and ends of iron and steel. It has six sets of chimes, and in the place of figures on its face it has the twelve letters, Glory be to God. The fine 14th century doorway, to which we come through a quaint trefoiled arch of the porch, brings us into a nave with a roof a little like a barn's. The preacher stands in what looks like half a pulpit, its stone pierced with trefoils and carved with bands of flowers.

Wroughton. Its pinnacled tower stands out boldly among the elms and sycamores looking across a lovely wooded vale, and perched at the other end of the nave is a small 15th century turret in which still hangs the sanctus bell, older than the Reformation.

The churchyard has a magnificent yew with branches spreading nearly 20 yards, and an ancient cross; and we noticed a small stone which since 1666 has borne this tribute to John Duck:

Who lived well to die never,
Died well to live ever.

The spacious church has 14th century nave and chancel, 15th century clerestory and aisles, and within its porch is a fine Norman doorway with worn beakheads. A king, a bishop, wimpled ladies, and other stone faces look down from the nave roof, and quaint gargoyles from the north aisle. The beautiful piscina has a water-lily and leaves carved in its basin, and the stone seats have fine canopies with little faces. There is an old table and two carved chairs, the remains of an ancient stone reredos, and a font which probably dates from the 15th century.

The curious brass of Will Sadler tells us that

Impartial Death which stops the breath of kings,
And beggars, and other mortal things,
Deprived us of the friend in strength of age
(That year the Armada in a furious rage
Threatened our ruin).

The widow lived 45 years without her William, dying in 1633 at "92 or more—a doer of God's will more than a sayer."

A mile or two behind Wroughton stands the bold front of Hackpen Hill, crowned by Barbury Castle, an Iron Age camp with double ramparts.

Wylye. The church is mainly 15th century but the chancel is of 13th century origin and the tower arch 14th century. The rector, Thomas Dampier, who was here from 1759 to 1831, put the candelabra in the nave the year before Waterloo. The silver chalice is more than four centuries old, and the pulpit was carved in Shakespeare's day. It has graceful stair-rails and is a wonderful piece of craftsmanship. In its top panels are four winged cherubs; in the middle panels are trees in arches, all but one burdened with fruit; in the bottom panels doves spread their wings and have olive branches in their beaks. The back is panelled, and has a dove, a tree, and at the top a gilded pelican in piety. The canopy is lavishly carved and in its centre is a golden sunflower. The lectern is the same age as the pulpit, and of the same rich design; and the sanctuary has three old armchairs with richly carved backs, one with two figures on it.

The 500-year-old tower is brave with battlements, pinnacles, gargoyles, and pierced windows, and over the porch is a carving of the Crucifixion now blurred by sun and wind and rain.

Yatesbury. It is 500 feet up near Calne. Its 800-year-old church is resting on those old sarsen stones, the hard greywethers of Stonehenge. It has a 15th century tower, an old cross, mass dials cut in its walls, a porch with ancient timbers in its roof, and a Norman arch set above its south door with a hideous animal at each end of it. Over the porch are two particularly fine old women at the rainpipes. Indoors the steps and doorways of the old roodloft are visible still. The chancel arch has four beautifully carved heads, serene and dignified.

Four ancient glass medallions shine in the windows, with the winged lion, the winged bull, the eagle, and the enchanting kneeling angel of the Four Evangelists, all in gold. Other fragments of glass have leaves, crowns, and flowers. The font is one of the best pieces of work left in Wiltshire by a Norman craftsman; leaves curl round the base of the bowl, and a graceful floral design runs round the top.

Yatton Keynell. The church was rebuilt in the 15th century, to which period belongs the tower, one of the five towers that are considered more beautiful than any others in Wiltshire and are distinctive as a group in England. The other four of this group are at West Kington, Westwood, Nettleton, and Devizes, and the top stage of each of these towers is covered with window tracery, the centre panel being pierced to let out the sound of the bells. The Yatton Keynell tower is tall and beautiful, with slender pinnacles, traceried windows, and panelled battlements. Indoors one face of the tower is covered with reliefs of golden cherubs and painted heraldry, one in memory of Abraham Light and his son Isaac, who lived here in the Commonwealth.

The church has much rich panelling in the window splays, under some of the arches, and on the chancel screen, where the stone carving is exquisite with delicate tracery and painted coats-of-arms. The capitals of all the piers are carved with flowers.

The roodloft stairway is cut through the pier of one of the arches, with a doorway barely 18 inches wide and five feet high. The chancel arch is 15th century and the tower arch 200 years older. There is a canopied piscina, a charming window in the 15th century porch, and several scratch-dials on the outer walls, where is also a consecration cross.

Zeals. A little village in grand hilly country near the Somerset and Dorset borders, its great house, halfway from Zeals to Mere, is older than its little church and far more historic. It is the home of an ancient Wiltshire family which gave one of its members to the scaffold in the Royalist rising under Colonel Penruddock; he was Colonel Hugh Grove, executed at Exeter in 1655. Here also hid Charles the Second one day when flying from Cromwell's men. The house has a fine gateway, and one of the rooms has a carved roof.

APPENDIX

Places of interest open to the public

(* Indicates property in the care of the Department of the Environment)
(† Indicates National Trust property)

Avebury: Avebury Manor
*Avebury stone circles and museum
*Silbury Hill
*Windmill Hill
Bradford-on-Avon: *Tithe Barn
Bratton: *Bratton Castle
*Westbury White Horse
Corsham: Corsham Court
Durrington: *Woodhenge
Horningsham: Longleat House
Lacock: †Lacock Abbey
Lydiard Tregoze: Lydiard Mansion
Salisbury: Malmesbury House
†Mompesson House
The Old Deanery
*Old Sarum
Stonehenge: *Stonehenge
Stourton: †Stourhead
Tisbury: *Old Wardour Castle
Wardour Castle
West Kennet: *Long Barrow
*The Sanctuary
Wilton: Wilton House

It is advisable for intending visitors to check times of opening as these occasionally vary.

WILTSHIRE TOWNS AND VILLAGES

In this key to our map of Wiltshire are all the towns and villages treated in this book.

Place	Map
Aldbourne	G4
Alderbury	F10
Alderton	B3
All Cannings	E6
Allington	C4
Allington (Newton)	F9
Alton Barnes	E6
Alton Priors	E6
Alvediston	D10
Amesbury	F8
Ansty	C10
Ashton Keynes	D2
Atworth	B5
Avebury	E5
Barford St Martin	E10
Baverstock	D10
Baydon	G4
Bemerton	E10
Berwick Bassett	E4
Berwick St James	E9
Berwick St John	C11
Berwick St Leonard	C9
Biddestone	B5
Bishop's Cannings	D6
Bishopstone	G3
Bishopstone (Wilton)	E10
Bishopstrow	C8
Blunsdon St Andrew	F2
Boscombe	F9
Box	B5
Boyton	C9
Bradenstoke	D4
Bradford-on-Avon	B6
Bratton	C7
Bremhill	D5
Brinkworth	D3
Britford	F10
Brixton Deverill	B9
Broad Chalke	D10
Broad Hinton	E4
Brokenborough	C3
Bromham	C5
Broughton Gifford	B6
Bulford	F8
Burbage	G6
Burcombe	E10
Calne	D5
Calstone	D5
Castle Combe	B4
Castle Eaton	F2
Charlton	C3
Charlton St Peter	E7
Cherhill	D5
Chilmark	D9
Chilton Foliat	H5
Chippenham	C4
Chirton	E6
Chisledon	F4
Chitterne	D8
Chittoe	C5
Cholderton	G8
Christian Malford	C4
Chute	H7
Clyffe Pypard	E4
Codford St Mary	D9
Codford St Peter	C9
Colerne	B5
Collingbourne Ducis	G7
Collingbourne Kingston	G7
Compton Bassett	D5
Compton Chamberlayne	D10
Coombe Bissett	E10
Corsham	B5
Corsley	B8
Corston	C3
Cricklade	E2
Crudwell	C2
Dauntsey	D3
Devizes	D6
Dinton	D10
Ditteridge	B5
Donhead St Andrew	C10
Donhead St Mary	C10
Downton	F11
Draycot Cerne	C4
Durnford	F9
Durrington	F8
East Coulston	C7
East Grafton	G6
East Kennett	E5
East Knoyle	B10
Easton	F6
Easton Grey	B3
Ebbesborne Wake	D10
Edington	C7
Enford	F7
Erlestoke	C7
Etchilhampton	D6
Everleigh	F7
Farley	G10
Fifield Bavant	D10
Figheldean	F8
Fisherton-de-la-Mere	D9
Fittleton	F7
Fonthill Gifford	C10
Fovant	D10
Froxfield	H5
Fyfield	F5
Garsdon	C3
Great Bedwyn	G6
Great Chalfield	B6
Great Cheverell	D7
Great Somerford	C3
Great Wishford	E9
Ham	H6
Hankerton	D2
Hannington	F2
Hardenhuish	C4
Heddington	D5
Heytesbury	C8
Highway	D4
Highworth	F2
Hill Deverill	B9